SECRECY AND OPEN GOVERNMENT

Also by K. G. Robertson

BRITISH AND AMERICAN APPROACHES TO INTELLIGENCE

PUBLIC SECRETS: A Study in the Development of Government Secrecy

Secrecy and Open Government

Why Governments Want You to Know

K. G. Robertson
Intelligence Management Consultant

First published 1999 by
MACMILLAN PRESS LTD
Houndmills, Basingstoke, Hampshire RG21 6XS
and London
Companies and representatives
throughout the world

ISBN 0–333–75367–4

A catalogue record for this book is available from the British Library.

This book is printed on paper suitable for recycling and made from fully managed and sustained forest sources.

10 9 8 7 6 5 4 3 2 1
08 07 06 05 04 03 02 01 00 99

Printed and bound in Great Britain by
Antony Rowe Ltd, Chippenham, Wiltshire

To my wife Ellen, with all my love

Contents

1 Introduction

This book is about democracy, power and secrets. It is also the story of how the UK came to abandon its secretive ways and adopt freedom of information. However, it is not a romantic tale but one of self-interest and struggle; it is the story of how power and the control of information are intertwined. Although it is full of ideals and references to democracy, values, liberties and rights, it does not accept that such ideals are the 'cause' of change and the introduction of 'open government'. Rather I argue that the nature of governance, the methods by which governments govern, has altered and changed the balance of power between different groups within the British state. Such changes in interests affected the incentives to control and release information. I argue that the recent decision to introduce freedom of information is not merely a reflection of the views of a particular political party or ideology but reflects a changed political environment with new incentives to manage information. Such changes range from new management structures in the National Health Service to a new crime-fighting role for the Security Service (MI5).

This book challenges the conventional wisdom that secrecy is best understood as a matter of values, of right and wrong. The relationship between values and interests is a complex one but all too often writers on secrecy refer only to values and never to power and interests. Such an approach is convenient for those who wish to believe in progress or 'inevitability' but it is of limited relevance to understanding the real causes of change.

In my book *Public Secrets* I argued that:

> It is the extent to which information is seen as part of the political struggle for office which determines the level of control of information. There are then two variables; the motive to exercise control of information and the ability to implement the degree of control desired.[1]

It is the structure of power, and the interests which it generates, which explains the incentives to compel others to keep secrets or to allow access. The more centralised and clearly hierarchical the structure of power, the more will be the incentive to compel others to keep secrets. The more decentralised and 'flat' the structure of power, the more will be the incentive to compel others to allow access. The balance of interest is the extent to which scrutiny by others – that is, some form of public access – enhances or diminishes politicians' sense of authority, of being in charge. The argument can be clarified by being expressed negatively: commitment to the value of openness or the legitimacy of secrecy has very little part to play in explaining variations between democracies; why one has more or less secrecy than another. This is not to say that values are irrelevant to democracy or to secrecy, as Tant believes I claim,[2] but that secrecy or openness can both be justified on the grounds that they contribute to 'good government', which is the principal justification of democracy.[3] They cannot both do so at the same time or in the same set of circumstances but they can contribute to democracy, depending upon how democracy is organised. In some forms of democracy it can at least be argued, without this being a contradiction in terms, that secrecy contributes to democracy, while it is equally appropriate to argue that in other forms of democracy openness greatly contributes to democracy. The value of secrecy and openness are secondary in that both are instrumental and must be judged in the light of their contribution to democracy. As I argued in *Public Secrets*, the creation of the official secret was legitimately seen as one solution to the problem of democratic government.[4] It is not necessary to my argument to assert that the British form of democracy is more democratic than others. Indeed, it is perfectly possible to argue that, even in the nineteenth century, it took a form that was a less perfect expression of democracy than in other nations. The point is this: given its form of democracy, secrecy was both comprehensible *and* legitimate. What legitimated the secrecy was not some notion that secrecy was a 'good thing' but that it contributed to the process by which elected representatives, ministers, and the institution of Parliament controlled the process of decision-making. They were the guardians of the popular will and if secrecy helped them to carry out the popular will then democracy actually legitimated the official secret. In some other nations, where democracy took a different expression, this was clearly not the case. If the way in which the popular will was expressed, the way in which democracy was organised was different, then in those nations secrecy would not contribute to democracy and would therefore be neither comprehensible nor legitimate.

The key to understanding the evolution of official secrecy in Britain was, and it will be argued remains, the way in which pressures to control or release information are mediated through a structure of power. This structure of power crucially involves relationships of authority between elected representatives and unelected officials although it also involves a range of complicated power relations such as that between government and the courts, and intelligence agencies and their consumers. However, governments do not operate in a vacuum. The influence of external factors has certainly increased over the last 20 years. The role of Europe, the European courts, the cold war, commercial electronic transactions, devolution, globalisation, and an increasingly 'individualistic' and sceptical culture, all create a different political environment.

In 1982 I argued that the question was whether freedom of information was a symptom of the end of democracy rather than its fruition and this question is even more pertinent today.[5] The institutions of government and the ideals of democracy are under scrutiny as never before. Political scientists in Europe and North America are prepared to argue that the loss of public confidence in the nation-state is such as to create a 'crisis of legitimacy'.[6] This is a view that can be found across the whole range of the ideological spectrum, from left to right. There are those who believe that the nation-state is no longer capable of delivering the welfare benefits promised by democracy and those who argue that the market is far more effective in delivering public services than the democratic state. The nation-state is seen as having exhausted its potential to deal with a whole range of domestic and global issues. On the domestic side, all governments are talking up the crisis of expenditure associated with changes in labour markets, ageing populations, and expanding opportunities for health care. On the international scene there is a whole range of issues – multinational companies; global warming; toxic waste; drug-trafficking; 'mad cow disease'; migration and refugee issues – that are seen as requiring a transnational response.

However, it is not only governments that are experiencing a crisis of confidence. There is also the fear that people have 'lost faith' and no longer share a sense of community, a set of shared ideals, a shared view of right and wrong, and that this has created a 'retreat into self'. Answers are seen as lying 'inside' us so that the only 'real' requirement is authenticity, being true to one's self, one's sense of personal integrity. This postmodern view of our culture is one in which individuals have little or no faith in institutions, science, or in the rational heritage of the Enlightenment.[7] One does not need to accept all of the philosophical or methodological issues associated with 'postmodern*ism*' to recognise that such concerns are echoed in the views of politicians, church leaders and the media. If individuals have become uncertain, see the world as increasingly 'risky', then it is hardly surprising that people wish to consume more and more information.[8] It is 'information' that enables the individual to try to make sense of the world, since no institution or experts can be trusted. One's future depends upon consuming, having access to, more and better information because it is only through access to information that one can safeguard one's individual destiny. The lack of faith in institutions means that it is only through access to information that one's private interests can be safeguarded.

I do recognise that many writers over many years, particularly in North America, have asserted that secrecy is incompatible with democracy, but such arguments have become more attractive to citizens as their faith in democracy has declined. That is the irony. It is also the case that governments have become less secretive as they have become greedier for information. The more 'efficient' the state becomes as a collector and processor of information, the greater is the argument in favour of access to official information on the grounds that the public have a right to know that records are accurate and decisions are fair. There is also the risk that as the state demands more information it may withhold or disclose that information in ways that are damaging to the rights of individuals. We must remember that the power to reveal can be as valuable as the power to conceal. Indeed, the power to disclose is merely the corollary of the power to keep secrets. Any removal of the state's duty to keep its secrets secret risks creating a state that is more powerful, not less. The only way to prevent such a situation is to create ever more regulation, monitoring, and review of official information. However, as we shall see in Chapter 3, it can be argued that such rules do not 'solve' this problem but merely create new, more sophisticated, mechanisms of manipulation. Creating rules legitimates government control of information as well as providing rights to the citizen.

However, there is another side to the argument. Democratic governments can regulate access to 'benefits', by seeking to divest themselves of responsibility for providing them! Hence, as the state seeks to take less responsibility for providing services, it is happy to let others take the blame when things go wrong, and it is therefore less interested in secrecy!

As I stated above, most writers find government secrecy problematic. They believe that democracy requires public access to official information and that the denial of such access is a symptom of the lack of democracy. The only issue that requires explanation is why some democratic governments have resisted the inevitable liberalisation of secrecy laws and why others have stubbornly refused to introduce freedom of information. Most writers conclude that 'backward' governments will not be able to maintain official secrecy in the face of steady and relentless pressure for change. Once some democracies introduce openness there is no hope for the remainder – like dominoes, they will fall. Experience elsewhere will demonstrate that secrecy is not necessary to good government and the last barrier to open government will crumble.

The assumption underlying much of this comparison is that time is the only factor explaining such variations. All democracies are destined to arrive at a common point so that the only factor to be explained is why some get there more slowly than others. The explanation of reform in the UK is that 'at long last', or some such similar phrase, Britain has come of age.[9] Like a natural process whose outcome is known (the irony is, of course, that in Darwinian theory this is a contradiction in terms) one can be in 'the front', 'lag behind', or be 'backward'. However, such an argument only makes sense if the goal is already known and one assumes that all states are travelling towards the same, known, goal. Phrases such as the 'triumph of democracy' or the 'end of history' all smack of the notion found in other discredited views of history: 'inevitability'. Historicism, even in its liberal form, does not appeal to this author. Another common, and more powerful, interpretation is that there exists a set of values associated with democracy but that it takes time for some states to remove the barriers to the fulfilment of such values.[10] This is also a teleological argument, one framed in terms of purpose, but this time the teleological element is acceptable because the purpose is a human one; people are attempting to implement a set of defined values. There is no mysterious force involved; it is simply that those who are committed to democracy will also, *ipso facto*, be committed to 'open government' or some similar value that implies a reduction in, if not the elimination of, secrecy. Thus any person, party, or nation, proclaiming itself to be democratic 'must', given the meaning of democracy, also become more open. The only factor remaining to be explained is why everyone cannot implement all the elements of democracy at once. It is rather like a journey; one may choose the destination but not be able to get there right away. In other words, even if everyone is committed to the same goal, the real world does not provide everyone with equal knowledge or equal resources. Not everyone will therefore get there at the same time.

Many readers may well find such views attractive but the notion of 'progress' can be misleading. Like all such explanations it is vulnerable to the charge that 'mind' does not evolve in a vacuum. It is also vulnerable to the charge of complacency. Because events appear to correspond with one's desires, then it is the fulfilment of those desires that explains such events. Another problem is that such a 'universal' theory fails to explain the considerable variations in the way in which governments have reformed official secrecy and in the timing of such changes. Constants such as 'secrecy is bad and openness is good' cannot explain variation. One possible counter to this view is that the spread of such ideas is itself variable and that this explains the variations in practice. However, for this to be accepted there must be, in turn, an explanation for the uneven spread of the idea of 'openness'. There would seem no good reason to believe that there are significant barriers to communication whereby some Western democracies would learn about this new principle later than others. Indeed, as we shall later, the literature is full of references to experience elsewhere and the principle has been known, and practised in at least one country, Sweden, since the eighteenth century.

In fact the problem lies in the premise underlying such an explanation; the normative approach to secrecy. Most of the writing on the subject of government secrecy has been based upon the notion that government policy on official information is a result of a commitment, or the lack of a commitment, to a given set of values. Because the approach is based upon deriving practice from a set of normative principles, authors feel free to express approval or disapproval, mainly disapproval, of government policies on official information. Indeed, many writers are open advocates of greater openness on the grounds that it is a 'necessary', or certainly desirable, feature of government. Given such assumptions it follows that failure to implement reform is seen as a failure of the political elite. The blame lies with people, politicians, who do not ascribe to 'correct thinking'. However, such an approach would not be taken very seriously if it were offered as the dominant, let alone sole, explanation of the rise of the welfare state or indeed any other main feature of contemporary democracy. Only the crudest analyst would argue that the welfare state was merely the result of 'progress' or was the result of a commitment to 'democratic values' – many other factors such as public demand, the needs of industry, tax revenues, the contradictions of capitalism, political ideologies, and party competition would be seen as being as, if not more, important.

If we are to understand the variations in timing and practice between Western democracies, we need to examine more than democratic values and people's commitment to them. To explain such variations we need to examine the structure of government and the structure of power in democratic societies.

This book, then, attempts to provide an analysis of the changes that have taken place in government control of information. The first two chapters provide an analysis of the normative approach and of the concept of surveillance. Then I examine the changes in British government followed by the debates over personal files, bugging, official secrecy, and intelligence. Finally, there is an examination of the Conservative and Labour government attempts to end 'the British tradition of secrecy'. The basic argument is that both the way in which Britain is governed and the tasks expected from the 'secret state' have changed, changed in such a way there are far fewer incentives to keep information secret than was the case even 20 years ago. Our politicians are neither more liberal nor more democratic than they once were; they have recognised that 'open government' no longer threatens their interests and may actually provide an effective way of managing the information greedy state.

2 The Morality of Secrecy: the Philosophy and Politics of State Secrecy

Three approaches to the issue of state secrecy will be examined: the philosophical, the political and surveillance theory.[1] It will be conceded from the outset that such divisions are somewhat arbitrary since there is a considerable degree of overlap between the philosophical and the political even if surveillance theory rather stands alone. Such overlap tends to reflect the fact that an approach, which I shall call 'the normative', tends to dominate all three, although it is less dominant within surveillance.

The most common approach to official secrecy is the one that I have labelled as the normative; the basic premise being that the values of contemporary society, particularly democratic industrial societies, are that openness is good and secrecy is bad.[2] Such writers believe that there are few, if any, justifications, for keeping information secret and wish to reduce secrecy to a minimum. The normative view argues that government should be accountable to the people and that all institutions of government should practise openness. There will be exceptions but such exceptions should be carefully defined so that secrecy is kept to a minimum.

Another approach is that secrecy is a product of the development of surveillance society. Weber, Foucault, Giddens, Dandeker and Lyon are major contributors to this perspective. However, although this tradition also tends towards the view that secrecy is bad, they do not believe that secrecy will be removed merely by persuading the elite or opinion-makers to adopt a more 'liberal' view of society.

My approach, which I shall call the realist, takes a different view. The realist sees secrecy as a reflection of power, not values, and believes that there are almost as many reasons for secrecy as for disclosure. The realist argues that it is underlying changes to the structure of state power and not shifts in values which give rise to changes in official secrecy. The realist is not a friend of secrecy, or proponent of greater secrecy, but neither is the realist opposed to it. The realist takes the view that secrecy is not a matter of conviction but of the balance of power between different forces within the political system. Changes in the degree of secrecy will only follow changes in the balance of power.

THE PHILOSOPHICAL APPROACH

Sissela Bok's book *Secrets* is an influential philosophical analysis of the concept of secrecy.[3] Bok defines secrecy as 'intentional concealment': that is, it involves the deliberate withholding, hiding, or concealment of information in order to prevent someone else from knowing, making use of, or revealing the information.[4] Bok also stresses her desire to avoid a definition that makes secrecy necessarily immoral or disreputable. She wishes to recognise that there may be 'good' secrets – the examples which she offers are 'the sacred' and 'personal' secrets – as well as 'bad'. The aim is a 'neutral definition of secrecy'.[5] However, although this is an admirable objective it remains to be seen whether ethical 'neutrality' is sustained throughout the analysis. Bok repeats her claim to neutrality in her discussion of the need for secrecy. She argues that secrecy is indispensable as a 'guard to intimacy', as protection for personal autonomy. The ability to hold back information can given the citizen some influence, some power, in conflicts with the state and it provides 'a safety valve for individuals in the midst of communal life'.[6] However, such 'good' secrets are all concerned with the preservation of the individual and tell us nothing about whether institutions can ever possess 'good' secrets. However, Bok does open up this possibility when she discusses the need for secrecy when making plans. She argues that the ability to envisage a future goal is a distinctively human, and fragile, capacity that requires the protection of some secrecy. She says that intentions which are transparent and predictable are more readily foiled and that

> Secrecy for plans is needed, not only to protect their formulation but also to develop them, perhaps to change them, at times to execute them, even to give them up. Secrecy guards projects that require creativity and prolonged work: the tentative and the fragile, unfinished tasks, probes and bargaining of all kinds. An elopement or peace initiative may be foiled if prematurely suspected; a symphony, a scientific experiment, or an invention falters if exposed too soon.[7]

The key point she emphasises is that with all these cases it is control over secrecy and openness which is crucial and not whether secrecy is inherently good or bad. The conclusion of this section on 'good' secrecy is that secrecy is fundamental to human needs; for maintaining a sense of identity, the ability to plan, to act, and for a sense of ownership. The main weakness of the argument so far is that the justification that secrecy is 'good' depends upon 'personal' secrecy that is closely akin to privacy. The balance of the argument is heavily biased towards the individual and away from the institutional or organisational needs for secrecy. This, as we shall see, reflects her view that secrecy is 'good' if it serves a moral purpose and 'bad' when it does not. A good secret is one that furthers a goal of which Bok approves, a bad secret is one which is used to protect a goal of which Bok does not approve. This is illustrated by her examples of good organisational secrets. She allows that secrecy may be important to organisational planning but her examples concern peace plans and treaties![8] A further criticism of her approach can be made because of the emphasis she places on the idea that the preservation of the integrity of the personality is 'good'. Such a notion is, as Foucault would argue, a construct that constraints as well as liberates. It implies that the assertion of the right to be an individual is one of the highest forms of liberation without recognising that it also isolates, weakens, and makes the self vulnerable. It is the very notion of the individual personality that allows manipulation, discipline and surveillance. She does recognise some negative effects of personal secrecy, in that it can shut off the individual from his or her fellow persons but her main argument concerns the harm that can be caused to others rather than to the individual *per se*. The only clear cut examples which she gives of harm to the person are that

1. secrecy can lead people to sustain false beliefs because they do not allow their beliefs to be challenged by others, and
2. secrecy can produce guilt because it prevents the individual from sharing their inner thoughts and thereby denies others the opportunity to place such thoughts into perspective.

However, we are given no criteria by which to judge when secrecy is likely to become pathological or 'excessive'.[9] That the love of secrecy, like the love of money, may become pathological is obviously a possibility but we are not given any basis to judge either our own or others' conduct to know when this line has been crossed. Bok admits that many people have seen all secrecy as bad because they believe that there is an 'absence of clear criteria for when secrecy is and is not injurious'.[10] In a sense personal secrecy merely adds to the guilt which the isolated, privatised, individual of modern culture may already feel about not being fully engaged with 'the other'. Bok is much happier when discussing the consequences of secrecy for others. Here there are 'objective', costs and benefits, consequences for identifiable groups of people. For example the school-bus driver who keeps secret the fact that his medical doctor has told him that he has a severe heart condition does not have a rightful claim to secrecy.[11] So far it is clear that Bok's main concern has been with the individual – with questions of personal secrecy. However, the important section of Bok's work for this volume is her discussion of 'collective practices of secrecy' or organisational secrecy.

The main thrust of Bok's analysis is that secrecy is particularly dangerous when those who employ it are holders of power for, in the absence of accountability and safeguards, secrecy makes such people even more powerful. The balance of the moral argument has dramatically switched so that what was seen as a mechanism of defence, *protecting* the integrity of the personality, is now a weapon of offence, associated with the aggrandisement of power. Bok struggles to find examples of 'good' secrecy in a collective context and, even when she does find one, it often depends upon personal privacy. One example refers to the confidentiality of medical records but such cases merely extend the duty of confidentiality from the individual to the collective; the individual voluntarily agrees to divulge personal secrets to the state and the state thereby takes on the duty to protect the right of the *individual* to keep his or her personal secrets, secret. One must conclude that were the state to obtain the information without consent then it would be under no obligation to keep such personal information confidential. Bok displays her true colours when she concludes that although there is a presumption in favour of the right to control personal information, the opposite is the case with collective secrecy:

> when those who exercise power claim control over secrecy and openness, it is up to them to show why giving them such control is necessary and what kind of safeguards they propose.[12]

One may ask – what has happened to the desire for neutrality? Why is it legitimate to make an a priori assumption that collective secrecy is less justifiable than individual secrecy or that secrecy necessarily leads to the abuse of power? Is the potential for the abuse of power, by misusing secrecy, greater in individual relationships than in organisations or are these matters of fact requiring evidence? If we are to apply a test of harm then we need to examine not merely the potential but the actuality: Is secret government worse than open? Is 'open' government worse than secret? Foucault encourages us to clash opposites which raises the possibility that, just as with the contrast between 'torture/imprisonment', 'open/democracy' may merely be another, perhaps even more effective, way of constraining subjects/citizens. But more of this later.

Bok's discussion of government secrecy is based upon three key premises:

1. Although individuals may have good reasons for keeping secrets, one cannot simply transfer such justifications to collective bodies or groups.
2. Although secrecy is neither good nor bad, there is a presumption against the legitimacy of collective secrecy, especially secrecy associated with the exercise of power.
3. The right to claim the protection of collective secrecy entails the duty to specify the mechanism of accountability and the particular set of circumstances in which secrecy is to be exercised.

Bok opens her discussion of 'Secrets of State'[13] with an analysis of the 'esoteric' tradition of state secrecy exemplified in the *arcana imperii*, the mysteries of state. Writers from the pre-modern era often sought to claim that running the state was no one's business but the rulers and those they selected to advise them. She argues that such a view is not entirely dead and lives on in concepts such as 'reason of state', the assertion of a general right, in certain circumstances, to act as the ruler sees fit. She further asserts that such a view can still sway, even overawe, the inhabitants of a state because of the rituals which governments use to surround themselves with an air of mystery. Pomp and pageant are not simply to impress the tourists but to separate, mark out, those who rule. Such rituals are designed to imply that rulers are 'different' and are therefore entitled to certain privileges, such as the right to keep secrets. However, Bok says, such rationales cannot survive once people become 'suspicious of secrecy and press for more open government'.[14] She does not seek to explain why people will become more suspicious or indeed, why they will inevitably demand more openness; such propositions are simply, it seems, a part of the 'modernisation' process. However, although Bok obviously believes that there are general grounds for suspicion of state secrecy, she does accept that smooth administration requires a degree of secrecy for deliberations, surprise (timing of events), and to maintain obligations to those who have supplied information to government on the understanding of confidentiality.[15] The problems arise, she says, in interpreting such principles in practice. This involves asking such questions as: who should be able to determine that secrecy is necessary? Under what circumstances should it be allowed and for how long?

These questions are best explored by looking at her arguments about particular issues. Bok has particular difficulties with the concept of military secrecy. She recognises that there are genuine problems of defence, war, and the need for self-preservation, and seeks to discover the 'proper limits' for such justifications.[16] She uses two quite different tactics. The first is to show that secrecy may not actually contribute to national security. This is to argue that secrecy is counter-productive and will not assist in achieving the 'agreed' requirements. The second is to argue that there are moral considerations that can never be set aside, so that even in times of 'national survival' one must ask the military to justify morally what they do. Secrecy should never be allowed to cover unethical conduct in the name of national security. Her conclusion is that only by having an open, public discussion of moral choices can a society avoid the 'burden of living with the results of clearly immoral or even questionable choices'.[17] However, when it comes to giving examples they are either those which few would find problematic, such as treating prisoners with decency, or they are highly contentious issues such as the morality of covert action.[18] There are few, if any, examples where the conduct is so obviously immoral that secrecy could never be justified as a protection for such conduct. Bok recognises the dilemma, that secrecy is necessary to protect military activities and yet secrecy can prevent discussion of the justifiability of such activities, but also realises that she can provide no formulae to resolve it. She can only appeal to the need for lively discussion and the questioning of all demands to protect information on the grounds of national security. However, one idea that is new and creative is a treaty to dismantle the 'secrecy race'.[19] Her proposal amounts to a recognition that, as with other types of 'weapons', secrecy will not be unilaterally abandoned since this would give other competing states too great an advantage. However, the problem with such treaties is verification. She does point out that satellites and other technological developments could provide the means by which such 'openness' treaties could be verified, but the idea is not developed beyond a couple of paragraphs of text. This is a pity, since the idea is worthy of further exploration.[20]

Bok comes to no hard and fast conclusions, and in her final chapter she acknowledges the complexity of the issues associated with secrecy. Given her initial premise that secrecy is not inherently wicked it is clear that each claim to secrecy must be examined on its merits. There is however, a major qualification to this in the case of governments; here the presumption is that secrecy is undesirable because of the danger of an alliance between power and secrecy. In the case of governments secrecy may be necessary but it should be kept to a minimum and constantly challenged. Only when governments are required to defend their claim to secrecy is this likely to happen. This is why democracies are less tolerant of secrecy – the people do not always need to know but they always need to know what is being kept secret and why.

THE POLITICAL APPROACH

British political scientists were relatively late in taking up the issue of open government. Indeed, there was little academic discussion of official secrecy until the beginning of the 1970s. There were journalists and political commentators who had written on specific cases and events but serious analysis of the issues was notably absent. The only academics[21] to have attempted such an analysis prior to the 1970s were Clive Parry,[22] who interestingly published in an American journal, and D. G. T. Williams, who published the justly famous volume, *Not in the Public Interest*.[23] This situation can be contrasted with the United States, where there exists a long tradition of academic interest in secrecy.[24] However, there is an understandable tendency for academics to become interested in a topic when reform is on the policy-makers' agenda. The Fulton Committee Report of 1968 and the Franks Committee Report[25] of 1972 laid the foundations for greater interest in the subject of official secrecy. The number of works by academics, journalists and interest groups has grown steadily from the 1970s to the present, reflecting a continuing, if usually unacknowledged, dialogue between commentators and policy-makers. However, this section is not designed to provide a catalogue of published works but to analyse approaches to the subject of official secrecy.

The first British political scientist to comment at length on the topic of government secrecy was Clive Parry.[26] However, his concern with official secrecy is coloured by the recent experience of the Second World War and by the cold war with the Soviet Union. He argues that all governments seek to keep certain matters secret but that:

> The whole western world has passed into an age when, for an unforeseeable long time, defence must be the supreme preoccupation of governments, when cold war may become hot war and when therefore every country must continuously have many of the features of an armed camp. If democracy is not to destroy itself in the process of ensuring its salvation, some technique other than that of non-information must be developed in order to ensure the continual democratic check upon executive arbitrariness and, what is perhaps more important, executive inefficiency.[27]

Parry recommends one aspect of British practice, 'the executive's taking of the legislature into its confidence very fully', on the grounds that a strength of the parliamentary system is the ability to meet in secret session. The main argument is that it provides an opportunity to air views, feelings, and anxieties without, as Sir Winston Churchill expressed it, the 'enemy reading what was said'.[28] The argument was not that a secret session enabled the government to divulge 'secret matters of fact' but that it gave an opportunity for the legislature to air its feelings without restraint. During the Second World War Parliament met in secret session some 65 times. However, Parry recognises that in constitutional terms this was a 'novelty' and that the Official Secrets Act (OSA) is of far greater consequence for British government. He rightly recognises the comprehensive nature of the 1911 OSA in that it covers all 'official' information and criminalises both the giver and receiver of unauthorised information. Although he comments that it would be 'easy to criticise [the] legislation as far reaching' he concludes by saying:

> Nevertheless, looking beyond trivialities, and even instances of injustice to individuals, it remains possible to commend the principle that the Official Secrets Acts are designed to protect – that official business is official and to be given publicity only in regular fashion.[29]

Parry concludes in a generally positive tone by arguing that Britain has succeeded, with the implication that other nations have not, in keeping the flow of information between the executive and the legislature relatively free because of the twin elements of secret session and official secrets legislation. For Parry, secrecy can help the flow of information because it can provide a protected framework within which relatively free discussion can take place. Of course, it must be conceded that his freedom of discussion is confined to an elite group, the executive and the legislature, and that their enjoyment of this privilege is at the expense of public ignorance. However, it is worth noting that Parry at least recognises the complexity of interest and institutions and examines the affect of secrecy upon their ability to exercise power and influence. This certainly contrasts with many later writers who would dismiss Parry's views as merely elitist and old-fashioned.[30]

Another early writer on this subject, D. G. T. Williams, argues that 'executive secrecy has been carried too far' in Britain, although he is careful to state that he is not disputing that there is a 'need in very many cases for executive secrecy'.[31] In the course of his book Williams identifies many of the institutions which encourage executive secrecy, including: the cold war, cabinet government, the need for a 'frank, speedy and efficient civil service', the role of the courts, and the concern with the loyalty of crown employees. However, he is concerned that the executive branch of British government is getting ever more powerful and that such factors are tending to hold back public ability to call the executive to account. He argues that the public are 'entitled in a democratic society to know a great deal of what is done by central government'.[32] Williams bases his criticism on a certain vision of democracy, one in which the public must be able to scrutinise the actions of government and be able to understand what governments have done and why. This is particularly so because of the expanding role and power of the modern state. The argument is a normative one but it is tinged with concern over the balance of power between legislature and executive, and between the citizen and the state. The basic principle behind his argument is that government *ought* to be open unless there are reasons otherwise. However, as we shall see, later writers find even this concern with institutional arrangements as being likely to place too much power in the hands of the executive. Any argument based on the idea that the executive requires a degree of secrecy is seen as dangerous, since the executive will exploit any and all such excuses to enhance secrecy.

It is not surprising that after the Franks Committee Report of 1972[33] there was increased interest in official secrecy.[34] What approach do such works adopt? The first post-Franks monograph on the subject of official secrecy was written by Ronald Wraith, then Senior Research Officer at the Royal Institute of Public Administration, and published in 1977.[35] Wraith argues that the 'British system is one which is no longer acceptable'. However, although Wraith clearly argues that secrecy and democracy are in conflict, he does attempt to move the debate forward by focusing on the impact of secrecy on routine administration and does not simply argue from principles. It is, he argues, the secrecy surrounding the countless acts of administration involving housing, education, social policy, and so on that is so damaging to Britain. This is a normative approach but the values are somewhat different from most other writers, as he does not focus on the macro level, the damage to 'democracy', but on the micro, the damage to individuals as 'clients' of the state. Such a strategy has the advantage of denying to the defender of secrecy any appeal to grand principles such as 'the national interest' or constitutional conventions. Secrecy must be judged from the bottom up and not the top down. This 'bottom-up' approach had, as we shall see, a certain appeal to the Conservative government of John Major.

During the 1970s and early 1980s several works were published that were highly critical of the British tradition of secrecy. Most of these were, at least in part, stimulated by debates over reform among pressure groups and political parties. The Liberal and Labour parties adopted freedom of information as a part of their official policies and two pressure groups, the Outer Circle Policy Group and the Freedom of Information Campaign, advocated major reform. All of these works basically take the same perspective, namely, that democracy requires public access to government information.[36] All such works also have two features in common: the rejection of the British tradition of secrecy; and the demand for US-style freedom of information legislation.[37]

One of the most prolific and influential British writers on secrecy issues is a Professor of Law, Patrick Birkinshaw.[38] Although much of his work is concerned with providing a valuable description of the whole range of secrecy and privacy legislation, in one of his more recent works he does provide a more general perspective. He makes two main points:

1. Freedom of information, despite the potential for abuse, works overseas and should not be denied to UK citizens. He states: 'Are we to believe that the British people are not mature enough to accept that responsibility?'[39]
2. Britain's obsession with official secrecy is characteristic of an outmoded concept of democracy: 'Section 2 OSA was a statement of imperial pride, social exclusiveness, the virtues of unquestioned tradition and culture and a resonant reinforcement of an antiquated *status quo*.'[40]

However, such arguments do not sit so well with some of the comments made in earlier works, where he states:

> Take away a government's preserve on information, and its preserve of when and what to release, then take away a fundamental bulwark of its power. This may be desirable or it may not. It is undeniable, however, that its impact is potentially profound.[41]

In this earlier work he follows the above by pointing to the dangers associated with such changes: the potential for the rise of new centres of power outside government such that government becomes 'all outside and no inside'. This could facilitate an acquisitive and inquisitive, even 'oppressive', society in which private bodies and the media could misuse access to damage the privacy of individuals. Birkinshaw would appear to have moved from a position that recognised the complexity of power and interests involved in government information to a purely normative position arguing about the character of the British people and leaders and the 'nature' of democracy. He gives no explanation of his conversion to the simple proposition that secrecy is wrong and freedom of information is good, but that a conversion has taken place seems clear. Perhaps one clue comes from the sense of disappointment that is evident in his analysis of the 1989 Official Secrets Act. He may have felt that if this was all that was to be granted then a more radical critique of the British tradition was justified. However, his earlier position is the one of substance. A sense of frustration may explain his shift to a more moralistic stance but it does not mean that power and interests have 'disappeared'.

Another critical work is that by John Baxter.[42] Although Baxter avoids explicitly stating a position on official secrecy, it is clear from his introduction that he is deeply worried by what he calls:

> the problem of keeping the vast structure of government under control, of making sure that those who affect our lives are in some way responsible, and ensuring that they do not take the opportunity to use the power at their disposal against those who, theoretically at least, have entrusted them with it.[43]

The values underlying his position are clear: the evils of abuse of power by government with its vast ability to collect, process, store and manipulate information contrasted with the virtues of representative democracy, government by the people, and the individual right to privacy. Nowhere in the introduction is any explanation, let alone 'defence', of official secrecy provided. It is only the 'rule of law', and rights such as 'privacy' and 'civil liberties', which offer protection against 'surveillance' 'domination' and abuse of power.[44]

Rosamund Thomas[45] and David Hooper[46] both published works that deal with cases brought under official secrets legislation. Hooper is a solicitor practising in London and his work, *Official Secrets*, does not pretend to be an academic study in that there is not a single source given for any statement made in the entire book. The message of the book is that there is 'too much secrecy in Britain' and that 'much may be learnt from other countries'.[47] Such statements place Hooper firmly in the 'normative' category.

Thomas's book covers much of the same ground, although it is aimed at a more scholarly market. The problem with *Espionage and Secrecy* is that it avoids all discussion of the general principles and merely concludes by stating that

> There is no easy answer to this dilemma (protecting national security and freedom of expression) and the attainment of such a balance. Many complex issues are involved ranging across the *criminal* law, the *civil* law, *international* and *constitutional* law, and the 'interests of the state,' to media ethics and national cultures.[48]

This list of 'factors' is already quite long but when Thomas goes on to refer to the added complication that 'European rulings and law' may 'diverge' from English tradition[49] the range and type of factors becomes so diverse and lengthy as to be almost unmanageable. To be useful an author needs not only to identify various factors but also to weigh and assess them. This Thomas declines to do. Although she avoids being readily classified as 'pro or anti secrecy', this is at the expense of clarity. Without some claims, hypotheses, views, one cannot agree or disagree with the author, and one cannot engage in any meaningful dialogue.

The final work specifically devoted to official secrecy is that by A. P. Tant. In his various writings on official secrecy Tant has engaged in a debate with those who have written on official secrecy in Britain and, in particular, with what he calls the 'Robertson Thesis'.[50] However, this is not the place to engage in a return debate with Tant. I shall focus on his views rather than what he has to say about mine.

Tant argues that official secrecy represents the 'elitist' tradition within the UK. What he means by this is that government is not accountable to the people, but only to the people's representatives.[51] Tant is not impressed with many of the arguments for freedom of information, since these are concerned with access to low politics, and not with access to high politics. By 'high politics' he means the major policy and strategic decisions which are taken at the highest level, the type of decisions which prime ministers and cabinet ministers believe win or lose elections. Freedom of information (that is, access to administrative documents after the decision has been taken) offers no threat to high politics and therefore there is little need to oppose such reforms in the UK, or anywhere else for that matter. The real issue, argues Tant, is not freedom of information but 'open government'. Open government means, to paraphrase US President Woodrow Wilson's famous phrase, 'open policies, openly arrived at'. Such a change would involve a participatory, rather than a consultative, democracy, in which the influence of the people could be brought to bear at all stages of decision-making.

However, the problem that Tant faces is to describe the nature of this 'participatory democracy'. It is all very well to identify certain general, abstract principles, but quite another to say how they would translate into mechanisms for granting and exercising power. Not only is the concept not operationalised, but we are not given any reference points by which to compare the model against current practice. The book is almost wholly concerned with the UK and, in particular, with the views of the British Labour Party, so that there is no comparison with any other democracy. Tant does not attempt to assess whether any democracy attains such an ideal or even whether any other system more closely approximates to his ideal. The UK is judged as elitist solely by reference to its own tradition and political failures and without comparison to any other democracy. This is a pity, since it is relatively easy to set up an ideal and then judge a nation as having failed to attain it.

It is also worrying that Tant sees 'Radicalism' and 'Socialism' as being two other ideals that have been 'undermined and sanitised' by the 'elitist nature of British government'.[52] Such an argument, that any reforming movement which fails does so because of 'elitism', appears dangerously close to being a tautology; such ideals fail because of elitism and the best evidence that Britain is elitist is that such ideals always fail. The only way of avoiding such a tautology is by comparative study but Tant does not carry out the systematic examination of whether other democracies are more open and whether this makes for greater accountability to the people. The United States and Sweden are both more open systems in the sense that there are institutional mechanisms for the discussion of policy before decisions are taken, but is there any evidence that either of those countries is thereby more 'democratic'? This obviously depends upon the meaning of democracy and there lies the rub. Tant's definition of democracy places the focus on participation but this is not the only way of conceptualising democracy. Raz argues that democracy is concerned with the quality of decisions (outcomes) and in this conceptualisation there is no *necessary* contradiction between secrecy and democracy. It is at least possible to ask whether secrecy is correlated with better or worse (however measured) decision-making. Here the comparison between Sweden (open), the United States (open) and Britain (secretive) seems less clear cut.

However, Tant is a radical who sees reform of secrecy as one significant measure that would reduce the elitist nature of British government. But as other writers (such as the early Birkinshaw) point out, all such reforms can have both costs and benefits. To argue that any one measure, even opening up decision-making, will make Britain 'democratic' is surely naïve. Such a reform would affect the balance of power but it might do so in surprising ways. Of course, it can also be argued that it is alterations in the balance of power that produce reforms of secrecy.

The last work to be considered focuses on the problems of 'secret intelligence' rather than on secrecy as such. Two academic lawyers, Ian Leigh and Lawrence Lustgarten, provide a comparative discussion of a wide range of issues associated with national security in the UK, Canada and Australia.[53] Their perspective is outlined in their opening chapter, where they argue for what they call a *democratic conception of national security*.[54] The meaning of this phrase is elaborated at some length but it rests upon the fundamental premise that there is a 'permanent and inescapable' tension between individual and state security,[55] since both the 'nation', particularly the democratic nation, and the individual require and deserve protection. The paradox, however, is that the 'state is simultaneously protector and threat to vital personal and political values'.[56] The paradox becomes particularly crucial, say Leigh and Lustgarten, as governments make the concept of national defence ever more elastic; national defence can become national security, which in turn can become national well-being, and finally, defence of the realm may end up being defence of party or narrow government interest. This 'slippage' from legitimate to non-legitimate meanings of defence poses a particular threat to individual liberty. It may lead to a reversal of the 'normal' such that legitimate opposition becomes illegitimate threat. A whole range of activities can then become marginalised by an ever-widening concept of national security. Their solution to this problem is to 'strip the concept (national security) down to its irreducible minimum'.[57] However, although this approach is based upon the ideal that reason can clearly identify such a minimum, one can question whether such attempts have ever succeeded in attaining consensus. To paraphrase from another definitional debate, that over terrorism, 'one man's national security is another man's lack of freedom'.

This review of works on aspects of official secrecy demonstrates that there is an overwhelming consensus, even if there are variations of emphasis, on three propositions:

1. secrecy is an evil that ought to be reduced;
2. governments ought to be made more accountable; and
3. the process of governing should be made more open.

All of the writers tend to operate within the liberal, normative tradition, in which democratic values provide the explanation of state secrecy. However, there is another important tradition, a more radical one, that emphasises the importance of power and challenges the 'rationalist' assumptions of many of the previous writers; the theory of the surveillance state. The following chapter explores this tradition.

3 Surveillance and Secrecy

As we saw in the last chapter, most philosophers and political scientists have taken a normative approach to official secrecy. The dominant argument has been that the values of a modern liberal democratic state require public access to government information, with secrecy being seen as a residue of a pre-modern, elitist and undemocratic culture. However, surveillance theorists have somewhat different attitudes to the secrecy 'problem', since their starting point is the work of Michel Foucault.

FOUCAULT

Foucault offers a fundamental challenge to the normal agenda for the discussion of government, secrecy, and power because he denies the liberating power of rationalism, humanism and liberalism. In Foucault's work 'modernity', 'progress', and 'humanism' have all produced new forms of subjugation, new forms of constraint on the self. All forms of power and truth give rise to forms of government that tend to ossify and harden categories so that the self becomes objectified. In so far as freedom comes from denying the rigidity of categories, the only liberating strategy is continual resistance to this process of objectification, the 'hardening of categories'. The obvious danger of this approach, that one cannot judge the ethical merits of different forms of government since there is no objective standpoint from which to make such judgements, has been commented upon by many writers. This means that the 'ordinary' critique of state surveillance found in liberal writings is of little interest to Foucault, because no amount of study can provide the 'truth' about how knowledge and power interact. Indeed, the very search for such 'objective' understanding gives rise to categorising people so as to count them, measure them, and punish them. To survey people, to place them under close scrutiny, is to subject them to the 'gaze' that objectifies and dehumanises the self. The social scientist, far from being a liberating force uncovering the misdeeds of the state, is in fact an essential partner of the state. The scientist legitimates the discourse of fact and knowledge upon which the authority of the modern state rests. This means that it is very dangerous to utilise Foucault as if his agenda was similar to other critics of bureaucracy such as Weber.[1] Weber is a product of the enlightenment tradition in which concepts such as freedom, ethics, vision, and the integrity of the individual are not only meaningful, but are the basis of the research agenda. Weber's antidote to bureaucracy, and its capacity to constrain, is a visionary leader mobilising support via a parliamentary political party. Foucault has no sympathy with such a remedy. It is only individuals, rejecting the attempt to place them in categories, who can seek to avoid constraint.

The reality is that Foucault's concept of surveillance has very little to do with our normal meaning of the term. As the English translator of Foucault's *Surveiller et Punir* readily admits, there is no 'adequate English equivalent' to the French word *surveiller*.[2] He recognises that the English words 'surveillance' and 'supervise' are too technical and restrictive and yet others such as 'inspect' or 'observe' are too neutral. The problems associated with the concept of surveillance are demonstrated by the diversity and richness of Foucault's characterisation of 'discipline':

1. Discipline requires enclosure, 'the specification of a place closed in upon itself', such as a workhouse, boarding school, military barracks, or factory.
2. Enclosure is not sufficient; the space must be partitioned so that each individual has his or her own place. This enables individuals to be located, supervised, assessed, and judged.
3. Spaces must be allocated to particular functions, allowing the distribution and partitioning of space in a rigorous manner: such as by task, as in a factory, or by disease, as in a hospital.
4. Within the enclosed space each individual occupies a position within the hierarchy, a rank. Schools are divided into upper and lower houses, prefects and non-prefects, pupils and teachers.[3]

In addition to spatial allocation and distribution discipline requires the regulation of activity. Here the elements are

1. the timetable, the precise allocation of activity in a temporal sequence;
2. establishing a rhythm to activity, not only when to march but also how to swing the arms, how large each step should be, how to hold the head and chest, and so on;
3. the co-ordination of bodily movements, the one with the other, when and how gestures are to be made;

4. defining how the body will use objects – for example, detailed rules on how to hold a rifle;
5. breaking down all movement into its smallest unit so that time and movement are used both economically and to their maximum.[4]

These ideas led Foucault to the conclusion that the 'perfect disciplinary apparatus would make it possible for a single gaze to see everything constantly (panopticism)'.[5] Backing up such a system, 'at its heart', is a penal mechanism, a kind of court with its own laws, offences, and forms of judgment. Such a 'court' is not only concerned with wilful acts of disobedience, but also with failures to achieve the required standard. However, the most perfect system of surveillance would have no need of punishment. Obedience is a product of the uncertainty over when you are being observed and when not. It is the belief that you may be under surveillance that freezes the soul and incapacitates the will. The beauty of such systems of surveillance is that they can be used by anyone and for whatever motive. The power does not belong to particular individuals, it is the power given to whomsoever is behind the screen, seeing without being seen. The power to deny invisibility leads people to internalise their own subjection so that there is no need for power to have 'any physical weight'.[6]

Despite the focus on surveillance and discipline Foucault devotes only relatively few paragraphs to 'policing'. He argues that the aim of policing is knowledge of 'everything that happens'. To make this concern with every 'particle of the social body' a reality, the police had to be 'given the instrument of permanent, exhaustive, omnipresent surveillance'.[7] The form of this instrument, says Foucault, was a system of magistrates, police officers, agents, and informers, with the aim being to move from the surveillance of 'settings', specific places or institutions, to a 'generalisable mechanism of panopticism'.[8]

However, in the case of policing, unlike the sections on punishment and prisons, he provides relatively little empirical material to support his analysis. There are only a few quotations from eighteenth-century French commentators and from Catherine the Great of Russia[9] but no examination of how, for example, the system of using informers changed from early modern to modern times.

There is no doubt of the impact and significance of Foucault, since all writers who address such issues make at least some reference to him.[10] However, the issue is how Foucault's ideas can help with the interpretation of official secrecy. It is obvious from the above account of his ideas that a great deal of what he has to say is only indirectly concerned with secrecy despite the emphasis on 'surveillance'. The question of whether and how one could provide a Foucauldian interpretation of secrecy must await an examination of other sociological approaches to surveillance.

GIDDENS

Anthony Giddens, in volume II of his *Critique of Historical Materialism: The Nation-State and Violence*,[11] argues that surveillance is a key feature of the development of the nation-state and its capacity to exercise domination. He believes that without the capacity to code and store information, which provides a resource to co-ordinate populations, the state could not exist.[12] He identifies two forms of surveillance, the 'accumulation of coded information' and the 'direct supervision of the activities of individuals'.[13] The former refers to the creation of a written record, in modern days taking an electronic form, and the storage of such information in records of all types; while the latter refers to the ability physically to observe other people which, of course, depends upon shared time and space. There are two other elements that need to be added to provide the basic Giddens model: locale and state. Locales provide the settings for interaction and include dwellings, cities, and even nation-states. Settings provide both a sense of the temporal sequencing of events and of the 'architecture' within which interaction takes place.[14] The state involves the monitoring of the 'reproduction of the social system' and the marshalling of authoritative resources, which particularly involves control of the means of violence, that is, administrative power.[15] These ideas are linked through Giddens' claim that

> Administrative power is based upon the regulation and co-ordination of human conduct through the manipulation of the settings in which it takes place. Surveillance as the coding of information is an essential element of such power.[16]

It would be too much of a digression to discuss all of Giddens' ideas on the emergence of the nation-state and 'modernity', but it is worth noting that one of the 'inventions' which most fascinates him is the timetable. The timetable is an expression of the ordering of life in 'regularised time-space settings'. It expresses the fact that organisations know who will be doing what and when.[17] The timetable is the result of the improved transport, communications (telegraph), and record-keeping (printing) of modern societies. Such innovations enormously enhance the surveillance capacity of the state and enable it to seek to regulate and bring under control much more of social life than could have been contemplated by earlier rulers. One aspect of such regulation is the 'policing of deviance' which is an expression of the nation-state's desire to monopolise the means of violence. This leads to the creation of specialist agencies directed at internal pacification. At the same time the idea of the autonomous individual, self-directed and self-reflexive, becomes established, which is the precondition for the idea of citizenship: 'for only if the individual is recognised as an autonomous agent does it become reasonable to regard that individual as politically responsible'.[18]

However, Giddens makes it clear that he does not believe that such rights simply evolve, or are granted by a beneficent state, rather they are the outcome of a sustained conflict. Indeed, he claims that surveillance is both enhanced by the granting of rights and that such rights give people a 'lever of struggle' which can used to counter efforts at control.[19] Because of such conflicts Giddens concludes that there exists a 'tendency' towards totalitarianism in the modern state.[20] He describes totalitarianism as involving an extreme form of surveillance which requires the population to possess identity cards, permits and papers; and that this, in turn, provides an expanded basis for the supervision of the population.[21] Although this is the first of his list of totalitarian characteristics, the importance of coercion and moral totalism are also recognised. Surveillance, however, does provide the fundamental basis for the deployment of the full apparatus of coercion against an unarmed or poorly armed population.

But, the question that needs to be addressed is: why is surveillance of such importance to the modern nation-state? Giddens answers this question in his final chapter. He argues that the capacity of the nation-state to penetrate the 'minutiae' of social life transforms the relationship between the ruled and the ruler. He argues: 'Surveillance is the necessary condition of the administrative power of states, whatever ends this power serves.'[22] Surveillance is both necessary to the provision of kinds of 'benefits' and yet the act of providing benefits generates ever more information. Without files there could be no welfare state and the welfare state in turn generates ever more information about the population. The management – control – function is a corollary of the paternalistic function of the modern sate. This is true whether it is the collection of information about industry to support regional grants or export licences or the provision of income support to the unemployed. The danger is that this linkage can be used to oppress the population by making the holding of the 'correct attitudes' a precondition for the receipt of benefits. It is also the case that by providing benefits, whether export licences or welfare payments, the state creates new forms of deviance. New 'crimes', such as fraud, are created by the system of benefits. This in turn creates pressure to create ever more elaborate systems of 'policing' to prevent such fraud. In other words, the capacity to survey the population is the condition for the democratic state with all of its willingness to allocate goods and services, and yet it is the allocation of such goods and services that generates incentives to increase surveillance. However, it is important to recognise that Giddens is aware that such tendencies give rise to opposition, either in the form of individual acts, 'crimes', or by generating social movements concerned with 'free speech and democracy' that seek to redress the balance. Such conflicts may actually threaten the 'governability' of society if people withdraw their co-operation and do not behave in the expected, required, manner.

DANDEKER

Christopher Dandeker is another writer who has been influenced by the writings of Weber and Foucault on bureaucracy and power.[23] His conceptualisation of surveillance is very similar to Giddens in that he describes it as consisting of three activities:

1. the collection and storage of information;
2. supervision by instruction or by the physical design of the natural or built environment; and
3. the monitoring of those under supervision in order to enforce compliance.[24]

However, although Dandeker very much follows Giddens in his conceptualising of surveillance, his aim is narrower in that he is attempting to use such ideas to help the understanding of specific institutions: the armed forces, police and business enterprises.

Dandeker states his aim as being to 'analyse the development of bureaucratic surveillance systems' and to show 'how these organisations expanded their surveillance functions'.[25] He goes on to claim that such surveillance systems give rulers the capacity to administer 'subject' populations and to 'will the future': that is, to identify trends and to take action to influence such trends. Dandeker identifies one of the crucial issues as being that the growth in control functions, the capacity of the state to penetrate society, does not mean a corresponding growth in the states' ability to use such capacity in the interests of the majority. He argues that in the modern world there are two main forms of bureaucratic surveillance: the rational-legal public bureaucracy, in which the subject population has the 'means of ensuring the accountability of bureaucracy';[26] and bureaucratic dictatorship, a system in which the bureaucracy need only fear the wrath of the ruler. Such capacity has enabled the modern nation-state to manage its eternal relations and to police (pacify) its subject population.[27] Such ideas, Dandeker hopes, will allow him to explore how 'police organisations were constructed' in the modern state.[28]

The question then arises of how Dandeker applies such models. Although he has a great deal to say about the military and business, it is his ideas on policing which are most relevant. The main conclusions which he draws are that the police have become more centralised, more national/regional in character rather than local, more subject to internal management and control, and more concerned with detection than with prevention. He concludes that current policing

> relies less on voluntary contributions from the public and more on the police's own autonomous investigate skills based on an infrastructure of administrative penetration of society and linked mechanisms for the collection, storage and processing of criminal records and intelligence data.[29]

He calls such policing 'pre-emptive', although he does not elaborate on what he means by this. He seems to imply that the police take action on the basis of their increased capacity to collect and store information to 'detect crime and react quickly to incidents' rather than to prevent crime by working with the community. But even such action depends upon receiving a complaint from a member of the public that would still seem to place 'the voluntary provision of information' at the core of the whole process. However, although one may agree with Dandeker that policing has changed, and in the direction he indicates, this still leaves open the question of the degree and significance of change. Dandeker appears to assume that the changes have been profound but such a conclusion requires more empirical support than he provides in his text. The claim is more about tendencies and possibilities than established fact. This raises the interesting question – why do Giddens and Dandeker find the notion that modern society is characterised by increasing surveillance so appealing?

Their fundamental thesis is that modern society is one in which surveillance is increasing and that information collection and storage are dominant characteristics of modernity. In order to examine this thesis we must be able to express the claim in a way that allows it to be challenged. There are problems in doing this, given that the argument is phrased in a very general way and given the lack of detailed empirical focus in the studies. Although both Dandeker and Giddens have many empirical examples, both historical and contemporary, their common approach is to announce a broad thesis that is then illustrated by a range of examples. Dandeker is less open to this criticism than Giddens but even Dandeker, as we saw with the example of policing, is happy to use illustrations from a variety of areas of social life. In addition, the testing of the claim is made difficult because of the uncertainty over the meaning of the concept of 'surveillance'. The ordinary usage of this concept implies negative moral connotations and a repressive system of control. It implies a highly active process in which those in authority place others under scrutiny such that virtually all activity is monitored. Giddens means no such thing when he uses the word 'surveillance'. On the other hand, the everyday meaning of 'collecting and storing' information has no particular moral connotation and would not necessarily be seen as oppressive. To use a concept with strong repressive and moral connotations to describe routine administrative practices certainly requires justification, and yet no such justification is offered. Rather, Giddens simply chooses to define away the everyday meaning of the concept of surveillance by giving it his own rather neutral and technical meaning. Why then are sociologists so attracted by this terminology?

There is no doubt that both Dandeker and Giddens are pointing to something real in contemporary society. People expect to be treated fairly and, as Weber demonstrated, this requires the bureaucratisation of social life. It is only through rational legal routines – through rules, files, and records – that fairness and equality can be guaranteed and yet this process also challenges our sense of individuality. We fear that 'red tape' means an ever-greater loss of autonomy, privacy and individuality. The individualistic nature of modern society means that people expect individual and fair treatment but the mechanisms necessary to achieve such a goal risk destroying that very sense of individuality. The expansion of record-keeping is a consequence of the growth of the welfare, interventionist, state. However, if the expansion of record-keeping is not the result of some strange desire on the part of bureaucrats to collect ever more records, for ever greater intrusion into people's lives, then why should we call it 'surveillance'? The normal usage of the term certainly implies an intention to place people under close scrutiny as part of a system of control, but this is not what either Giddens or Dandeker really wish to imply.

In my opinion most people would not see the collection and storage of data as being morally repugnant if the data collection is seen as functional, serving a purpose of which they approve, and as long as the use of the data was limited to that approved purpose. Most of the anxieties associated with data collection and storage tend to focus on privacy, the concern that people have to control access to their personal secrets. But this is an aspect which both Giddens and Dandeker ignore. To focus on privacy would shift the whole frame of their analysis away from the collector, the state and its agents, to the object of collection, the individual and his or her sense of self. It would shift the debate from the macro to the micro level examining when people express fears about the collection and storage of information and away from their focus on capacity, the ability of organised groups, particularly the state, to gather data. It would also require an examination of the process of resistance to the surveillance state and the very extensive social and political movements that have campaigned on behalf of the individual to assert their rights and liberties. The danger is that the picture which sociologists have painted is partial and biased because it assumes that the process of surveillance does not generate an equally important process of resistance.

What would a Foucauldian analysis of this issue look like? The answer must surely lie not in the formal bureaucratic rules and rationality of the Weberian tradition, with its emphasis on power and interests, but with an analysis of how secrecy is a part of the *natural discipline* of contemporary democracy. Such an analysis would show how contemporary liberal democracy creates the setting within which secrecy is normal. The fact that bureaucracy both demands information from, and denies information to, its clients creates a taken-for-granted expectation that information control is an integral part of the mechanism by which benefits and services are obtained. It is the internalisation of the role of 'client' which gives bureaucracy the 'right' to keep secrets. The system of queuing, form-filling, waiting in outer officers, partitions, glass divisions, desks, computer terminals turned away from the client, files which – even if opened – are impossible to read because to the client they are upside down, all make for a setting in which secrecy is normal. From this perspective the study of secrecy would require detailed studies of the way in which micro processes created a setting within which secrecy could flourish. This would be a very different type of study from any previously undertaken.

Given this agenda, it may seem surprising that Foucault has been so influential, as he has not been used by students of surveillance to carry out such an exercise. It is perhaps ironic that it has been the large-scale concepts of modernity and capitalism that have been used to construct the history of modern surveillance. But this is to take a broad brush to undercover small particles. A Foucauldian analysis would not only identify how the setting of administration had changed, but would also look at how it had stimulated different types of resistance. Foucault is fascinated by the criminal, mad person and 'deviant' as a form of rebel against modernity and discipline. It would be interesting to look at the number of people who fill in forms incorrectly and otherwise engage in a form of sabotage against bureaucratic discipline. A recent report in *The Times* indicated that as many as one-quarter of all university application forms were incorrectly completed, with applicants leaving off, for example: the date, course code, their references, and their home address.[30] Such discussion brings us to the final writer to be considered here, David Lyon, who not only writes about surveillance but also resistance to surveillance, or what he calls 'counter-surveillance'.

LYON

David Lyon sets himself the important task of 'softening the scaremongering alarms about surveillance society' through recognising that the processes that seem to constrain us can also enable us to participate.[31] He gives the example of the National (Social) Insurance number which enables people to receive unemployment benefits, although it also, he claims, enables people to be 'tracked'; he does not specify, however, by whom, how, or for what purpose. This opening may be seen as mere 'passing remarks' but, on another reading, it could be argued that the 'benefit' of surveillance is given a recognisable face while the 'tracking' function is left unspecified and mysterious. This can be seen as a very minimal softening of scaremongering! Although producing a 'balance sheet' of costs and benefits can be seen as a softening of the concept of the 'surveillance society', the fact that only the benefits are clarified while the costs are left dark and hidden could, on some readings, be seen as a classic scaremongering technique. The real question, of course, is whether this opening sentence sets the tone for the book. Lyon defines the 'surveillance society as being the collection, storing, retrieving and processing of precise details of our personal lives in government and private computer databases'.[32]

He goes on to describe this process as being 'not exactly spying' but merely the information traces that result from 'mundane, ordinary, and taken-for-granted activities' such as banking, driving a car and applying for state benefits.[33] This system of bureaucratic information processing is, he says, not unambiguously good or bad. However, people are anxious because much of the information is stored in unknown places and without their knowledge. Lyon recognises that the concerns associated with surveillance go far beyond traditional concerns with privacy, 'Big Brother', and democracy. He refers to the work of Mark Poster, who asks the question: 'if the world acts upon the information contained in electronic databases then what becomes of the real self, the image we have of ourselves in the everyday world?'[34] The world acts on the 'bits' of information it possess and is totally disinterested in our self-images and concerns. Poster goes on to argue that the postmodern world is a world of 'knowledge' in which the 'eternal' truths of science, democracy and technology have collapsed, leaving us with an ambivalent attitude towards knowledge systems. Such knowledge can come to constitute both the problem and the solution in that science and technology both empower the individual, giving control over the natural world, but also become the problem in that the we lose any sense of personal identity and sense of being in control of our lives. We control nature but not any part of our personal world. However, Lyon rightly poses the question of whether the problems posed by the 'new' surveillance and technology really are new or whether they are merely an extension of the traditional problems of bureaucracy, power, and information control?[35] His answer is that the problems are new. He argues that technology has altered people's control of information about themselves and that this change in their ability to determine what is disclosed and to whom is 'highly significant'.[36]

Throughout his work Lyon is careful continually to point out the two faces of surveillance: 'it may be viewed either from the perspective of social control or from that of social participation'.[37] These two faces reflect the fact that modern forms of organisation, ranging from the factory to representative government, could not function without records and the means for storing and accessing the data they contain. The enhanced means of communication and information processing are vital to enable people to participate as consumers, voters, workers, trade unionists, and any of the other roles that arise from membership of large modern organisations. On the other hand, records also create new forms of discipline which mean that the deviant, disobedient, or those merely under-performing, can be identified. So great is the surveillance capacity, or our fear of that capacity, that we internalise organisational norms and expectations; rules are accepted and become taken for granted.[38] However, Lyon points out that this fear of surveillance also gives rise to resistance. This does not refer only to protests against surveillance organised by various civil liberties groups, but also to what Lyon calls 'counter-surveillance'; that is, using technology to inhibit the technology itself. This can involve placing security measures against the misuse of data or using the technology of record-keeping to require data-users to register and be monitored. One disappointing aspect of his discussion of 'counter-surveillance' is the absence of what I would call 'everyday forms of resistance' such as refusing to register or fill in forms correctly, using cash instead of credit cards, using a false identity when communicating on the electronic network, and 'ticking the box' which enables you to restrict distribution of marketing data from one firm to another. It is also possible to 'escape' from surveillance by refusing to participate, although this obviously has costs in that one risks denying oneself access to the goods and services on offer or paying more for such services. But this is the other face of the Janus of modern society. It would be interesting to carry out research into both the forms and extent of what I have called 'everyday resistance'.

One other seemingly important form of resistance is to try to maintain personal secrecy, an aspect of privacy. Lyon makes the often-made point about the complex and elusive nature of the concept of privacy but there is no doubt that contemporary notions of 'privacy' have their roots in the process of individuation. Notions of personhood and individuality exist only as a part of social relationships and so privacy is a socially constructed phenomenon. We can only understand the meaning of privacy if we know the social context within which it is being asserted, the relationships of power and dependency, wealth and poverty, knowledge and ignorance, within which the 'right' to privacy is being claimed or denied. However, Lyon claims that there is a generally accepted tendency in modern society for people to 'retreat' to the private household as a part of their strategy for coping with the stresses and strains of life; Lyon informs us that in some quarters this is called 'cocooning'.[39] The relevance of this part of Lyon's work is his attack on the notion that personal secrecy is a solution to the surveillance society. Lyon is unconvinced by the argument that state secrecy can be countered by personal secrecy.

However, let us be clear about the debate. As far back as the work of Edward Shils, *The Torment of Secrecy*, social commentators have argued that there is a relationship between the public and the private, and secrecy and openness. Totalitarianism, says Friedrich, is characterised by that which should be private, information about individuals, being open; and that which should be open, government information, being secret. Democracy is characterised, at least ideally, by personal privacy and open government.[40]

Lyon sees such approaches as part of a 'liberal' tradition in which notions of privacy are intimately tied to property rights, the market-place, and utilitarian philosophy. He is sceptical of the argument that the market-place should determine the flow of data, through giving people 'rights' over their own data so that companies or governments could be fined or sued if they misuse such data. He rightly points out that such an approach leaves intact the inequalities of power which would mean that the poorest would be least able to defend their rights to personal information. The market/property solution, with its inequalities and defects, obviously needs to be compared with alternative solutions. To adopt a solution which 'ignores' inequalities of wealth and power by arguing for a normative solution to these issues creates its own difficulties. However, Lyon recognises that the 'traditional' solution to such problems, a normative order of 'trust' within which social interaction and communication takes place, is irrelevant to an entirely mechanical process by which machines transmit data without regard to such social niceties. Machines neither 'gossip' nor accept information on conditions of 'trust'.

However, Lyon is reluctant to abandon a normative solution, particularly given his position, as stated in his preface, that his 'own route through these troubled waters is guided by converging traditions of Christian social thought'.[41] His solution to these problems is to utilise notions such as human dignity and freedom as the basis for constructing a normative order to regulate surveillance.[42] Lyon argues that most of the commentary on surveillance has been aimed at avoiding dystopia, a nightmare world, rather than attempting to provide a vision of what the world could be like, a positive vision of the future. To start from the negative is, for Lyon, to start at the wrong place. We should begin by trying to articulate the world in which we would like to live and then see how technology can contribute to that vision. His aim is to construct a normative order based upon a positive vision of the future.

Lyon offers three key ingredients: participation, personhood, and purpose.[43] Participation as a value would be enshrined in making computer networks 'common carriers', public utilities, and by requiring such public utilities to ensure fairness, to act in the best interests of data-subjects. Personhood is to be enshrined by requiring data-holders to be 'caring and protective'. They should be required to include more than just information that concerns them but also information that we wish to include. It might be information about why we are applying for a loan or why we are temporarily unemployed. Purpose refers to the need constantly to question whether we are happy with the purpose behind the construction of a particular data bank or surveillance system. We should take responsibility for such matters and not simply allow the market or bureaucratic interests to determine what is permissible. We have placed restrictions on genetic experimentation on the grounds that what is possible is not necessarily desirable and we should do the same thing with information technology.

It hardly needs to be said at this stage that this normative approach to the problem is not persuasive to me. If norms are appealed to because they are capable of inhibiting the powerful, then two questions arise: why should either governments or corporations, both obvious power-holders, support such measures and why will they abide by them? It may be credible to suggest that norms can regulate the private sector, since one can envisage socialist political parties seeing such recommendations as a part of a tradition of regulation. One is tempted to argue that there may be those who wish to bring the means of collection, distribution and exchange under common ownership. However, nationalisation seems out of fashion, even among left-wing political parties, and such measures would greatly increase the cost and complexity of governing. I am also sceptical of whether including 'nice things' about us would really reduce people's fears about the impact of this technology. Finally, I am sceptical that imposing limits on such a basic and fundamental technology would work. Limits on genetic manipulation, particularly on human genes, is somewhat less radical than attempting to limit the spread of television monitoring of public and private spaces and the electronic processing of data. There are of course, already existing limits imposed by data protection legislation in many countries, but Lyon is not explicit or clear about what further limits he would wish to see. The argument that whatever those limits may be they should be vigorously debated is unexceptional, but without some fairly concrete suggestions from Lyon as to the nature and scope of these limits debate is likely to slip back into well-worn and predictable paths.

CONCLUSION

The concept of the 'surveillance state' challenges the idea that democracy provides a basis for protecting the citizen against the 'secret state'. Many of the problems of privacy, civil rights, and access to information are seen as symptoms of a 'greedy state' that cannot be challenged by such traditional methods. The contemporary state is information hungry and 'reform' has more to do with managing information than with preserving or enhancing freedom. This is a much more pessimistic view than that taken by most political scientists or legal scholars. However, I shall argue that although the emphasis on power is the correct basis for analysis, much of the sociological writing on surveillance creates a false picture of an overly centralised, bureaucratic and uniform state. The imagery of surveillance risks creating a picture of sinister forces manipulating citizens for some often vague, and unspecified, purpose. Although governments seek to protect, and even enhance, their power, it is not to achieve hegemony or dominance: it is because they live and work in an environment of competing interests. It is the fragmented and diverse nature of the interests in democratic states that give rise to anxieties about power. However, there is one interest that contemporary democratic politicians are less afraid of than their predecessors: the power of officials. This, as we shall see, is a crucial development in understanding secrecy.

4 The End of Whitehall? Reform of the British Civil Service

INTRODUCTION

The question 'has the British system of government, particularly its system of public administration, undergone a revolution?' is one of the most hotly debated issues in British political studies. This is because the organisation of government – the roles of Parliament, ministers and civil servants – is crucial to understanding the 'reality' of democracy. It is also central to the somewhat lengthier debate over 'modernising Britain' which has once again taken on a constitutional focus with the debates over devolution, reform of Parliament, a Bill of Rights, and proportional representation. The lack of a 'modern' constitution has led some critics to argue that Britain has 'fallen behind', although the exact nature and significance of such comparisons is often left unspecified. The monarchy, courts, Parliament, and civil service, have been variously criticised for being antiquated and unable to provide the quality of decision-making that a modern nation requires. This is certainly not a new issue in Britain. It is a discussion with a very long history that seems able to re-invent itself by shifting emphasis and by targeting different institutions. However, such shifts seem to reflect the latest 'scandal' more than any coherent or ideologically driven agenda.

However, it is clear that in the 1980s the Thatcher Government saw the British civil service as an obstacle to national prosperity rather than as an asset. It therefore determined to shake up the civil service so as to 'liberate' the nation from the shackles of bureaucracy. For some writers the Thatcher and Major eras virtually transformed the way we are governed.[1] However, for others, the changes in the civil service are marginal and cosmetic, a part of the Thatcher rhetoric of change but with little real substance.

What is perhaps more interesting is that virtually all writers agree that the basic direction of change seems likely to continue irrespective of the party in power. If the test of significance is not only the degree of change but also its irreversibility, then a revolution has indeed occurred. This then raises the interesting question of whether the reasons for this change go far beyond the anti-spending, anti-waste, and anti-bureaucratic views of a particular prime minister. This would be especially so if we found that there were signs of similar change elsewhere. To talk of a global phenomenon, a 'crisis of governance', is a bold step but there *may* be some common factors affecting public administration, the role of government, and the movement for greater openness, that are worth discussing.

There is no argument that 'the British constitution' has been changing, although there is considerable debate, as we shall see, over whether the changes are 'revolutionary' in nature. The impact of the reforms under a series of Conservative governments between 1979 and 1997 is still under evaluation, but all authors acknowledge that the British civil service has changed. For example, Geoffrey Fry, who had been 'dismissive' of earlier reforms, sees Next Steps as potentially a 'counter-revolution' that threatens to produce the 'break-up of the civil service'.[2] Other writers use similarly dramatic terminology to describe the effect – 'the hollowing out of the state'; 'an organisational hybrid'; 'federalised civil service'; 'fragmentation'; and 'decentralisation'.[3] A further impression of the range of views on the reforms can be found in the quotations below:

> In the Next Steps initiative, we have the germ of the possibility for real and radical change in the civil service. Yet the initiative's potential is already being dulled and routinised.[4]

> The speed at which the civil service has been reformed has been remarkable. With the exception of wartime, never has the civil service changed so rapidly.[5]

> The reformers may be disgruntled at the lack of academic enthusiasm for their activities, but there is a limit to the number of times that we can be told that the existing washing powder washes whiter, even whiter, ever more whiter.[6]

A useful summary of this 'revolution' is provided in the monograph by Campbell and Wilson, *The End of Whitehall*.[7] This work, like the earlier 'classic' on the Treasury by Heclo and Wildavsky,[8] is by two American academics who conducted a series of interviews with civil servants and politicians.[9] Campbell and Wilson identify several important elements of the 'Whitehall model' that they believe are undergoing transformation. These are:

- the monopoly of the civil service on advising ministers has been broken;
- there is machinery in place at the centre of Whitehall, in the prime minister's office, where civil service advice can be contested;
- civil servants may be less inclined to 'speak truth unto power' as advancement has become dependent upon being people that politicians 'can work with';
- the civil service is less isolated from the outside world in terms of both its appointments and its contacts;
- politicians have changed their character, in that many more are likely to be career politicians; and
- the Next Steps programme, and other earlier reforms, raises major problems of delegation and accountability, discretion and control.[10]

However, it is important to recognise that reform of the civil service is not a new issue. Apart from the early reforms of the 1870s and 1920s designed to create a professional, career bureaucracy staffed with experts,[11] there has been, since the 1950s, an on-going debate over whether Britain has the kind of constitution necessary to a modern state. There were several influential works – Andrew Shonfield's *Modern Capitalism* (1965), E. M. Nicholson's *The System* (1967), Hugh Thomas's *Crisis in the Civil Service* (1968), and Lord Fulton's Report on *The Civil Service* (1968) – all of which concluded that the system of government, including the organisation of the civil service, was inadequate for a modern and competitive Britain.[12] The emphasis in these works was on creating a more 'rational' way of making decisions by improving the quality of civil service recruitment, training, management, and expertise. The idea that generalists trained in the Classics at one of the 'elite' universities best ran the civil service was seen as archaic and damaging to Britain's performance at home and abroad. The attack was directed against an amateurish, class-ridden system that was to be replaced by a more technocratic and meritocratic system. However, despite both Government and Opposition acceptance of the Fulton Committee recommendations, changes were introduced in a piecemeal fashion and the impact was limited.[13] Although a new unified pay and grading structure was designed to create more opportunities for specialists, the top positions continued to be dominated by generalists. A new grade, the Administration Trainee, was also introduced to try to reduce the dominance of Oxbridge graduates, but this too had only a limited impact.

However, there is one interesting aspect of the Fulton Report, which re-emerges later, and that is its admiration of the Swedish model of public administration. The Fulton Committee recommended 'hiving off a wide variety of activities' to administrative boards, a form of administration characteristic of a pre-democratic, nineteenth-century Britain – and of Sweden.[14] But although some experiments of this type were carried out (Harold Wilson privatised office cleaning) they were limited in nature.

It was not until the Thatcher era, post-1979, that a new effort was made at fundamental civil service reform. There are several reasons why the Conservative government of 1979 saw reform of the civil service as a priority, the main one being the anti-'big government' ideology which had come to dominate Conservative Party thinking.[15] State intervention, public spending, Keynesian economics and government regulation were policies that were seen as having failed. The emphasis was on releasing individuals from constraint, on liberating the spirit of enterprise, and this required getting government 'off the backs of people'. Such attitudes were obviously less inclined to see the means by which government was delivered, the civil service, as being a part of a circle of virtue and rather more inclined to see it as an object of suspicion, as a potential obstacle to the process of 'liberation'. Another factor influencing Mrs Thatcher was a number of books by former civil servants and Labour ministers which tended to show the civil service in a less than flattering light.[16]

Finally, there is the influence of 'public choice' theory, associated with writers such as Niskanen, which argues that bureaucrats are not disinterested servants but interested parties committed to budget-maximising.[17] As Fry argues, 'Mrs. Thatcher closely associated the "gentleman in Whitehall" with the prolonged experiment in democratic socialism which had been "a miserable failure in every respect".'[18] Given Mrs Thatcher's self-image, that of a radical committed to shattering the postwar consensus, it is hardly surprising that she anticipated resistance from the higher reaches of the civil service, which was seen as having been one of the more important means by which this consensus had been constructed and implemented. Given the initial economic concerns of the 1979 Conservative government, particularly on reducing the level of public expenditure, it was anticipated that this would bring it into conflict with civil servants, who were seen as committed to preserving their job prospects by maintaining high levels of government expenditure. In addition to the desire to cut overall levels of expenditure there was also the expectation that major savings could be achieved by cutting out waste and by finding more cost-effective ways of doing things. Such policies would be bound to lead to a cut in civil service numbers.[19]

However, one can also argue that the reforms were not the product of a particular party ideology, or even the personality of a particular prime minister, Mrs Thatcher. As we saw, debates over delegation and centralisation, and over a specialist or generalist civil service, certainly go as far back as the Fulton Committee Report of 1968.[20] Although there were general factors influencing the reform process, including a sense of hostility to 'big government' and statist policies of virtually any kind, equally important was the accumulative process of change which has its roots both before and after the Fulton debates. Radicalism was as much a result of a sense of frustration that all previous efforts to create a more responsive, efficient and effective civil service had not worked, as of ideology.[21]

NEXT STEPS

The 'radical' reforms, resulting in Next Steps and contracting out, emerged from earlier efforts at reform, such as the 1980 Management Information System for Ministers (MINIS) and the 1982 Financial Management Initiative (FMI). Both of these initiatives were based upon a sense that departments had become so large, and spent so much money, that there was little effective understanding of what was going on in them, and that the mechanisms of controlling vast bureaucracies were outdated and inadequate. This was a sense that crossed the political party divide.[22] Of course the sense that public bureaucracies were not adequately under control was exacerbated by the perception that there was an inexorable rise in the cost of the public sector. This sense that costs were rising beyond what democracies could afford was again not confined to any one of the ideological poles; there were those on both the left and the right who predicted a 'fiscal crisis' for the democratic state. Also relevant to an understanding of the change in approach is the perceived contrast between the public and private sectors and the sophistication of their respective management theories and practices. No longer were the virtues of public duty, sophistication and general intelligence considered to be sufficient to manage a public bureaucracy. Again, this complaint echoes those expressed in the Fulton Committee Report but this merely reinforces the point that, although the changes were radical in aim, the problems being tackled were of long-standing concern.

The Thatcher government's first measure directly targeted at the civil service was the Scrutiny Programme. The Efficiency Unit was under the auspices of Sir Derek Rayner (now Lord Rayner), the former joint managing director of one of Britain's leading high-street retailers, Marks & Spencer.[23] The aims of the programme were ambitious: not only was Sir Derek to save money by reducing waste and inefficiency, he was also to change the management culture of Whitehall.[24] Although Rayner was head of the Efficiency Unit, he had no legal power to compel departments to produce papers or even to co-operate with the exercise, but the fact that the exercise was known to have the full and enthusiastic backing of the prime minister meant that the absence of such legal powers was no inhibition.

There is no doubt that savings were made and that some inefficiencies were eliminated by the unit.[25] However, all commentators argue that its impact on management was of even greater importance. Rayner's aim was to introduce 'best practice' from the private sector, which meant giving employees clear objectives and the responsibility for attaining them. However, he recognised that such reforms could not be 'imposed' and that people must have a sense of 'owning' the search for savings. He therefore required each department to select its own areas for investigation, to appoint its own team to carry out the investigation, and to report directly to the minister as well as to the unit. Rayner recognised that whether anything was done with the reports crucially depended upon the support of the relevant minister.

In 1980 there was one department, the Department of the Environment, which did have a minister who shared such attitudes, Michael Heseltine. He introduced the Management Information System for Ministers (MINIS) which was designed explicitly to introduce some of the 'best practice' from the private sector. The aim was to create a structure of responsibility in which the tasks, the objectives, were clearly defined and costed so that everyone would know who was doing what and why. Heseltine believed that people in departments often did not know the precise nature of their responsibilities and did not have a precise idea of their budget or their costs.[26] As well as drawing on business experience, Heseltine also acknowledges the help he received from Rayner in developing his scheme. However, other departments had 'few takers and absolutely no enthusiasm' for the scheme.[27]

The government response to this disinterest was to launch, in 1982, the Financial Management Initiative (FMI), the aims of which were very similar to those of Rayner and Heseltine: to set clear objectives and measure performance; to assign clear responsibility for assessing 'value for money'; and to provide the information necessary to the effective performance of responsibilities.[28] An important element of the system was the requirement that departments provide regular reports on their progress. By 1984 most had adopted some form of management information system, although, according to Fry, under different names to preserve their sense of self-respect.[29]

What effect did such measures have? One was improvement in productivity, even if it is hard to quantify these gains. However, the more significant aspect, because it encouraged further developments, was the creation of cost centres within departments that enabled the production of more accurate information on who was doing what and at what cost. Accurate information and clear lines of responsibility are crucial if one wishes to market test, hive off, or even privatise, elements of government administration. However, as Pyper concludes, 'FMI was something of a disappointment to the government'.[30] In part this was a problem of developing scales by which to measure performance, given that the government is often a monopoly supplier of unique, collective services. In addition many services are not located within a single department but straddle two or more, making it difficult to judge the effectiveness of one independently of the other. Such problems do not only affect the technical aspect of 'measurement' under FMI but the whole nature of what it means to talk of 'managing' public services.[31]

However, no one was convinced that the reforms had achieved their objectives; neither those in government nor those outside, such as academic commentators, believed that the reforms had 'modernised' the British state.[32] This provided an impetus to consider even more 'radical' measures.

The failure of attempts to increase efficiency through greater decentralisation and delegation failed for several reasons, one of the main reasons being the conflict between delegation and financial control. The Treasury rightly argued that delegation and decentralisation could lead to an increase in public spending as each section, agency, or department sought to develop its resources, activities and personnel.[33] Its response to this fear was to place ceilings on the resources allocated to each department. However, although this did limit the growth in spending, it also undermined departmental autonomy. 'Managers' found that they had relatively little flexibility to alter their department's activities, structure, or personnel, because of the tight rein imposed by the Treasury. Zifcak argues that although there were a number of experiments in delegating budgets, the main consequence of FMI was to enhance Treasury control.[34] The reason for this was that many of the main costs, such as the number of personnel, accommodation, and wages, remained fixed. Furthermore, departments were not allowed to carry over any savings to the next financial year. Managers found this particularly inhibiting; it provided little or no incentive to improve efficiency.[35]

There were also problems with the management information system, MINIS. This was a device imported from the private sector as a tool for strategic management so as to provide top managers with a way of assessing whether objectives were being met. However, although it did generate a great deal of information about departmental activities and did identify some waste – for example duplication of effort[36] – its usefulness was limited because of the nature of the 'top' managers: that is, ministers. Although ensuring 'value for money' has taken on increasing importance because of the worries over total public expenditure, ministers are still appointed by a prime minister who has won, and would no doubt like to continue to win, elections. A cabinet of efficient managers is no doubt a pleasant surprise to any prime minister, but if the actions and policies of ministers do not instil confidence in the public, do not make people 'feel good', then there is little point in having power. The task is to achieve results and to do so in a way that inspires confidence and enhances party popularity. If efficiency gets in the way of politics, then managerial virtues will be sacrificed. This is the hierarchy of values according to which a minister, and a government, survives or falls. However, it is important to note that this is what we, as the electorate, would wish. This hierarchy is not a result of some self-interested motive in 'survival' or remaining in office for its own sake because of self-esteem or love of ministerial perks. The rationale, the justification, of democracy is that ministers act in response to what we the nation, the people, or even the party, 'want'. The electorate is not much interested in politicians whose main virtue lies in being good housekeepers.

The problem, then, was that much of the effort at reform was undermined by more 'important' interests; that politicians act in ways that will secure the support of the electorate. This was reinforced by the government perception that the public priorities were to limit public expenditure and the overall tax burden.

The failure of the reforms led to the next major development, Next Steps. This programme gets its name from the title of a report published in 1988 by the Efficiency Unit.[37] The stated aim was nothing short of creating a 'different way of conducting government business'.[38]

The principle reform associated with Next Steps was the creation of a series of agencies. These were designed to give managers a far greater degree of autonomy than any of the previous reforms. Although they were to remain under the central policy-making umbrella of a department, they were no longer to be part of a unified, central hierarchy. Some authors, for example Fry, have argued that there are important continuities with the earlier recommendation of the Fulton Committee that public administration should be performed by a series of 'boards' rather than by the existing unified system of ministries.[39]

The basic assumption behind Next Steps is that one can separate policy functions from the delivery of services so that those involved in delivery can be progressively transferred to semi-autonomous agencies: the key phrase being 'semi-autonomous', since it is not suggested that the agencies will be independent boards. This was a step too far for the Treasury, which was worried that it would lose central financial control.

An agency is headed by a chief executive who is able to exercise a degree of discretion while operating under a plan agreed with the relevant ministry. The expectation, reinforced in a statement by the prime minister on the day of publication (18 February 1988), is that those working in agencies would continue to be civil servants. The other commitment was that the lines of responsibility, to ministers, the national Audit Office, and the Parliamentary Commissioner for Administration (the Ombudsman) would also continue to apply. Sir Peter Kemp, the project manager, estimated that 95 per cent of civil servants are involved in the delivery of services and his aim was to have three-quarters of all civil servants working in agencies. It is claimed that 67 per cent of staff now work in agencies, very close to the target figure.[40] However, before providing a more detailed analysis of some of the issues associated with the current changes, it is worth considering the last element of the packet of changes: market-testing. Although market-testing is not a new idea[41], the scale of change is considerable; Rhodes estimates that 50 per cent of the public sector has been privatised, along with 650 000 employees.[42] However, as Elizabeth Mellon points out, agencification and market-testing are not the same things. Although contracting for services can be part of the agreement between an agency and a department, it can often be no more than a formal accounting procedure rather than any real relationship of supplier and purchaser:[43] the reason for this being that agency heads actually have very limited autonomy. They cannot determine many of the key variables affecting whether or how a service is delivered. This is neatly summarised in the following quotation from an agency head: 'if "freedoms" are synonymous with "shackles", then I have them to the extent that prisoners can hobble in leg irons'.[44]

However, the pattern is not uniform. In some cases market-testing may mean no more than that one or two specific functions are subject to testing, with the existing employees not only being allowed to apply but encouraged to do so. In other cases, such as the National Health Service, the whole sector has been subject to competition and forced to accept 'the legitimacy of purchaser and client demands on their activities'.[45] Even in this case there are still many unanswered questions about what a market or quasi-market means. As Ferlie *et al.* point out, there may not be alternative suppliers and there may no way for unsuccessful producers to 'exit'.[46] Also competition may be as much about quality of service as it is about effectiveness or cost. Consumers may not feel able to judge the effectiveness of different acute surgical units but feel very competent to judge whether those delivering the service, from telephonists to doctors, are approachable and responsive. There is also the complication that even if some quantifiable improvement is detected after the introduction of market-testing, this may be a product of changes in management which actually have very little to do with the quasi-market. That is, the improvement could have been attained by adopting the new management techniques without pretending that a market existed. Furthermore, even where a contract has been agreed, an important aspect of which is an agreed budget, there remains the question of what happens if there is a shortfall or over-runs? Given that most in-house tenders from agencies have been successful and that most agencies have no commercial freedom, what is the meaning of the contract? As Harrison suggests,[47] it may be a way of changing culture rather than a means of increasing efficiency or achieving cost savings. It helps those involved to identify what they do and what it costs and to see themselves as suppliers with clients or customers but may have little impact on efficiency or performance. If there is only one agency supplying a service, then a department will still be obliged to enter a contract, however poorly the service is provided.

Talbot concludes that it is very difficult to evaluate the impact of Next Steps and market-testing because both are occurring at more or less the same time. The relationship between privatisation and the process of agencification is also far from clear. As Talbot shows, some have been privatised before the review process associated with agencification has been completed and others have been asked to consider privatisation after they have been made agencies.[48]

It is clear that although market-testing and 'hiving off' are potentially linked to decentralisation (Next Steps) there is no necessary relationship between them. Ideas such as contractual relationships between agencies and ministries, the identification of budgets and resources, and the setting of objectives, may help to create the conditions under which it is easier to identify possible targets for privatisation, but in most cases this will not be an option because of the nature of the service provided. Where the service impacts on the public, and the government is a monopoly supplier, then the need to deliver uniform, fair, and equal provision, creates strong disincentives against privatisation. The retention of some form of political input into administration is likely to outweigh any cost or efficiency benefits. Certainly many managers of agencies have commented that they enjoy little real discretion to alter any of the key variables that could change the way they perform their duties. However, in addition to these practical problems there are some fundamental debates associated with recent reform: the division between policy-making and policy execution; political neutrality; and accountability. These will be discussed in their order of importance to the present argument.

A NEW TYPE OF CIVIL SERVICE?

One of the great debates in the 1980s was over whether senior levels of the civil service were becoming politicised under Mrs Thatcher. Perhaps the strongest expression of this concern came from F. F. Ridley, who, in a series of articles, voiced disquiet that not only were appointments and promotions being affected by whether civil servants were 'one of us' but by the fact that commitment, even enthusiasm, was now being expected, if not required, from individual civil servants. It was the idea that civil servants had to be 'converts' which aroused Ridley to passion. He states:

> What we may end up with, I fear, is a system of loyal apparatchiks... Unless one practices saying 'no' while democracy is still alive, one is unlikely to say it at the last moment, when one's livelihood, if not one's life, is at stake.[49]

and again:

> Senior civil servants are increasingly called on to expand their minister's policies publicly... though they probably don't believe a word of it. What is more serious is the use made of senior civil servants to sell government policies, thus the government's political standing and (it hopes) its electoral chances.[50]

Some may find the passion of the language refreshing but few would share Ridley's conviction that Mrs Thatcher changed the rules as radically or as fundamentally as he implies. It is surely obvious that all ministers would prefer civil servants to express some conviction in their work, for conviction is linked to motivation and motivation to performance. It would be a very strange organisation in which it was not. As Theakston argues, when discussing the Labour Party's experience in office:

> Analyses that focus on adversarial relations between ministers and civil servants... oversimplify and distort. Relations are complex and fluid, and the lines of division are more often to be found not between the political and bureaucratic elements in government but *within* them, as alliances of ministers *and* officials compete with each other to advance particular goals or defend common interests.[51] (Author's emphasis)

However, the problems arise when ministers appear to expect civil servants to carry out actions designed to further the short-term political advantage of the government. It is clear from the Scott Inquiry that civil servants were expected to provide answers to parliamentary questions that were less than forthcoming.[52] Civil servants interviewed by Campbell and Wilson[53] complained that ministers were not interested in advice – unless it confirmed their chosen policy! However, many of these problems are not new. Civil servants have been expected to provide misleading answers to parliamentary questions by every modern government.[54] The convention has always been that ministers need not provide more information than they judge politically necessary and civil servants have been expected to operate within that convention. When authors talk of civil servants being expected to collaborate in the misleading of Parliament it often means no more than that civil servants are being expected to uphold the long-established practice of not saying more than is necessary, of providing the minimum of information rather than the complete story. Either all governments are guilty or none are.

Fry also comments that neutrality, carrying out policies with equal professionalism for any party and for any government policy, is linked to the self-interest of civil servants. Some programmes and policies pose a much greater threat to their interests than do others. Governments that view the civil service as a symptom of 'big government' and wish to reduce numbers and privileges are likely to arouse opposition. Radical governments, of whatever political persuasion, are much more likely to 'fear' opposition from the civil service and will wish to see evidence that those entrusted with implementing policies are actually doing so. It was not so long ago, under Labour prime minister Harold Wilson, that cabinet ministers were writing about 'obstruction' from the civil service.[55] Although fears of politicisation were certainly common during Mrs Thatcher's period of office, there is little evidence that the structure of relationship between government and civil servants had substantially changed. As Pyper argues, the evidence points to a Thatcher bias in favour of personalities rather than because of any shared party political views.[56]

There are also more fundamental arguments for scepticism. Commentators are perfectly free to express their dislike of Thatcher's policies but they cannot expect civil servants to act as some kind of internal opposition to those policies. They have neither the legitimacy nor authority for such a role.

The second area of controversy surrounds the supposed division between policy-making and policy implementation. Such a division, as we saw earlier, underlines the thinking behind programmes such as Next Steps. However, all writers agree that this distinction is a hard one to draw in any pure or *a priori* sense.[57] The lines depend upon the way the tasks of ministers, senior civil servants, agency heads, policy advisers, the cabinet, and interest groups are defined. If one does not know what role these people are to play then one cannot construct opaque, let alone clear, divisions between policy formulation and implementation. The problem is further complicated by whether it is better to concentrate strategic decision-making, or long-range planning, in a central core body. It is perfectly possible to construct organisations based upon very horizontal, collegial, lines of decision-making to create what Burns and Stalker call an 'organic' form of organisation.[58] This form of organisation is contrasted with the more traditional, Weberian, bureaucratic model, which Burns and Stalker describe as a mechanical form of organisation. The choice depends upon the nature of one's environment, one's market situation, and how innovative, and risk-taking, one wishes to be. The public sector is normally seen as an environment in which the Weberian virtues of universality, impartiality, and rule adherence are appropriate, but given the diversity of public sector activities it is unlikely that one form of organisation is appropriate for all sectors. This is, of course, part of the problem – how to construct general constitutional principles and yet allow for the enormous diversity of tasks which modern governments perform.

The conventional view of the role of civil servants is that they are 'policy advisers'. The noble role is to 'tell the truth to power', that is, to offer careful, independent, objective and impartial assessments of any policy that ministers might which to carry out. This is the role that civil servants see as having the highest status and as being the most rewarding. Managing a department, even one with a large budget and staff, was seen as a far less interesting and rewarding role.[59] However, the key issue is whether the boundaries between these functions have changed but this is a hard question to answer. This is partly a matter of flux – things are in the process of change – but also of the diversity of experience within the more decentralised civil service. Perhaps the only way forward, and certainly a popular method among other writers, is to proceed by example.[60] At least the diversity can be illustrated. Ferlie *et al.*, after studying the National Health Service (NHS) conclude that:

> one way of conceiving of the new public management is as the unbundling of large vertically integrated public sector organisations into a flotilla of quasi-autonomous organisations. The strategic apex of these devolved organisations assumes greater significance as it operates with an enhanced range of delegated powers and can potentially be seen as a major power source, reshaping the local organisation along strategic lines... Strategy development was found to be an important function for these [NHS] boards.[61]

The implication here is that the creation of quasi-autonomous organisations can create many centres with some responsibility for long-range and strategic planning. The case of the Prison Service and the Home Office is a well-known example of the difficulties of separating policy from administration. After the victory of the Labour Party in

1997, the leader of the Conservative Party, John Major, resigned and a leadership contest was held. During this election for a new leader of the Conservative Party, Ann Widdecombe, a former Home Office minister, made what many commentators described as a blistering personal attack on one of the candidates, Michael Howard, MP, the former Home Secretary.[62] The row centred on the resignation of Derek Lewis, the former head of the Prison Service, after a series of embarrassing incidents involving the security and treatment of prisoners. Widdecombe's main complaint centred on the allegation that Michael Howard had misled the House of Commons over the circumstances surrounding the dismissal of the Governor of Parkhurst Prison and the resignation of Derek Lewis. However, the most relevant point is Widdecombe's claim that, if the errors in the running the Prison Service were such as to require the resignation of Mr Lewis, then they were sufficiently serious to require the resignation of ministers. Widdecombe is adamant that ministers should not be able to hide behind the uncertain boundary between policy and operations. The Home Secretary's actions 'created a false distinction between policy and operations that has reverberated around the whole of Whitehall, not just the Home Office.'[63] This is an issue, the boundary between policy and administration, which has altered the interest in controlling information. At the moment the civil service is in transition but the direction is clear – ministers will respond to uncertainty by divesting themselves of responsibility and by giving up the control over information that went with that responsibility.

CONCLUSION

To find one formula which maximises, or at least does not sacrifice, effectiveness, efficiency, managerial autonomy, political responsiveness, and accountability would seem an impossible task. If there is no one method which maximises all of these attributes, then one must construct a decision matrix: Are some values more important than others? Is there a minimum below which none can fall? Do you wish to try to cluster some to reinforce those values, even if this weakens others? The major problem with the reform of the British civil service is that there has been no clear strategy providing such a matrix. It has rather been a case of incremental reform, building on a perceived series of 'failures'. The end result may be radical, even revolutionary change, but still lack coherence and a clear objective. This makes it difficult to judge the reforms, as there are no clear criteria by which to do so. In the next chapter we shall see how these reforms have affected an issue closely linked to secrecy, accountability.

5 Accountable Government?

THE IDEA OF ACCOUNTABILITY

The concept of accountability is one of the most crucial to contemporary debates about the state, democracy and governance. This reflects not only the normative dimension of the concept of democracy but also the changing relationship between the citizen and government.

Until the Fulton Report, and the concerns over official secrecy that it generated,[1] the fears about governance focused on procedural issues associated with the exercise of authority. It was the potential for the abuse of power associated with rise of the large, centralised, bureaucratic state that concerned most commentators.[2] In an earlier generation of texts on the British state there are few references to the concept of accountability. For example, there are no indexed references to accountability in the classic constitutional law texts of the 1970s and even books on official secrecy published in the 1970s and 1980s contain few, if any references, to the concept.[3] In the 1980s and 1990s, as we shall see below, there has been a virtual flood of books on the issue. But what is accountability? There are several senses to this concept.

The traditional view of accountability, that used by many lawyers or political scientists, is well expressed by Oliver and Drewry, who

> take accountability to mean the duty to give explanations or justifications for action and then to make amends if it should turn out that something has gone wrong.[4]

The key ingredients of the idea of accountability are: (1) a set of rules, a normative dimension, that requires or obliges someone (2) to offer a verbal or written statement of events and their part in them. However, (3) such a statement may not only seek to explain but provide an ethical justification of their action and (4) such statements are part of a process of scrutiny in which grievances or complaints are handled and 'errors' detected. The end result of the process is (5) a product such as remedial action, compensation, or even a simple promise not to 'do it again'.

It is also important to recognise that this process of 'giving an account' takes place in public. Even 'internal' mechanisms of accountability are only meaningful if they conform to certain universal standards and can therefore be defended in public. In no sense could there be a 'private' system of accountability – this would be a contradiction in terms.

However, political scientists are not the only social scientists to be interested in accountability. The Canadian sociologist, Richard Ericson, has examined the notion of accountability in relationship to policing. In a series of works he has argued that the structure of laws and administrative rules concerning 'policing' are a resource rather than a determinant of outcomes.[5] Rules provide a means for legitimating the decisions that are in one's interests. In this radical approach, to be 'accountable' means using rules to provide 'covers, rationalisations, and justifications of actions'.[6] The public rules are there to protect the organisation from having to expose its 'recipe rules', its operating rules, that are a part of its private, hidden, sub-culture and which actually do guide conduct.[7] In this sense 'to be accountable' means operating within an organisation that provides the resources for those in positions of power to justify what they do to those without power. Of course, the public rules, as opposed to the private, recipe rules, do constrain the members of the organisation but only to a limited degree. They constrain the range of justifications that they can give and do create areas of vulnerability where conduct falls outside that range.

Ericson argues that the tendency among governments and police agencies to create an ever-growing number and diversity of rules only produces a proliferation of rationalisations. Such rules were no doubt responses to previous embarrassments or 'legitimation crises' but the end result is an expansion in both the number and diversity of opportunities to find some rule that mitigates, if not justifies, what has been done. Far from challenging the powerful, greater accountability actually enhances their ability to manipulate public perceptions of their actions.

However, the problem this more radical approach faces is that it is deeply counter-intuitive. If more rules merely provided more opportunities for the powerful to justify their actions then one would expect liberal critics to be opposed to, and conservatives to be in favour of, developing ever more detailed rules – but the opposite is the case. This may simply demonstrate how misinformed and wrong-headed people can be, but it does create an enormous, at least initial, credibility burden.

So what is the crucial point that Ericson has missed? I would argue that it is this: more detailed rules do provide opportunities for 'negotiation' and to legitimate malfeasance of office, but the existence of rules also forces the issue into the public arena and this more than outweighs any possible benefits to the power-holder. Ericson is right to point to the double-sided consequence of rule proliferation but wrong to underestimate the disinfecting qualities of sunlight. The crucial point about accountability is that the process of justification and blaming, story-telling and criticism, takes place in public and this increases the probability that some action will be taken to redress the grievance. It may complicate the next occasion at which a similar event takes place, because there is now a body of 'justifications/rules' in place, but without the rules there would be a reduced chance that any public negotiation would take place and reduced probability of amends being made. The rules are not merely about establishing 'truth', but about creating mechanisms for the resolution of disputes. Rules do assist the latter, even if Ericson is right to say that rules can be a screen as well as a source of illumination.

THE 'NEW' CIVIL SERVICE AND THE ACCOUNTABILITY OF MINISTERS

Commentators have also noted that there are differing interpretations of the notion of accountability as applied to British government. Nevil Johnson argues that the convention of ministerial responsibility, one of the traditional pillars of the unwritten constitution, is not about holding people responsible for their actions but a method of defining roles; it defines *what* ministers are responsible for, rather than to *whom* they are accountable.[8] However, as Dowding, surely correctly, points out, this is too limited an interpretation of the nature of accountability and would be unlikely to create fear in the breasts of ministers.[9] If there were no notion of blame, and therefore of holding to account, then parliamentary questioning would hold no terror.[10]

Dowding also provides a useful summary of the various forms of accountability:

- *redirecting* – it's not me, it's them (particularly useful with the growth of quangos, agencies and other non-governmental bodies (NGOs));
- *reporting* – giving the facts: this happened then, and was done by this or that section;
- *explaining or justifying* – we did what was right or reasonable;
- *amendatory* – accepting that something needs to be put right;
- *sacrificial* – the minster accepts blame and resigns.

Dowding argues that the reason why there are so many, though often linked, senses of accountability is that the UK has an underdeveloped body of public law. This means that there is no statute clearly laying out the duties and responsibilities of ministers. It is only through an evolving process involving Parliament, Select Committees, Committees of Inquiry, judicial review, government and the public that the 'current' notion of ministerial responsibility is defined.

One of the most important recent contributions to this process of defining 'responsibility' is the Scott Report on arms sales.[11] The 'reporting' function is a well-recognised element of accountability but Scott gives it a new importance by stressing the obligation on ministers to provide *full information*. To Scott, answers that are incomplete, misleading, untruthful, or partial, are failures to perform the duties of a minister and are therefore failures in accountability. Vernon Bogdanor argues that Sir Richard gives new emphases to the concept of ministerial responsibility by stressing the obligation to (1) not 'knowingly' mislead and (2) not 'unreasonably' withhold information. The first of these, the duty not to mislead, is the more established of the two and is included in the Civil Service Code.

However, this still proved to be one of the more controversial aspects of the Scott Report, because of the element of judgement associated with whether a minister intended to deceive or mislead. An examination of the facts surrounding a particular event is rarely likely to provide conclusive evidence as to the state of mind of a minister. The possible resignation of William Waldegrave, Minister of State at the Foreign Office, 1988–90, hinged upon when a change in arms sales guidelines amounted to a change in arms sales policy. Waldegrave had repeatedly told Parliament that there was no change in arms sales policy and yet Sir Richard found that the changes were such as to amount to a change in policy. Sir Richard concluded that Waldegrave believed that the then guidelines were sufficiently flexible and could therefore accommodate a range of interpretations without this amounting to a 'change of policy'.[12]

The second element of accountability identified by Scott is that ministers have a duty to provide as full and accurate information as possible. This, according to Bogdanor, does not preclude 'deliberate untruths' – lies – in certain very exceptional circumstances such as when a minister is asked about interest rates or Northern Ireland. There are higher values, such as preserving life, than truth-telling. However, ministers need to be wary of appealing to these higher values, since such appeals only succeed if they command widespread acceptance. They can quickly become tarnished if they are flavoured with the spice of party or personal advantage. However, the more common problem is not the rare instance when a deliberate untruth is told but when incomplete information is provided. It is part of the traditional conventions that ministers do not need to give more information than is necessary. In *Public Secrets* I argued that when answering questions in the House of Commons: 'The degree of detail contained within these explanations [Ministers' replies] is not, however, determined by anything other than the needs of the government.'[13]

The interesting point is that in the 1960s and 1970s all attempts to find a lever to force governments to provide full(er) information were seen to have foundered on the rock of party discipline. The House of Commons could not force ministers to provide more information than they wished because the only 'real' sanction was to make the issue a matter of confidence and bring down the government. Parties were seen as being wary of committing suicide. What has changed? If ministers are to be expected to put providing full information above party advantage it would seem that times have indeed changed. The other possible interpretation is that Sir Richard has engaged in the expression of pious hopes that are only likely to produce, as with the hopes of parliamentary reformers in the 1960s, disappointment.[14]

In my earlier work I stated that 'Parliament has failed to expose the government and lay bare the information upon which government policies are based, and this is because such a tactic would be seen as a usurpation of the Cabinet's right to govern.'[15] The rock upon which previous reforms have foundered is the need for party discipline within an oppositional system of representative democracy. Have matters changed so much that this is no longer the reality? As we shall see, things have changed, although the degree and nature of change are open to debate. There now does seem to be a sense, even among politicians and prime ministers, that the government is no longer capable of controlling events because public expectations are so high, demands so diverse, and interests so conflicting. One cannot maximise all the key elements, one cannot accept ultimate responsibility and maximise autonomy and seek to share responsibility and maximise participation. If complexity means that the risk of things going wrong (or at least not going well) is increased then there is an enhanced incentive to spread the risk – that is, to encourage consultation. If other bodies (such as the European Union, multinational companies, or the media) are seen as 'sharing' sovereignty, thereby reducing the capacity to act autonomously, then there is a reduced incentive to claim to 'be in charge'. Why take responsibility if you believe that you do not have the capacity to act autonomously? Perceptions of increased complexity and reduced capacity do appear to have altered the desire of democratic governments to see themselves to be as 'powerful' as their predecessors. What you cannot control, you share. If this is true for power, it is also likely to apply to information. If you no longer see yourself as enjoying a monopoly of power, why continue with a monopoly over information?

But how do these general issues relate to reforms of the civil service? As we saw in the previous chapter, Conservative reforms of the British state gave rise to many controversies and one of the most important is the impact on accountability. The concern with 'accountability' is now both quantitatively and qualitatively at an all-time high. However, this should not mislead us into thinking that related issues have not been debated for many decades. The 'reality' or otherwise of ministerial responsibility; the judicial review of administration; mechanisms of redress and grievance; and the scrutiny of the executive by parliament – these are all old chestnuts of British public administration.

But there is no doubt that the debate over accountability has been intensified by reforms such as Next Steps. Commentators were lining up to point out that such changes could undermine the traditional mechanisms of civil service accountability to ministers, and ministerial accountability to Parliament.[16] This issue, though, is far from straightforward. For those who have argued that ministerial responsibility is a myth or, at least, a very inadequate part of the British constitution, there can be no basis for arguing that Next Steps is damaging to accountability on the grounds that it erodes ministerial responsibility – one cannot erode something which does not exist.[17]

Oonagh McDonald is one author who cannot quite make up her mind about this issue.[18] She constantly casts doubt on the 'reality of ministerial accountability' through phrases such as 'the government insists nothing has changed' (implying that it obviously has and that such denials are obsfucations), the concept remains 'a key concept in constitutional orthodoxy' (the implication being that 'orthodoxies' are as much myth as meaningful tradition), and chapter sub-titles such as 'Ministerial Accountability – a Myth?'. However, in the section on 'Myth' she cannot bring herself to dismiss the idea of ministerial responsibility as entirely mythical. Rather, she piles up the doubts and then argues for a reformulation of the existing position on the grounds that 'neither the sense in which ministers are responsible to

Parliament, nor the range of activities for which they are accountable, have been properly considered.'[19]

Peter Hennessy also suggests that the concept is somewhat illusive, calling it the equivalent of the search for the Holy Grail, but he does appear to accept that there is substance to the concept by arguing that 'responsibility' is not merely about 'giving an account' but expresses something about structures of *power*.[20] This is similar to Nevil Johnson's idea discussed earlier.[21]

However, one would expect those on the sceptical end of the spectrum to welcome an initiative such as Next Steps precisely because it ignores the 'hoary old myth', that is, ministerial responsibility. Similarly, one would expect those who see ministerial responsibility as having some substance, even if requiring clarification, to argue that Next Steps is dangerous on the grounds that it damages existing mechanisms of accountability.[22]

The main anxieties associated with the agencification of the civil service are

1. that there are inadequate mechanisms by which the new agencies can be held to account, and
2. there is no substance to the notion of accountability if there are no consequences, resignation, dismissal and so on, associated with being held to account.

The first issue is associated with the change in management structure by which the 'traditional' lines of responsibility via department heads, permanent secretaries, and ministers are replaced by a more confused pattern in which agency heads are said to be both autonomous and a part of the existing ministry structure. The Cabinet Secretary, Sir Robin Butler described this as a system that was 'unified, but not uniform'.[23]

One of the early problems created by this 'diversity' centred on the question of who was responsible for replying to MPs' questions. The government insistence that despite agencification the civil service remained a service responsible (accountable) to ministers who were accountable to Parliament, meant that MPs found themselves unable to interrogate the people who were now responsible for 'operational matters' – that is, precisely those day-to-day decisions most likely to affect their constituents. When challenged on this issue, the government responded by asserting that the minister would determine whether the issue concerned a 'strategic, resource or operational matter'.[24] If the issue were operational, then the chief executive would be asked to reply to MPs and a copy could be placed in the House of Commons Library. However, although other MPs could read this reply, they were hardly likely to learn of its existence. This system came under criticism in the Treasury and Civil Service Select Committee for its 'lack of accessibility' but the government took almost a year to revise its procedures and agree to the publication of such replies in a supplement to *Hansard*.[25] There were also concerns over the lines of accountability concerning financial management. The new agencies were designed to have greater autonomy in financial matters and yet the permanent secretary of each department was designated as sole accounting officer and therefore the only person accountable to the Parliamentary Public Accounts Committee (PAC). The PAC is the oldest and most prestigious of the parliamentary committees for it directly interrogates the designated accounting officer concerning the management of public finances. This was the only occasion in which civil servants were directly accountable to Parliament. The financial autonomy of agencies obviously created a problem for this system – if the agencies were autonomous then the permanent secretary could not be sole accounting officer. The government's response was to make chief executives designated accounting officers in two differing senses. Where there was genuine financial independence, such as with The Stationery Office, the agency chief would be appointed the accounting officer who would be answerable in his or her own right. Where agencies were funded largely through a department vote, then chiefs would be designated agency accounting officers and would be accompanied by the permanent secretary when answering to the PAC.

The creation of agencies has led, then, to a variety of fears that existing conventions will be rendered inappropriate or inadequate. There is the fear that ministers will argue that they are not the 'appropriate' person to 'give an account', since they are not responsible for day-to-day operations. Any uncertainty or confusion in the lines of responsibility is likely to be exploited by ministers when it suits their political or personal advantage. The proliferation of agencies, quangos and privatised bodies provides enhanced scope for the use of this tactic. The second anxiety is that ministers will argue that even when they are obliged to 'tell the story' of what happened in their department they will use, or even abuse, the autonomy of agencies to argue that they are not to blame for any error. They were not in control since the agency, division or whatever, had operational responsibility for this matter. The minister becomes a witness to events but, as with a witness to a murder, you can provide an account of what happened without being the murderer! The creation of a more complex civil service may also provide enhanced incentives for ministers to argue that they are not 'to blame' even when they are willing to accept that 'something needs to be done': this that 'needs to be done' being anything other than something that affects their standing such as setting up an inquiry or changing the framework within which others act. The reforms may also reduce the incentives to resign, thereby reducing the number of 'sacrificial resignations'. Any confusion over lines of responsibility is likely to be viewed sympathetically by Cabinet colleagues as being a 'good reason' not to resign. The reforms decrease the political affects of error and therefore increase the tendency to avoid accepting *moral responsibility*.

However, there are those who have taken a different viewpoint and have argued that there is potential in Next Steps for improved accountability. This is not simply a result of the publication of more information, performance indicators and so on, but because of the framework documents that create agencies. The framework document defines the functions of the agency and the policies it is to pursue, and sets performance targets. A typical document describes aims and objectives; the relationship between the chief executive and the minister and between the chief executive and permanent secretary; financial arrangements; terms of service and pay; and arrangements for review. The chief executive is then responsible for implementation and there are often elements of his or her salary related to performance. Although the chief may be appointed from within the existing department or civil service, the post is often advertised and appointments have been made from the private sector. One major change in the character of the civil service has been the move away from fixed grades and salaries towards 'flexible' and performance-related pay. The fact that people in different agencies might receive different pay, for doing what would certainly in the 1950s and 1960s have been seen as the same job, is a major departure.

Framework documents always contain the possibility for review and renegotiation – a newly elected government could review all such agreements, but in addition framework agreements require the negotiation on an annual basis of more precise performance targets, which must be negotiated between the department and chief executive each year. The publication of performance targets means that it is, at least in theory, possible to provide a much more accurate assessment of effectiveness and efficiency. This is important to the work of Parliament in general, to select committees, and to the National Audit Office which have responsibility to check on 'value for money' under the 1983 National Audit Act.[26] The formulation of specific, and explicit, requirements, aims and objectives, and performance targets for both the agency and individuals, provides a basis for the judgement of value for money.

However, as Oliver and Drewry point out, there are dangers of distortions being created by the fact that what is audited is what can be measured, and this provides incentives to chief executives and individuals to maximise these at the expense of other factors such as 'quality'.[27] Oliver and Drewry provide the amusing example of the bus-driver who sometimes does not stop and pick up passengers because doing so makes it more difficult to meet punctuality targets! However, as the authors rightly point out, it is surely possible to create a framework in which appropriate weight is given to context, and to qualitative factors, so as to minimise such distortions.[28] The key issues are surely those identified by Woodhouse, who argues that framework documents can only contribute to accountability if they are 'formal, open and clear'.[29]

CONCLUSION

As we saw in Chapter 4, changes in the civil service have further complicated conventions, such as ministerial responsibility, that were already under attack. From the Fulton Committee onwards there were many voices arguing that the growth in size, complexity and diversity of the modern state meant that no government, even one composed of 90 ministers, could hope to know, let alone control, what was taking place. However, changes such as contracting out and agencification have given an enormous further impetus to those arguing that existing mechanisms are inadequate. Even the Conservatives felt obliged – as a result, I would argue, of their own reforms – to experiment with what they called 'open government'. This means that even the most traditional of ministers can see that freedom of information is less costly than it once was – less costly to them.

6 Data Protection, Privacy and Limited Rights of Access

This chapter, and the next, deals with official secrecy in Britain *before* the introduction of Freedom of Information legislation. These chapters examine the background to reform and analyse the changes to official secrecy introduced under the previous Conservative government. This is a necessary step to understanding the freedom of information proposals of the new Labour government under Prime Minister Tony Blair. It is also important to recognise that Freedom of Information is not a new idea and has been the subject of debate since the 1970s. To understand why it has been introduced now it is necessary to understand what came before and why the process has been, in the eyes of the many critics of British official secrecy, so slow. The process of reform has been piecemeal and gradual, reflecting government anxieties that changing the structure of government control of information would involve changing power relationships in Whitehall and beyond. Successive British governments were aware of a variety of pressures for change, from Europe, scandals, backbench MPs, and civil liberties groups, but they were not willing to introduce a coherent information policy for fear that this would radically alter the structure of political power. They therefore adopted piecemeal reform.

However, these pressures would never, in my view, have forced a British government to introduce freedom of information legislation. The process of piecemeal reform could have gone on indefinitely despite the fact that there were rising costs because of the variety of bits and pieces of legislation granting some form of access, review or accountability. Something else happened, as we shall see in a later chapter, to alter such calculations, to alter the balance of risk in continuing with piecemeal reform or introducing a coherent system of information management in the form of freedom of information legislation. However, before examining recent developments it is necessary to understand the evolution of the control of official information during the 1970s and 1980s and this is the subject of the next three chapters. This chapter examines three issues:

1. the first piece of legislation giving people a right of access to broad categories of data, the Data Protection Act;
2. the right of access to, and disclosure of, personal files; and
3. the right of access to local government information.

In one sense, Britain has had freedom of information legislation for many years. What we have not had, and will not have until the White Paper proposals become law, is a comprehensive and coherent right of access to official information. However, governments have been, as we shall see, relatively happy to grant rights of access when such access did not threaten to alter the structure of power within which they governed.

DATA PROTECTION

The first piece of legislation giving a British citizen a statutory right of access to information was the Consumer Credit Act 1974. This Act, however, only gave the individual the right to see his or her personal file if it was held by a *private* sector credit reference agency. It had no implications for official information. Nevertheless, the principle that citizens should have access to their own personal files is an important one. The argument that there can be few, if any, grounds for withholding information which describes a named individual from that same named individual is surely compelling. Personal files are used by both private and public bodies to make decisions that directly, and often severely, affect the interests of individuals. It is therefore imperative that they contain accurate and timely information and that they do not contain information which adversely affects the rights of the citizen, such as information on religious or political opinions. The person in the best position to know whether the information is accurate, or to complain that it is in some way prejudicial, is the individual concerned.

Although this principle was first recognised in 1974, its application to other areas has been slow. Its most significant extension came with the Data Protection Act 1984 (DPA). However, it is claimed that the British government only introduced the DPA for commercial reasons and because of developments in other European countries.[1] This may explain why the Act suffers from limited terms of reference. It only applies to information held and recorded by 'equipment operating automatically', which effectively means information stored on computer. Manual records are therefore not covered. Also, the legislation only applies to information about individuals: the data subject must be an identifiable 'living individual', so corporations or other organised groups are not covered. However, the Act does apply to both private and public bodies. It identifies eight principles that underlie the legislation:

1. the information shall be obtained and processed fairly and lawfully;
2. data shall be held only for a specified and lawful purpose;
3. it shall not be disclosed in any manner incompatible with those purposes;
4. the data shall be adequate, relevant and not more than is necessary for the purpose;
5. the data shall be accurate and kept up to date;
6. it shall not be kept for longer than necessary;
7. individuals shall be entitled to know that personal data is being held on them and to have access to any such data; and
8. appropriate security measures must be taken to protect unauthorised access to the data.[2]

A Data Protection Registrar is appointed to register data users – it is a criminal offence not to register – and to regulate the interpretation of the legislation by data users. The register, which is available in most main public libraries, contains information about:

- who holds the data, the identity of the data holder;
- the purposes for which the data is being held;
- the sources from which the user may obtain the information held in the data;
- a list of those to whom the data holder may disclose data;
- a list of the overseas countries to which data may be transferred; and
- a contact address for individuals seeking to request access to their personal data.

The Act also has an important number of exemptions, relating to security, crime and revenue-raising. However, it is important to point out, as does Bryan Niblett, that in all cases, except that of national security, the requirement to register still applies.[3] National security is grounds for a blanket exemption and a certificate from a relevant minister is final and conclusive evidence that the data is so exempt.[4] The Data Protection Registrar, who is charged with the enforcement of the Act's provisions, has no right to inspect such security databases to ensure that good practice is being implemented. A subject can also be denied access to specific files if these are held for the prevention or detection of crime, the apprehension or prosecution of offenders and the assessment or collection of any tax or duty. In addition, not only are such files exempt from disclosure, a person need not be told that any data on them is held by an authority and data may be disclosed to an appropriate agency, without the consent of the individual, if the purpose is the prevention of crime or collection of any tax. However, it is important to point out that the data is only exempt if its release would, for example, impair the investigation of crime. It is not, as with national security, a blanket exemption for all police files. This means that if a police force has computerised files containing personal data that do not concern the investigation or prosecution of crime then the normal provisions would cover such files. However, it is clear that the Data Protection Act has a limited effect on this, most sensitive, category of files. Such files are sensitive both in the information they contain (for example, suspicion of associating with known criminals), and in the purposes for which they are used (for example disclosure of tax files to the Security Service).

However, data protection is not a static area and there are important developments in the EU that will affect the United Kingdom. In 1995 the EU agreed a new directive on data protection to cover manual, as well as computerised, personal data.[5] The new requirements contained in the directive include

- imposing stricter conditions for the processing of sensitive information, such as medical data;
- obliging data users to give individuals certain information when data about them are collected;
- giving individuals the right to object to information about them being used for direct marketing; and
- applying data protection controls to personal information held in certain manual filing systems.[6]

The directive includes a positive obligation on data holders to inform 'subjects' about the use of the data and how to complain. At the moment complaints procedures depend upon the Data Protection Registrar carrying out an 'active publicity campaign' informing people of their rights. The new EU directive places the obligation to inform people on the data holder. However, one of the rules has been relaxed in that data can be transferred to countries with no recognised data protection legislation in certain circumstances. Transfer to such countries will be allowed only if they provide satisfactory assurances concerning the quality and security of their data systems.

PERSONAL FILES

In recent years the right to inspect personal files has been gradually extended, although without any apparent guiding rationale or strategy. The Access to Personal Files Act 1987 gives individuals the right to inspect personal files held by local government housing and social service departments. Later, in 1989, the provisions were extended under the Education Act 1980 to cover education. In 1988 the Access to Medical Reports Act gave individuals the right to inspect reports written by doctor for insurance companies or employers and the Access to Health Records Act 1990 gave patients the right to inspect a wide range of records generated by health professionals.[7] Records can be withheld if release of the information would be likely to cause serious harm to the patient. Where the DPA applies, then it must be used rather than the Access to Health Records Act. However, the legislation covering access to personal information is diverse and confused. The confusion comes about because of four main issues:

1. Some rights of access derive from statute while others, such as the Citizen's Charter, derive from government discretion. Where a right of access depends upon discretion it is non-enforceable in a court of law and can be altered or removed at the will of the government.
2. There is potential for conflict between different legislation, since some measures provide rights of access while others prohibit disclosure. Generally, a right of access has to give way if there is other legislation prohibiting disclosure. Both the Data Protection Act and Citizen's Charter provide explicit provision to this effect.
3. There are different laws covering local government and national government that may become even more complicated by different rules covering devolved assemblies in Scotland and Wales.
4. The methods of application, charging, and appeal are not uniform and there is even less common practice between agencies as to the quality and manageability of their record-keeping. The Audit Commission found that almost half of all hospital records were incomplete or too bulky to work with.[8]

The Conservative government had promised in its *Open Government* White Paper of 1993 to introduce a comprehensive Bill covering all aspects of personal records but, by the time of the election in 1997, no such Bill had been printed. The Labour government's promise to introduce freedom of information legislation will, as we shall see, include a right of access to personal information.

RECORDS, VETTING AND THE DISCLOSURE OF PERSONAL INFORMATION

Although access to personal data is an important issue, it is not the only 'privacy' debate. One of the major recent controversies has focused on the right to disclose information about individuals considered to be dangerous to the public. Although 'vetting' by employers, both public and private, has a long history, the argument that schools, medical practitioners, and other social services should be warned about the presence of certain categories of offender has raised new concerns over the balance between social protection and the rights of the individual. However, this debate needs to be put into context in that disclosure of personal information by government agencies is not new.

One of the key issues is that associated with the disclosure of criminal records to a variety of organisations and public bodies. Hebenton and Thomas identify two key purposes for which police records are disclosed: (1) to report convictions to certain categories of employers; and (2) to carry out the vetting of employees in connection with employment decisions.[9] The list of employers to be notified of offences includes: medical and dental practitioners, midwives, teachers and others having the care of children, drivers of public service vehicles, holders of air crew licences, applicants under the Gaming Act 1968, and taxi drivers, as well as those involved in aspects of the criminal justice system, the largest single group affected being those concerned with the welfare of children. Although Hebenton and Thomas do not provide any estimate of the number of people in this category – it must be hundreds of thousands – they do point out that the addition of taxi drivers to the list meant the addition of 85 000 new individuals.[10]

In October 1996 the then Home Secretary, Michael Howard, proposed to create a new Criminal Records Agency for England and Wales that would allow employers to get information about the past history of job applicants. Under the Police Act 1997 new provisions were created that allow individuals applying for certain positions to apply to the police for a 'criminal record certificate'.[11] There are three types of certificate. The first lists unspent convictions, those convictions involving prison sentences of under 30 months which lapse after a number of years and are then 'spent' or show no convictions. However, such convictions will no longer be regarded as 'spent' for jobs involving children or other vulnerable people. These posts would require the second type of certificate, a 'full' certificate that would give all convictions and cautions. A registered person such as an officer of a local authority must countersign such a certificate. A third type is the 'enhanced certificate', which will be issued to those applying for jobs involving people who have regular, unsupervised access to children, those wishing to foster children, applicants for gaming or lottery licences, candidates to become judges or magistrates or to other positions specified by the secretary of state. The certificate would include cautions, minor offences, and spent offences. It is an offence for the 'registered person', such as an adoption agency, to disclose the information contained in the certificate to any other person or body.

A recent case, which provides an indication of how the rights of certain individuals, particularly sex offenders, are being eroded on the grounds of public safety, took place before the High Court in July 1997. The court ruled that police were right to warn the owner of a caravan site that a couple with convictions for rape and indecent assault were moving to the area on the grounds that they might pose a risk to children holidaying in the area. Fearing for their safety, the couple moved on. The Lord Chief Justice ruled that a blanket policy of revealing identities would be objectionable, but where there was a clear risk the public had a right to know. Paul Cavadino, the principal officer of the National Association for the Care and Rehabilitation of Offenders, argued for a code of practice to regulate such actions. He believes that disclosure should be restricted to 'the most exceptional circumstances'.[12] The debate over disclosure will intensify with the creation of the Sex Offenders Register in the autumn of 1997. This requires all sex offenders to provide basic information, including their current address, to the authorities.

Similarly, the vetting of employees has a long history and affects a large number of people. In evidence to the Home Affairs Committee, the Home Office stated that in 1989 there had been over 500 000 searches of criminal records as part of government employment checks. The Home Office argued that the large number of checks resulted from the increased employment of contract staff and that such checks were necessary on 'national security grounds'.[13] However, as the Select Committee states:

> We find it hard to believe that over half a million people were taken into Government employment directly or indirectly in 1989 who had access to 'classified material' to the extent that revealing it would harm national security.[14]

Even allowing for the number of contract staff, and of transfers as well as first appointments, the figure does seem unreasonably high if the justification is truly the protection of national security.

There is an argument to be made that no risk to national security can be tolerated and that any dubious person in the eyes of the civil service, one with a criminal record, must be weeded out. However, although such a strategy may reduce the risk of breach of trust, it certainly increases the risk that a suitably qualified person may be denied a post. If access to criminal records is not used to deny employment, or is not at least a factor in such decisions, then why consult the record in the first place? The issue that needs to be addressed is whether the public accepts that this balance of risk is the correct one. Do the public think it right that someone be given a job when there may be information which can be accessed, although it is not available to all categories of employer, which may suggest that their character has a 'defect'? If they do, then they will support the existing system. However, one can phrase the question in another way, which may well produce a quite different answer – does the public think it right that the government should be able to exclude people on the basis that they might commit a breach of trust when ordinary employers have no such right? If the person is applying for a post that entails access to national security information then the balance of risk may well be in favour of caution, but to justify such checks on the basis that they might have access to 'classified' information is not acceptable. Many employers would argue that their employees enjoy access to 'confidential information' but they are not entitled to access police records.

This problem is compounded because the British government, in addition to police files, also has access to information provided by the Security Service under its positive vetting procedures. The denial of employment or promotion because of information held in a security file may be extremely harmful to a particular individual and yet there is no way to challenge the accuracy of such 'security' files.[15]

RIGHT OF ACCESS TO LOCAL GOVERNMENT INFORMATION

The legislation covering public access to local government reinforces the argument about values and power. The first, and most obvious, point is that Parliament, when legislating for local authorities, is legislating for bodies over which it is sovereign. It is Parliament that determines the legal framework within which local government operates. The second point is that ministers are not accountable for the actions of local authorities or for the decisions taken by local government officers. Although the actions of local authorities do have implications for the government, especially since local government spends a significant proportion of public revenue, the relationship between local government and the rise and fall of ministers or political parties is far from clear cut. The cabinet, therefore, has a different structure of interests when considering what is good for local government from when considering what is good for national government. Governments can be much freer in requiring others to disclose information when the implications of that information are not seen as affecting their political fortunes. Although Birkinshaw argues that 'there is an immediate irony that it [the Local Government (Access to Information) Act 1985] was passed with the approval of the Government, which had steadfastly refused such legislation for itself',[16] I see no irony, just self-interest.

The main legislation covering access to local authority information is the Local Government (Access to Information) Act 1985. This legislation provides access not only to documents but also to council meetings[17] and to background papers. It therefore has provisions that provide a degree of open government. Openness refers to those provisions giving the public the right to know about, and participate in, decisions before they are taken. Freedom of information generally grants a right of access to documents *after* decisions have been taken. The legislation is therefore a potentially very powerful basis for exposing the plans, debates, and politics of UK local authorities. The right of access is also enforceable in the courts.

However, the right of access is not unfettered. The legislation exempts 15 categories of information. These fall under several main headings: the privacy of individuals; the rights of employees and office-holders; financial, commercial or legal data; and the prevention of crime.[18] Information concerning the education, adoption and fostering of children and information concerning contracts or prospective contracts, if such information would damage the commercial interests of the council or identify those tendering, is also exempt. The Act also requires councils to publish advance notice of meetings with their place and time and to provide copies of the agenda. Such provisions can only be avoided in the case of an 'emergency' and the nature of this emergency must be specified in the subsequent minutes for public inspection.

As discussed above, the legislation also provides public access to 'background papers' – that is those papers or reports which 'disclose any facts or matters on which, in the opinion of the proper officer, the report or an important part of the report is based and have, in his opinion, been relied on to a material extent in preparing the report'.[19] It is unfortunate that there appears to have been no study carried out into the effects of this provision on local government decision-making, given the apparent significance of the legislation in providing access to material before decisions are taken or meetings held.[20] This 'open government' provision ought, if advocates of the public right to know are to be believed, to have provided a major stimulus to local democracy.

An important part of all access legislation is the cost of applying and the mechanisms for appeal. There is no provision in the Act for setting a framework for charges, time limits for the processing of applications, or mechanisms for adjudicating disputes. If an application is refused, then the citizen can either appeal to his or her elected councillor or to the local government ombudsman, but there is no designated authority such as an information ombudsman or commissioner. Although the White Paper on Open Government proposed creating a national code for openness in local government, to be policed by the local government ombudsmen, no national code has been produced and it has been left up to individual authorities to issue their own codes.

The contrast between the access provisions in local government and the reluctance of governments to apply the same principles to themselves is further evidence that the problem did not lie in any ideological or fundamental objections but a result of the differing interests involved. Open government was good for local government because it did not affect the election prospects of MPs or cabinet ministers; it was bad for national government because it affected the balance of power between Parliament, ministers and civil servants. It was never a matter of democratic theory or elitist attitudes; it was power that was at stake.

CONCLUSION

Several factors have influenced legislation covering secret state activities that impinge upon the citizen: public disquiet associated with human rights such as privacy; commercial pressures; European human rights rulings and council directives; and changing fashions in law enforcement. However, underlying all of these is the issue of controlling the 'information rich' state. The more government provides social, economic and other benefits, the more information it demands from us and the more this threatens our sense of being in control of our 'personal secrets'. The growth of the greedy state has changed the balance of risk so that we are unable to maintain control over our personal information if we wish to enjoy the products of the welfare state. This expansion is not simply a matter of size but of the range of services, regulations, and functions that the state performs. It may attract some to try to reduce this problem by cutting the range of benefits, licences, and regulations so that the state becomes less greedy for information. However, to deny ourselves welfare and other benefits in order to preserve privacy seems unlikely to attract many citizens.

Those who attack the 'surveillance state' are right to be concerned about the changing relationship between the citizen and the state but their remedy of ever more controls, more watchers over the watchers, ironically creates more bureaucracy and generates yet more need for information. To turn the clock back to an earlier era in which people could live 'private lives' is impossible. We attack the symptoms – ever more data, regulation, surveillance, 'policing', and files – but no one can switch off the bureaucratic demand for information, for to do so would significantly impoverish us all. Our response is to try to make this greedy, information rich state more visible, and more transparent. However, there are similarities with the problem of traffic management – the more cars, the more regulation, and the more regulation, the more need to regulate the regulators, but none of us will give up our cars!

7 Listening In

The Interception of Communications Act 1985 was the first piece of legislation to place the activities of the secret state under a form of regulation. However, the basic aim of this Act, and of other subsequent intelligence legislation, was to give legal protection to existing practices and not to satisfy any perceived public anxieties by inhibiting or restricting the agencies. Although the stimulus for legalising interception and domestic intelligence lay in a series of embarrassing events, the basic intent of the legislation was not to constrain or limit such activities but to 'normalise' them. Other countries, such as Canada and the United States, felt compelled by public anxiety to place restrictions on the activities of domestic intelligence agencies but the British government felt under no such pressure. The aim of the British reforms was to provide a minimal form of accountability while legalising existing practice. The basic formula found in the Interception of Communications Act 1985 has been followed in all subsequent intelligence, the only exception to this being the new parliamentary body, the Intelligence and Security Committee, created by the Intelligence Services Act 1994.[1] The motive behind such legislation has not been civil libertarian but managerial: managing the fall-out from the European Court of Human Rights; managing the complexities arising from the end of the cold war; and managing the complexities of using intelligence in more open environments such as courts of law.

The issue of telephone tapping was first discussed in Parliament in 1952 after the public controversy generated by a visit by a group of local councillors to a telephone exchange. During their visit they had been shown how taps were placed on telephones.[2] This led to questions in the House of Commons during which the Home Secretary, Sir David Maxwell Fyfe, stated that the government had the power to intercept: 'It is a power that has been used by every government, of whatever political persuasion, since the telephone was invented, and is a Prerogative power.'[3]

Another scandal broke in 1956 when the prosecution revealed that they had tape recordings of conversations between a client and his barrister that allegedly showed wrongdoing on the part of the barrister. The contents of the recording were provided to the Bar Council and questions were asked in the House of Commons.[4] The subsequent controversy led to the Birkett Committee, which reported in 1957.

The report confirmed the view expressed by Maxwell-Fyfe that the government relied upon the claim of royal prerogative in order to justify interference with mail and telephone communications.[5] The Committee accepted that the state had the right to interfere with communications even though the statutory, common law, or even prerogative authority for such conduct was not clear. Even in 1979, after adverse British court comment on the *Malone* case,[6] the government did not see any need for new legislation. It was only with the European Court of Human Rights ruling on *Malone* that reform became compelling.[7]

However, it is important to recognise that the objective of the 1985 Act was to enable, rather than to restrict the interception of communications. The aim was to create a legal framework within which existing practices would continue. Both the British courts and the European Court of Human Rights had attacked the absence of a legal framework rather than the practices themselves.

The basic principle of the legislation is that all interceptions must be authorised by a warrant from the secretary of state. A warrant may be issued on any of three grounds:

1. protection of national security
2. prevention of serious crime or disorder
3. protection of the economic well-being of the nation.[8]

However, the last criterion is qualified, in that interceptions on the grounds of economic well-being are allowed only if the information concerns the acts or intentions of persons outside the UK. Also an address, person, or premises must be specified, although ‘person’ is defined as including corporate bodies. Since organisations may have multiple telephone receivers, and different branches at different places, a single warrant may cover several interceptions. In the case of international communications no identification of a person or address is required, only the type of material to be examined is specified by the secretary of state. This allows the kind of vacuuming of the airwaves which modern equipment provides. The safeguard is that only information of the type specified in the warrant can be retained. Although the legislation does define a mandate, a list of tasks, it is framed in such a way as to permit governments to do everything they had done before.

The procedures involved are also enabling. The authority to issue a warrant is given to a minister, and not to an independent person such as a judge. Although the minister must consider whether other methods of obtaining the information are available, the final decision on this matter lies with the minister and is not subject to external review. However, in order to satisfy the European Convention on Human Rights it is not sufficient to create procedures for determining when interception may take place; it is also necessary to have some system of oversight or review.

The standards likely to be acceptable to the European Court of Human Rights were indicated during the review of German procedures that occurred in the *Klass* case.[9] The Court decided that German procedures, involving oversight by a parliamentary committee, did not infringe the Convention, given the safeguards against abuse that they contained. The British legislation did not, however, create a German-style parliamentary committee, but created a uniquely British solution in the form of a commissioner and a tribunal. The commissioner is required to keep the operation of the warrant system under review. The commissioner's main role is to ensure that the legal provisions of the Act are being observed. His or her task is to assess whether the secretary of state had reasonable grounds for believing a warrant was necessary.[10] This means that the policy, purposes, and definition of the national or public interest are those of the secretary of state. The commissioner is not entitled to ask whether it is, in principle, 'a good thing' that the telephones of certain groups should be monitored. The issue is only whether the secretary of state 'could reasonably take the view that in that case the warrant was necessary'. The commissioner is also obliged to make an annual report to the prime minister.[11] The report is published after checking to ensure that no matters prejudicial to 'security, prevention of crime, and economic well-being' are present, the same criteria as those used for warrants.[12]

With all posts such as 'commissioner' the main point of interest is whether the incumbent feels any need to establish a role as 'public watchdog'. Although this may happen at any stage, there is a natural tendency to search for clues in the early statements and reports. After all, neither the media nor the public are likely to have much idea about the role or function of the commissioner. Although the legislation provides the framework, it is the practice – the nature of the issues, style and language in the commissioner's reports – that define the character of the office. The first report, by Lord Justice Lloyd, is written in a calm, 'technical', style with no hint of sensationalism or publicity-seeking. It is clear that Lloyd saw no need to garner popular support by making any sensationalist comments. The only 'problem' issue identified in the report concerns the power to modify a warrant if a person moves house or changes their telephone number. Given that a warrant may cover an organisation, or 'combination of persons', and can apply to either 'persons' or a named address, Lloyd concludes that it is vital that a change of address should not be used to create what is effectively a new target. It ought to be made clear whether the warrant was targeted against an individual as a member of an organisation or against the individual as such. If the former, then changes in home address are not modifications but new targets. In the latter case they are not. However, despite this reasoning, Lloyd allows that this can be done in the case of terrorism, since it is 'a special case'. This rather technical discussion of the meaning of 'person', 'address' and 'organisation' is of importance but it is hardly the stuff of media controversy likely to excite questions in the House of Commons. The commissioner concludes his first report by stating that he is 'impressed with the value of the intelligence obtained' and that all concerned 'observe the spirit, as well as the letter, of the law'.[13]

The commissioner has wide powers to review procedures and to make recommendations but he is, by virtue of his appointment and principal role, acting as an internal monitor rather than as a public or parliamentary 'watchdog'. If the early reports are, as I have argued, 'designed' to be reassuring, one may well ask whether the later reports under Lord Nolan are any different. The answer is, unsurprisingly, no. The latest report identifies some errors but they are relatively minor errors of a procedural or technical nature.[14] For example, the Foreign Office, without apparently seeking legal advice, believed it could post-date renewals for warrants. However, the legal adviser to GCHQ – how some at GCHQ must have enjoyed this – pointed out that the Act did not allow 'post-dating' and all warrants had to be signed afresh by the secretary of state. Lord Nolan 'reminds' departments of the need to seek advice before changing procedures. He also identifies one or two other errors which, while disturbing for individuals, are inevitable and of little consequence. A one-digit error may mean that your phone is tapped instead of a drug dealer or IRA safe house, but they are hardly likely to end up raiding your garage as a result. The public benefit of such taps clearly outweighs the potential, very small risk that one technical error, such as a wrong digit in a telephone number, could lead to an inadvertent infringement of someone's privacy. The commissioner is clearly satisfied that all concerned are 'doing their best' and that errors of this type are inevitable, however much people strive for accuracy, and that the only way to eliminate such errors would be to stop all telephone tapping. Lord Nolan is clearly asking us to make a judgement of public cost and benefit: if we wish to remove any possibility of error, and the risk that some consequences *may* flow from such errors, then we must stop collecting intelligence by this means. If, on the other hand, we wish to enjoy the benefits of intelligence, we can only strive to reduce the possibility of error while accepting that a few will occur. This is certainly a debate any democracy ought to have, but it would be much more likely to take place if such issues were not buried in dry legal language.

However, the commissioner is not the only 'watchdog', in that there is also a tribunal that has responsibility to investigate complaints from members of the public.

The tribunal consists of five members of the legal profession of not 'less than ten years' standing'.[15] The main role of the tribunal is to allow an opportunity to the public to express grievances and to obtain recompense. It must investigate any complaint from a member of the public that they have unjustifiably been the subject of interception provided it is not 'frivolous or vexatious'. The tribunal must examine whether a warrant has been issued and whether it was justified. If it finds that procedures have not been followed, then it *must*: inform the complainant; inform the prime minister; quash the warrant; destroy any records; and pay compensation. However, the statement that no malpractice has been found does not tell the complainant whether no interception has taken place or whether they are the subject of an authorised warrant. The statement that no *unauthorised* interception took place does not tell the citizen whether or not they have been subject to monitoring. However, I find it hard to see how it could be any different. To provide a definitive answer would alert criminals to the circumstances in which intercepts are granted. Very quickly one would begin to detect patterns that, in addition to being of interest to academics, would be of great interest to criminals, drug dealers, and terrorists. The balance of interest has to be against confirming or denying the existence of any intercept. The argument that providing reasons would only encourage litigious citizens to take further legal measures, is not an option, since no review or appeal against the tribunal's decision is allowed; it has final and absolute jurisdiction. The Annual Report for 1997, after more than 10 years, confirms that 'no complaint has yet been upheld'.[16]

Two further features of the legislation are worthy of comment. The first is that the tribunal and commissioner have no role to play in the case of an illegal interception by a government official – that is, one carried out without a warrant. The government argued that since such illegal acts would be subject to criminal prosecution, they would be investigated by the police and be under the control of the Director of Public Prosecutions. This still leaves open the question of whether such prosecutions would be resisted on the grounds that it would not be in the public interest to prosecute. However, such a decision would be extremely damaging to any government were it to be revealed. Although some commentators have encouraged public belief that illegal tapping does take place, and that intelligence and security agencies feel free to act outside the law, there is little evidence to support the view that this is anything but rare.[17] It would be surprising if it were common, given the very considerable latitude the Act provides. Another reason for scepticism is that the intelligence agencies have not been immune from leaks and this would seem to be a prime candidate for 'whistle-blowing' if it were common. The compelling argument is that government agencies are unlikely to risk doing things in an unlawful way if the law is so permissive that it imposes little or no inconvenience upon them. The second comment is that the Act only covers the interception of communications by means of the post or telephone, it does not cover the use of other aural or visual surveillance devices.

However, this area, surveillance and privacy, is continuing to develop, especially with the recent enthusiasm for 'intelligence-led' policing. The Police Act 1997 creates, as the radical civil liberties group Statewatch expressed it, a new regime for police to 'bug and burgle'.[18] The Act gives a chief constable the authority to authorise 'entry and interference with property and wireless telegraphy' when it is likely to be of 'substantial value in the prevention or detection of serious crime' and when the information 'cannot reasonably be achieved by other means'.[19] The Act also creates the post of the commissioner who will review complaints from the public; but in this case, the Commissioner is also the authorising authority. The reason for this difference is that, unlike the intelligence agencies, there is no secretary of state to approve warrants and it was felt that the police, customs or other law enforcement bodies should not be self-authorising. However, the mechanism of complaint is the same as with the earlier legislation.

The perception of rising crime, of new world *disorder*, has meant that surveillance technology is being applied to a wider range of activities. This required the government to place the use of such technology on a statutory basis. If evidence is to be used in a court of law, then the means by which such evidence has been collected must be regulated.

8 Official Secrecy

Britain has often been described as the most secretive of the Western democracies.[1] The Official Secrets Act of 1911 (OSA 1911), with its infamous Section 2 was seen as an oppressive piece of legislation, since it made the unauthorised disclosure of official information, about anything, to anyone, for whatever reason, a criminal offence. Section 2 of the 1911 Act was finally replaced, after many failed attempts, by a new OSA in 1989. However, most commentators have argued that the reforms were disappointing and some have argued that the new Act is worse than the old.[2] It is easy to understand the sense of disappointment, as the new OSA 1989 does not recognise any positive right of public access to information and it also does not recognise the defence that 'leaks' can be justified by reference to the public interest. Critics such as Palmer argue that the 'Act leaves unchanged the ethos of secrecy in the United Kingdom',[3] and a special issue of the journal *Parliamentary Affairs* includes articles that are highly critical of the Thatcher government's attitude towards official information.[4]

These writers explain the 'limited and minimal' changes to official secrecy as reflecting a lack of commitment to democratic values by recent Conservative governments. However, as we have seen, there is an alternative explanation to this, the dominant, normative approach. It is one that examines not ideology, but the changing structure and interests of the British state. If ideology is the basis of one's explanation, it must be admitted that it is somewhat ironic that it has been Conservative governments that have produced more change in the way the 'secret state' is organised than any previous administration – and this includes information policy.[5]

BACKGROUND TO REFORM

The demand in the UK for reform of government secrecy is not new. One could argue that the beginning of the end for the 1911 Act was the Fulton Committee Report of 1968 on reform of the civil service. One aspect of government practice that the Fulton Report singled out for specific criticism was the degree of secrecy surrounding government business. It states that 'the administrative process is surrounded by too much secrecy. The public interest would be better served if there were a greater amount of openness.'[6] The argument was that the quality of decision-making would be greatly improved if there were wider consultation and availability of information. The argument that this would also improve democracy is rather secondary. The government response was to issue a White Paper on *Information and the Public Interest*,[7] but its only significant recommendation was that governments should make more information available through the publication of Green Papers that were designed to lay out the policy options at an earlier stage than was done in the traditional White Paper. However, the 1969 White Paper was not concerned with reform of official secrets legislation; that task was given to a Select Committee chaired by Lord Franks.

Lord Franks produced his report, reviewing official secrets legislation, in 1971. It recommended what became one of the standard elements of reform proposals – the narrowing of the area protected by the criminal law. Criminal penalties, Franks argued, should apply only to areas associated with defence and internal security, foreign relations, currency, policing, and information entrusted to the government in confidence. The basis of prosecution was to be the system of government classification consisting of the following categories: restricted, confidential, secret and top secret. Information marked *secret*, *top secret* or *defence-confidential* was to be protected by the criminal law and a statement by a minister that the information had been properly classified was to be final. Neither a judge nor a jury was to have a say as to whether the classification was reasonable or in the public interest. The main merit of this approach was said to lie in its transparency and precision. All civil servants would know that they would be liable to prosecution were they to release a document marked with one of the three headings, without authorisation. Although the Franks Report was debated in Parliament, no legislation came before the House of Commons before a new, Labour, government was elected in 1974. However, despite the Franks Report, Theakston argues that the Labour Party 'paid little attention to official secrecy' between 1970 and 1974.[8]

In addition to the recommendations for reform coming from official bodies there was also pressure arising from a series of Official Secrets Act court cases. Such cases had resulted either in acquittal or in the judge issuing only token punishments and were seen as evidence that the existing law was ineffective.[9] The media went much further and described one such trial as a 'Whitehall farce'. There was also pressure from groups such as Justice, the British Section of the International Commission of Jurists, and from groups explicitly committed to FOI, such as the Outer Circle Policy Unit, and the Campaign for Freedom of Information.[10] The last group even managed to gain support from some retired senior civil servants. The experience of other countries, particularly that of the United States, Canada and Australia, was a major influence on pressure groups.[11] The argument was that if other countries, particularly former members of the Commonwealth with strongly British-influenced political systems, could introduce reform, then there was no reason for Britain to resist. However, as we shall see, although this may appear to be a compelling argument it is one fraught with complexity.

The Franks' proposals influenced two attempts at reform, one by a Labour government in 1978 and the other by a Conservative government in 1979. However, neither of these two government efforts at reform was successful: the first because of the calling of a general election; and the second because revelations concerning Anthony Blunt and Soviet espionage were made during debate on the 1979 Bill, which led to its with drawal. It was deeply embarrassing to the government that, in the midst of a major public scandal, it was attempting to pass a law that was seen as keeping all such matters secret.

The next major effect on government policy was the series of 'revelations' and scandals associated with intelligence. Sarah Tisdall and Clive Ponting were charged under the Official Secrets Act 1911 and Peter Wright (MI5) and Cathy Massiter (MI5) produced embarrassing revelations about their employer.[12] These cases had an impact not only on official secrets but, as we shall see in a later chapter, also on the government's approach to the management of intelligence.

Both Sarah Tisdall and Clive Ponting were charged under Section 2 of the OSA 1911 but Tisdall was found guilty whereas Ponting was acquitted.[13] Tisdall, a young junior clerk in the Foreign Office sent documents to the *Guardian* newspaper that gave details of the arrival of cruise missiles at Greenham Common. She was sentenced to six months in prison but the editor of the *Guardian* was not charged with the offence of knowingly receiving information that had been disclosed without authority. The other interesting aspect of the case is that the *Guardian* felt obliged to hand over the original documents after the court ruled that the documents were not protected under privilege because of 'national security'. The case of Clive Ponting also involved the unauthorised disclosure of documents but Ponting gave his documents concerning the sinking of the Argentine naval ship, the *Belgrano*, during the Falklands conflict to a backbench MP. In law this made no difference and the judge dismissed his defence that he was acting in the public interest. Despite this, Clive Ponting was found not guilty.

The Massiter case had a greater impact on the Security Service Act of 1985 than on official secrets. However, the fact that a former MI5 officer could, without the approval or consent of her employer, appear on television and discuss the activities of her service obviously raised questions over the effectiveness of official secrets legislation. Allied to the Wright case (see below) there was a threat that revelations by former employees would produce a crisis of confidence in the intelligence services.

The Wright case had an enormous impact on government attitudes to official secrets legislation. Despite the commonly held view, even endorsed by the Franks Report, that the British Official Secrets Act was 'draconian', it had been ineffective in preventing a former MI5 officer from publishing a book about his secret service career. It also exposed the difficulties in using the civil law to prevent publication or to recover the profits made from publishing exposés.[14] Once again, as in the nineteenth century, the government appeared impotent to prevent the publication of matters it considered to be state secrets. The picture of people coming off aircraft carrying copies of *Spycatcher* while British newspapers were denied, by court order, from publishing any of the allegations created an air of farce. It also created some very uncomfortable moments in Parliament. Although Wright's motive for publication was to continue an internal debate over whether the former head of MI5, Sir Roger Hollis, had been a Soviet spy, the press and Parliament focused on his claim of an alleged plot within MI5 to overthrow the former Labour prime minister, Harold Wilson. The fact that this is one of the relatively brief and poorly documented sections of the book did not detract from the constitutional importance of the issue.

The allegations of Massiter and Wright caused considerable disquiet, even among senior politicians such as Merlyn Rees, a former Labour Home Secretary with responsibility for MI5 and Sir Edward Heath, the former Conservative prime minister.[15] It seemed as if Wright and Massiter were threatening to undermine the public confidence in intelligence through their public statements and that there was little the government could do to stop them.

There is no doubt that the cumulative affect of Fulton, Franks, and Wright was to create a sense within government that official secrets legislation would benefit from reform. However, the problem was how to reform the secrecy laws without this appearing to undermine or contradict other constitutional conventions. As always, there were difficult decisions over the balance of risk between continuity and reform. In Chapters Ten and Twelve, on Intelligence and Open Government, we shall see that it was not until the relationship between the state and its citizens, the state and other states, and the state and its employees, had changed that the risk of radical reform was considered.

However, pressure came not only from external events, scandals and trials, but also from backbench MPs. The Private Member's Bill seeking to reform official secrecy which elicited greatest support among both parliamentarians and the press, was that proposed by the backbench Conservative MP Richard Shepherd in November 1987. The Shepherd Bill proposed that the basic offence should become the intentional or reckless disclosure of information contrary to duty. It sought to penalise the disclosure of information that

1. would endanger national interests or the safety of a citizen; defence; international relations; security and intelligence;
2. would aid commission of an offence or impede law enforcement; or
3. had been provided to the government under statutory obligation.

Although releasing information in these categories would be a criminal offence, the defence that the release was in the public interest was available. The defence is narrowed in that certain circumstances must pertain for it to be valid. The defendant must believe the information indicated crime, fraud, or misconduct and must have taken reasonable steps to comply with procedures. A minister is given the power to certify that information was properly classified and so falls within a protected category. The right to challenge such classification is not given to a jury or judge but to the Judicial Committee of the Privy Council. During the debate on the Bill, held in January 1988, the Home Secretary asked MPs not to support the proposal. He stated that the government was actively engaged in a review and promised to produce a White Paper by the end of June 1988. He beat his deadline by 32 hours – the White Paper was presented and debated at 3.31 pm on 29 June.

THE 1989 OFFICIAL SECRETS ACT

The Official Secrets Act 1989 only replaces Section 2 of the 1911 Act. It leaves the espionage provisions of the old Section 1 untouched.[16]

This means that the main purpose of the Act is the same as the old Section 2: to punish those who disclose information without authority; that is, to punish the civil servant that leaks. The legislation is not concerned with changing public access to information and creates no new right of public access. The intent is the same as with the 1911 Act, to control civil servants even if this means denying access to the public.[17]

The 1989 Act is, however, based upon new principles. The only information given the protection of the criminal law is that falling within certain limited categories. The basis for protecting certain categories is stated to be the harm that will result from disclosure rather than any breach of duty by a Crown employee. However, the fact that civil servants are now only liable to criminal sanctions if they disclose certain limited types of information does not prevent the government from imposing other penalties. A civil servant who leaks information not protected by the criminal law may still be transferred, demoted, or dismissed. There is no protection, in the language of the USA, for the 'whistle-blower'.

The main provision of the Act is to create four main categories of protected information. These are:

1. security and intelligence
2. defence
3. international relations
4. crime.[18]

The government stated that these categories were selected on the basis of the harm to the nation that would result from unauthorised disclosure. There are two categories that are surprising by their absence: cabinet documents, and economic information. Only if the content of cabinet or economic documents falls within the above categories is there the protection of the criminal law. They are, of course, protected by internal disciplinary sanctions.

One of the other main surprises was allowing the jury to determine whether the test of harm had been met. In all previous government proposals, including the Franks Report of 1972, a ministerial certificate that information was properly secret, determined that disclosure was contrary to the national interest. The minister's decision was to be final and absolute.[19] The 1989 Act is surprising in its willingness to rely upon an institution, the jury, which had demonstrated a willingness to reject official interpretations. The jury acquitted the civil servant Clive

Ponting despite his admission that he had handed over documents without authority. His plea, that his action was in the 'interests of the state' because his decision to hand over documents to an MP was based upon his duty to inform Parliament, was rejected by the judge. The judge ruled that the phrase 'in the interests of the state' meant the 'policies of the government of the day' and not what Ponting, or anyone else, thought they ought to be. This ruling meant that Ponting had no legal defence to the charge and yet he was acquitted by the jury.[20]

It is too early to say how juries will react to their new responsibility but there must be a real probability that they will, on occasion, exercise their responsibilities in a manner quite opposite to the desires of a government.

The 'test of harm' principle was defined in the White Paper on Official Secrets as unauthorised disclosures that cause 'damage to the public interest'. This is obviously a very broad and vague phrase but the government promised that each category would be protected only if concrete and specific damage could be demonstrated. The test of harm would therefore not be general but specific to each category. However, there are three areas where *any* disclosure is deemed harmful and where no specific or concrete test applies:

1. All security and intelligence leaks are deemed harmful if they are made by an employee of those services or to someone notified that they are covered by this provision due to the nature of their work (OSA 1989, Section 1).
2. All leaks concerning the interception of communications and information obtained by a warrant whether under the Interception of Communications Act 1985 or the Security Service Act 1989 (OSA 1989, Section 4).
3. A leak of information obtained in confidence from another state *may* be presumed to be damaging (OSA 1989, Section 3, subsection (3)).

In the case of other sections there is at least some test which must be met, such as the requirement that international relations be endangered or obstructed by an unauthorised disclosure, even if the tests may be rather hard to apply. It is hard to think of a leak concerning international affairs that could not be described as having 'obstructed' such relations.

Another controversial feature of the legislation is that no general defence of 'disclosure in the public interest' is allowed. This was a topic of considerable adverse comment in the media and in the House of Commons. Many MPs considered such a defence was essential to allow Crown servants to expose wrongdoing.[21] However, the government argued that other remedies were available to civil servants who felt that their conscience conflicted with their duty. They can appeal to their head of department and ultimately to the head of the civil service, the Secretary to the Cabinet. In the case of intelligence officers, a special mechanism had been introduced with the creation, in November 1987, of the post of staff counsellor for the intelligence services. The counsellor is available to any member of the intelligence services who has 'anxieties relating to his or her service'. However, this mechanism does not depend upon any legal powers or duties and the counsellor is not obliged to report to Parliament or even the prime minister. He or she is therefore not in the position of the Canadian or American inspector generals who have clear statutory duties.[22] The first holder of the office is a former senior civil servant, Sir Philip Woodfield.[23] His experience of the Whitehall machine may make him able to assess complaints, and to judge how best to proceed, but the results that he achieves will depend solely upon good will and personal skills.[24] This was seen by many MPs, including some Conservatives, as a rather weak plank upon which to reject the idea of a public interest defence. This important issue will be explored in more depth later in this chapter.

The protection of security and intelligence information is absolute. The Act even goes so far as to make it a criminal offence to 'make any statement which purports to be a disclosure' or that 'is intended to be taken by others as a disclosure'. In other words, even telling people nonsense is an offence if you intend them to believe it to be a disclosure about your intelligence work. The justification for this is that, in order to provide evidence as to the truth or otherwise of any claim made by an intelligence officer, the Crown may either have to drop a prosecution because it is unwilling to make any further disclosures or be forced to make other potentially damaging disclosures in order to refute the original claim. This problem has arisen in two recent cases involving former employees of the intelligence services: David Shayler, a former Security Service employee and Richard Tomlinson, a former employee of the Secret Intelligence Service. Both Shayler and Tomlinson argue that their decision to tell their story is justified by the 'wrongdoing' of their former employers.

Tomlinson, who has been erroneously described in the press as the first person to be charged under the 1989 Official Secrets Act, was dismissed from the service and was denied an opportunity to take his case to an industrial tribunal.[25] His complaint over his dismissal was reviewed by the Intelligence Services Tribunal but was rejected.[26] Tomlinson, it is alleged, sent a synopsis of a book concerning his time with MI6 to a publisher in Australia. This led to the charge of disclosing 'without lawful authority, information to another which had been in your possession by virtue of being a member of SIS'.

David Shayler, also a former intelligence employee, has not yet been charged with any offence, although he sold his story, supposedly describing aspects of life at MI5, to the British newspaper, the *Mail on Sunday*. Shayler argues that MI5 were retaining files on those who had been 'of interest' because of their association with 'subversion'. The files held on left-wing activists, Shayler claims, included the names of current ministers of the Labour government. Jack Straw, the Home Secretary, obtained an injunction against the newspaper, although he felt unable to go to court to prevent further supposed revelations in the same newspaper. He stated, in a letter to the *Daily Telegraph*, that he could not obtain an injunction against that particular story since it did not contain material likely to damage national security. Given that the terms of the injunction refereed to 'matters damaging to national security', there was no civil remedy available to him. However, this debate over civil remedies does not affect the possibility of criminal charges.

What these cases do show are firstly, the difficulty of preventing publication, especially if publication is abroad; and secondly, the complex issues affecting any decision to prosecute. Although employees or ex-employees of intelligence agencies are liable to charges, it is quite another matter to decide that a prosecution is in the public interest. In the case of unauthorised disclosures by former intelligence officers the onus of proof is virtually placed on the defendant because no *mens rea*, deliberate intent, is required for a successful prosecution. This means that more damage to national security may result from a trial than from tolerating 'whistle-blowers'.[27] It depends on the credibility of the ex-employee, the nature of the supposed revelations, and the degree of disclosure imposed on the prosecution to prove its case. Even an 'illiberal' measure such as the 1989 OSA does not solve the problems raised by the 'politics of secrecy'.

The final point concerning the OSA 1989, although security and intelligence issues will be examined in more detail in later chapters, is that all prosecutions, as with the previous Act of 1911, are subject to the consent of the Attorney General. This allows consideration to be given to whether a prosecution is in the public interest. This protects Crown servants from trivial matters, such as disclosing the colour of Security Service stationery (one hopes this is too trivial to be the subject of a prosecution!), being the subject of prosecution.

As stated earlier, the 'public interest' debate is of such importance that it deserves further discussion. The most eloquent advocate of such a defence is Yvonne Cripps. Cripps admits that the concept of the public interest is an 'elusive one'[28] but she also argues that the courts and the judiciary are able 'to assess, against a background of time and place, where the public interest lies in given cases'.[29] It is also clear from the introduction to her book, and from the cases selected to 'illustrate' the issues in the subsequent chapters, that Cripps has considerable sympathy with those who feel 'compelled' to disclose. The cases she selects are: (1) Crimshaw and Leig of the National Coal Board; (2) Trevor Brown of the Atomic Weapons Research Establishment; (3) Frank Snepp of the CIA; (4) Detective Inspector John Trench of the City of Glasgow Police Force; (5) Stanley Adams of Hoffman-La Roche; (6) Dougal Mackenzie of British Steel. However, these are all examples likely to arouse our sympathy, since they involve individuals playing the role of David against Goliath. All of the allegations – revealing waste in nationalised industries (1 and 6); nuclear safety at an atomic weapons centre (2); a case of wrongful imprisonment for murder (4); a major pharmaceutical company's contravention of the competition laws of the EU (5) – involve large corporations or public authorities engaged in waste, abuse of power or the endangerment of public safety. The images associated with such cases tend to be heroic and noble. At no point does Cripps provide anything that could be construed as 'the other side of the story'; all that she does provide is a general statement that 'it may not be appropriate for an employee to decide the public interest' even where the case does arouse our sympathy.[30] Her argument is not about the merits of disclosure, examining the costs and benefits, but concerns the procedural point that whoever does decide the merits, it should not be the employer or employee but some external assessor such as a judge.[31]

Of course one can argue that in a legal text it is precisely procedural matters that ought to be addressed, but – and this is crucial – the construction of procedures is dependant upon a certain ethical or normative view about the issue being formalised. If we think disclosure to be 'bad', we are not likely to construct the same set of procedural rules as when we see it as 'good'. The procedures may be relatively ethically neutral but the objective of such procedures cannot be. That is, we must be clear as to whether the procedures will 'encourage' people to disclose information in certain situations or 'discourage' them. Cripps chooses to avoid this issue in the body of her text. The values underlying her views only become clear in the book's conclusion. She states that 'it is increasingly recognised that needless secrecy may be damaging';[32] welcomes the introduction of statutory rights of access to information;[33] criticises the 1993 White Paper on *Open Government*;[34] and expresses the hope that experience with a code of practice on open government will bring about 'a generalised freedom of information Act similar to that in the United States'.[35]

Cripps recognises the complexity of the issues and the diversity of statute and case law surrounding breaches of confidence, but she is clearly an advocate of greater protection for those claiming 'public interest disclosure'. Cripps is working within the tradition that I have identified as the 'normative', which argues that 'democracy', the 'public interest', and 'good government' are principles from which certain clear rights can be deduced. Only in passing, in one sentence, does Cripps recognise that other factors may be equally, if not more important, when she states that: 'It is possible that the "Next Steps" programme may yield beneficial results with regard to the availability of information.'[36] However, it is a pity that this argument is neither developed nor explored. As we have seen, it is a key point.

It is quite clear from this survey that the intention behind the 1989 reforms was to concede as little as possible while regaining some legitimacy for prosecuting certain cases such as those involving intelligence officers. The aim was certainly not to create a new basis for the management of official information or to create a new relationship between the citizen and the state. It was an attempt to deal with an old problem, how to discipline civil servants who acted 'disloyally', in a more effective manner. It is not until the more fundamental civil service reforms of the 1980s and 1990s that we see signs of radical change in attitudes to information control.

9 Defending the Realm: MI5

The Security Service Act of 1989 cannot readily be attributed to any external pressure, parliamentary demands, or major scandal. It is a measure that has more to do with internal governmental calculations than with the nature of public debate. Although there had been public discussion of reform and expressions of disquiet over the legal, constitutional, and parliamentary position of the Security Service for some decades, there did not appear to be any irresistible pressure for change. Why then did the government, for the first time in British history, place MI5 in the public, legal, domain?

THE BACKGROUND

Successive British governments have reacted to 'scandals', failures, and breaches of security, by a series of patchy and inadequate attempts to create a proper structure for ensuring that intelligence fulfils the needs of a modern state. This is particularly true in the domestic sphere, where the lack of adequate mechanisms, even some appearance of ministerial responsibility, encouraged accountability by 'leaks'.[1] Historically the main scandals have concerned penetration by agents of the Soviet Union. This is quite different from the concern with domestic abuse of intelligence that generated demands for accountability in the USA.[2] Thus, for 40 years, the fundamental issue bringing intelligence into the public domain was the accusation that agents of the Soviet Union had penetrated British intelligence. However, this form of 'scandal' led attention towards issues such as recruitment, counter-intelligence, and management, and not towards the use or abuse of intelligence at home or abroad. When it was suggested to Mrs Thatcher that Britain should undertake US-style reforms of intelligence, her reply was as follows: 'I do not answer for the United States, but I ask him to consider which has the more effective security service (prolonged laughter).'[3] The laughter of MPs, one assumes Conservative members enjoying the prime minister's reply, may seem less than justified, but it does reflect important attitudes to the supposed harm caused by the restrictions imposed on the FBI.

However, even when debates have occurred following a security scandal, they have focused more on the handling of the affair than on the organisation or activities of the intelligence services. In the past, ministers or former ministers, of whichever party, made only the most general statements on the activities or organisation of intelligence. For example, during the debate that followed Mrs Thatcher's admission of the treachery of Anthony Blunt, statements typically took the following form:

> Clearly the public services are an attractive target for Soviet penetration and the Security Service especially so... Procedures for recruitment, vetting and monitoring members of the public services who have access to classified information have been much extended and approved [since 1940].[4]

and

> I can tell the House – there is no reason why it should not have been said earlier – that my Right Hon. Friend the then Home Secretary did change the nature of recruitment into the Security Service and the way in which it was conducted.[5]

Details are conspicuous by their absence. No statement on the nature of previous recruitment procedures or on the current practices, merely a statement that people do get recruited and that things have changed.

However, there is one body which came into existence as early as 1964, the Security Commission, that enjoys extensive powers of investigation and reporting. The Security Commission's function is to act as an independent review body after a breach of security has occurred. Its mandate is to investigate breaches of security that have been brought to light by a court case, or by some other public incident such as a defection, and to make recommendations. However, it can only undertake such a task when requested to do so by the prime minister, it cannot initiate investigations at its own behest or at the request of parliament. Although Parliament is able to put pressure on the prime minister to hold some form of inquiry, it cannot determine its terms of reference.

The Security Commission was created in January 1964 by the prime minister, Sir Alec Douglas-Home, in consultation with the leader of the Opposition, Harold Wilson, following a serious of security scandals culminating in the Profumo Affair.[6] In the debate on Lord Denning's Report on Profumo the main reason given for the creation of a standing commission on security was that the setting up of a tribunal of inquiry was too cumbersome for any but the most serious of cases.[7]

A tribunal is a quasi-judicial body whose proceedings have the appearance of a trial. It was felt that this was not necessarily fair to those individuals being investigated, since it might damage reputations without their having recourse to a reply. The government therefore argued that a permanent body of investigators, with experience of security, and appointed by the prime minister, would be more appropriate. Harold Wilson argued that, although he was sympathetic to the idea of a standing commission on security, he would rather that such cases were dealt with by a Select Committee of the House of Commons.[8] Such a committee, Wilson argued, would have the advantage that it could operate in private, call for witnesses and papers, and avoid being seen as a 'trial' of persons with the risk to reputations which any such investigation implied. He also rejected the criticism that a Select Committee would inevitably be partisan and divide along political lines. However, most members on the government benches argued that such a Select Committee would be bound to divide on party lines and that this was not the best way of arriving at the truth in security cases which concerned the defence of the realm. A few days later, however, the concept of a security commission was accepted by the Leader of the Opposition as a desirable step, provided that: all references to the commission were made known to the House; and provided it did not curtail the right of the House to debate and question ministers.[9] The Security Commission, a non-statutory body, came into being in January 1965. The commission describes its terms of reference as being to investigate and report upon the circumstances in which a breach of security is known to have occurred in the public service, and upon any related failure of departmental security arrangements or neglect of duty.[10] The commission, whose chair is always a retired judge, is drawn from those with relevant experience of government service. This, unlike the new parliamentary committee, can include former senior military officers and civil servants. The Security Commission's reports were, until the reports of the Intelligence and Security Committee, created in 1994, the best source available on the management of the British intelligence services.[11] The reports are surprisingly detailed as to the circumstances that led to a breach of security, the behaviour of the relevant departments, including the intelligence services, and in making recommendations for changes in practice. A good example of the commission's capacity to be independent of the government is their report on Michael Bettaney.[12] This was the first time it had had to investigate a breach of security involving an MI5 officer and it utilised the opportunity to extend the investigation beyond Bettaney's treachery, considering evidence from members of the security service:

> of a more general character relating to the internal organisation and management of the Security Service. Some of this evidence, coming from both present members of the Service at various levels and from former members, has been highly critical. In the unusual circumstances of this investigation we thought it appropriate to encourage witnesses to express any criticisms they had on this subject with complete candour and to assure them that any criticisms adopted in our Report would not be attributed to individuals.[13]

the Report thus contains general conclusions on the management of MI5 and makes the following striking statement:

> No doubt security considerations dictate that the Service should be to a large extent a *self-contained and substantially autonomous organisation*. But the very fact of the Service's comparative isolation makes it more important that those responsible at the higher levels for management should maintain a self-critical attitude and be constantly alert to the need to keep the Service's organisation, practices and procedures under review [emphasis added].[14]

The report goes on to criticise the director-general of the service for his failure to meet the substance of their recommendations concerning management structure and practices in his published reply to their criticisms. The Commission comes very close to accusing the director-general of complacency when it states:

> The commentary [by the Director] on the individual recommendations seems to amount, in effect, to a claim that existing practices in the Security Service already meet the substance of the requirements [on personnel management]... We cannot accept that this is so.[15]

The Commission demonstrated that independent examination, even by a relatively 'tame' body, could be a valuable tool of management – as well as a source of embarrassment.

The Security Commission only operates after the fact and it is not a permanent review body. However, the fact that it has normally operated only after the fact is not as serious a defect as it may appear. Given the number and type of 'breaches of security', it actually managed to cover most of the main intelligence agencies: security in GCHQ, the Defence Intelligence Service, the armed services, various ministries, and the Security Service itself. However, its terms of reference, breaches of security, did limit what it could achieve. The absence of any independent review body did, however, cause problems to Mrs Thatcher, even though her instinct was to oppose any and all such developments. Mrs Thatcher used the Commission as a means of dealing with the accusations of Soviet penetration contained in Chapman Pincher's *Their Trade is Treachery*. This book claimed that the former head of MI5, Sir Roger Hollis, had been a Soviet agent. Mrs Thatcher, in a statement to the House of Commons on 26 March 1981, stated that she had decided to ask the Security Commission to undertake a review of 'security procedures and practices currently followed in the public service'.[16] This was a highly unorthodox use of the Security Commission, since it hardly concerned a specific breach of security. Indeed, Mrs Thatcher never accepted that any breach of security had occurred, since she never accepted that the evidence against Hollis was persuasive or conclusive. The only conclusion that can be drawn is that this review was a means of deflecting criticism that no mechanism existed whereby dissatisfied members of the intelligence community could communicate their grievances or anxieties over alleged Soviet penetration. Perhaps she hoped that such a device would deflect the 'young turks' from going public or pressing their demands for a thorough investigation. We know, of course, that this failed and ultimately led to the *Spycatcher* saga.[17] However, the problem of disaffected employees did lead, in November 1987, to the creation of another new mechanism but this time one internal to the intelligence services themselves, a part-time 'ombudsman' for the intelligence services. Its first head was Sir Philip Woodfield, a former senior civil servant in the Home and Northern Ireland Offices, who was to 'be available for consultation by any member of the intelligence services who has anxieties relating to the work of his or her service'.[18] This move was in response to the complaints from former members of MI5, such as Cathy Massiter, that there was no independent person with whom they could discuss their personal or ethical problems. However, recent cases, such as David Shayler, show that this mechanism is no guarantee against employees 'going public'.[19]

Another avenue of investigation, but one facing considerable opposition from government, was the Parliamentary Select Committee. In 1992 the Home Affairs Select Committee published a report on the 'Accountability of the Security Service'.[20] It recommended creating a new Parliamentary Select Committee on the Security Service to oversee value-for-money and general policy issues. However, the government did not approve of either the inquiry or its conclusions. The

Home Secretary, Kenneth Clarke, argued that the security service fell 'outside the ambit of the Committee' and that 'some forms of parliamentary scrutiny can weaken effectiveness'.[21] He did not allow any representative of MI5 to appear before the committee, and its conclusions were weakened as a result. The lack of co-operation necessarily meant that the report consists of some conclusions derived from first principles and a rather sketchy review of some overseas practice.

The only other committees to have even flirted with these issues have been those dealing with public records and the special branches of UK police forces.[22] The suggestion that a parliamentary committee be allowed to examine the intelligence services was always rejected. The government used to argue that, although effectiveness and safety need not be jeopardised by parliamentary discussion of broad policy, 'successive Governments have concluded that the distinction which this argument implies between policy and operations cannot easily be defined in relation to security and intelligence matters'.[23] As we have seen, this issue, the distinction between policy and operations, is one that is increasingly problematic in today's civil service. It is also obvious that the government did change its mind on this issue because it allowed a form of parliamentary review in the Intelligence Services Act 1994.[24]

Underlying such resistance was the view that it was better to risk the perception that intelligence abuses did, perhaps occasionally, occur than to risk the perception that intelligence was a tool of government: better that the public believes that it was sometimes out of control than that they believe that it was a tool of political or party rule. However, the problem that this created was that independence for MI5 was incompatible with the traditional mechanisms of ministerial accountability. Ministerial control can only exist if there are mechanisms that make such control a reality. The traditional mechanisms of MI5 control were spelt out in the famous directive issued by the Home Secretary, Sir David Maxwell-Fyfe, in 1952. It stated that

> In your appointment as Director-General of the Security Service you will be responsible to the Home Secretary personally. The Security Service is not, however, a part of the Home Office. On appropriate occasion you will have a right of direct access to the Prime Minister.[25]

Lord Denning, in his report on the Profumo Affair, interpreted this to mean that:

1. The Head of the Security Service is responsible directly to the Home Secretary for the efficient and proper working of the Service and *not* in the ordinary way to the Prime Minister [emphasis in original].
2. The Security Service is, however, not a department of the Home Office. It operates independently under its own Director-General, but he can and does seek direction and guidance from the Home Secretary, subject always to the proviso that its activities must be absolutely free from any political bias or influence.
3. The Head of the Security Service may approach the Prime Minister on matters of supreme importance and delicacy, but this is not to say that the Prime Minister has any direct responsibility for the Security Service. He has certainly none in day-to-day matters. It would be a mistake for the Prime Minister to take such responsibility because he cannot in practice exercise adequate supervision, and he has not the secretariat for the purpose.[26]

The statement that the prime minister has 'no secretariat for the purpose' is the most interesting. In the case of foreign intelligence, the Cabinet Office is the institution of central co-ordination and analysis. There is a structure, the Joint Intelligence Committee, which deals with tasking, analysis, and dissemination of the product, but no equivalent mechanism has ever been claimed for domestic intelligence.[27] Without such a structure for domestic intelligence it is very hard to maintain that ministerial responsibility was a reality. The traditional account of MI5 had little credibility within the British constitutional framework. Even after the statute of 1989 (see below) there are still grounds for viewing MI5 as largely autonomous.

So why did the government finally place MI5 on a statutory basis? The first reason, as we have seen, is that the management and control structures for MI5 were less than perfect. It was also a pre-emptive strike. The government may have calculated that reform was inevitable and, rather than wait and be compelled to introduce very much more radical legislation, it decided to introduce its own legislation first. Overseas experience was also relevant but not in any simple way. There is a tendency for many commentators in the UK to look to the USA for 'models' of how to deal with intelligence and open government but in fact it was the experience of the Old Commonwealth, Canada and Australia, which was more influential on government thinking. The message which Whitehall was being given was that intelligence services could live with some form of public scrutiny and that there were, indeed, even some advantages to be gained. For example, it allows an opportunity for a service to mount an effective political campaign, instead of merely one behind closed doors, to maintain budgets and mandates by enlisting the support of the oversight body.[28] However, such 'political factors' were less important than the changes taking place in the operational focus of the service. Events in the former Soviet Union and Eastern Europe had not reached their climax at the time of the proposals, but the Security Service may still have been astute enough to recognise that other topics, such as terrorism and drug trafficking, were a useful addition to the traditional focus on espionage.

In 1992 the government announced that responsibility for monitoring Irish Republican extremism was to be transferred from the Metropolitan Police Special Branch to MI5.[29] The immediate justification for the change was the apparent lack of police intelligence on Irish Republicans active on the mainland.[30] However, it may have been weaknesses in analysis or the strategic use of intelligence rather than inadequacies of collection, which brought about the shift. Another important factor influencing the passing of legislation may have been developments in Europe, particularly the growing importance of police co-operation. The growth of *euro-copism* and criminal justice co-operation may have stimulated the service into protecting its strategic position as the main international player: MI5 has always seen itself as having a much more sophisticated and well-developed network of links with foreign agencies than have the British police. It may have wished to protect this position by taking on a more visible security role, since it would have been much more difficult, if not impossible, for it to have taken on the role of counter-terrorism while cloaked in secrecy. Finally, there is the impact of 'scandal,' particularly the revelations of two former employees, Cathy Massiter and Peter Wright.

Massiter revealed in a television programme, *20/20 Vision*,[31] that the British peace movement, the Campaign for Nuclear Disarmament (CND), had been under investigation by the Security Service. Allegations were also made that various pressure groups, trade unions, and 'extremist' political organisations, were under surveillance. It was even claimed that, for a time in the 1970s, the National Council for Civil Liberties (NCCL), now renamed the Liberty Trust, had also been classed as a subversive organisation and that therefore the names of active members were kept on file. Following the revelations the NCCL brought a case under the European Convention on Human Rights. In April 1990 the ministers of the Council of Europe decided that the classification of the organisation as 'subversive' was contrary to the Convention.[32]

It has been claimed that the court cases arising from these revelations was the principle cause of reform,[33] but unlike the *Malone* case, the implications were not so profound as to *require* a fundamental rethink of security intelligence practices.[34] The criticisms could have been satisfied by clarifying the definition of subversion. However, although such cases added to the publicity surrounding the Service it was the *Spycatcher* affair that brought it into everyday discussion. Peter Wright was a member of the Security Service and had caused considerable embarrassment to the UK government by his decision to publish his 'memoirs' in Australia. The subsequent legal battles, principally in Australia and the UK but also in other countries, made the mystery surrounding the existence and basic activities of the Service look rather ridiculous. This is not the place to undertake a detailed analysis of the Affair but it is important to recognise that measures protecting intelligence information in the new Official Secrets Act and the placing of the Security Service on a statutory basis, are two sides of a coin. The tough provisions on the secrecy of intelligence are seen as being balanced by the more open approach to the Security Service. Both aspects were influenced by the way in which the Security Service had lost its 'suit of armour' and had become an object of public discussion. The end of the total blanket of secrecy meant that information had to be managed.

THE SECURITY SERVICE ACT 1989

The 1989 Act defines the function of the Security Service as

> the protection of national security and, in particular, its protection against threats from espionage, terrorism and sabotage, from the activities of agents of foreign powers and from actions intended to overthrow or undermine parliamentary democracy by political, industrial or violent means. It shall also safeguard the economic well-being of the UK against threats posed by the actions or intentions of persons outside the British islands.[35]

Critics immediately expressed doubts over the meaning of phrases such as 'undermining parliamentary democracy' and the use of 'political or industrial' means. Such concepts allow considerable latitude to the government in deciding who and what constitutes a threat to the state.

No doubt, this was the intention. The government followed previous statements on the activities of the service and on the nature of subversion by its use of general and rather imprecise concepts.[36] The management of MI5 is placed in the hands of the Director-General, who is appointed by the prime minister and is responsible for its efficiency and for ensuring that only 'necessary' information is collected and for ensuring that information is not improperly disclosed. The assigning of tasks is the responsibility of the secretary of state, which would normally mean the Home Secretary or the prime minister but could also include the Foreign Secretary or the Chancellor of the Exchequer. There is no mechanism specified in the Act that would allow the Director-General to resist an instruction that he or she considered to be outside the scope of his or her remit. The only recourse available would be an appeal to the prime minister and failing that, resignation.

The 'watchdog' mechanisms are the same as those used in the Interception of Communications Act 1985: a commissioner and a tribunal. Once again the commissioner is to be a former holder of 'high judicial office' and is to be appointed by the prime minister. He or she is to review the exercise of power by the secretary of state, to report to the prime minister (at least annually or when matters arise), and to assist the tribunal to investigate some types of complaints. The commissioner, the Rt Hon. Lord Justice Stuart-Smith, issued his first annual report in March 1991.[37] The reports of the Security Service commissioner are of considerably greater interest than those of the Interception of Communications commissioner. In Stuart-Smith's reports are names such as Patricia Hewitt, Harriet Harman, and Vanessa Redgrave as well as lesser-known, but interesting cases, such as David Esbester. However, it is worth while to begin with the commissioner's own description of his role. He describes his task as being to review the issuing of warrants but only in so far as they are reasonable; that is, that the secretary of state 'could properly have come to the conclusion which he did.'[38] He further states that it is not his function to substitute his judgement for that of the secretary of state on the question of whether a warrant is necessary. He argues that the justification of whether a warrant is necessary is 'one of fact and degree, more easily recognised when being considered than defined in advance.'[39] The only circumstance in which the secretary of state's judgement is likely to be challenged is when a party or narrow government interest is *clearly* being furthered. This is an area requiring the most sensitive of judgements, since the distinction between national and party interest is often extremely difficult to draw. The conclusion is that 'powers have been exercised properly'.[40]

The commissioner has since published a total of seven reports.[41] Many items deal only with relatively minor technical and procedural issues but there are matters of greater substance to be found. One category concerns intrusive police operations and the other the concerns of citizens who fear that they have been 'of interest' to MI5 at some point in their lives. The first of these anxieties reflects the anomaly identified by the Intelligence and Security Committee concerning the legal powers of MI5 and those enjoyed by the police. The second reflects the high degree of anxiety felt by individuals who suspect that they may be the target of MI5 activity when neither they, nor their activities, pose the remotest threat to the security of the state. Such anxieties are intensified when individuals suspect that they may have been denied some benefit or opportunity because of the use made of MI5 reports, for instance in the process of employment vetting.

Although the monitoring of warrants to search and seize property is one of the main functions of the commissioner, he does not provide details of the number of warrants issued. He states that this would 'not be in the national interest'. He does provide the total number of complaints: there were 44, of which 35 had been investigated, but he states, 'No determination has been made in favour of a complainant'.[42]

The pattern of the reports is again very similar to that found in the reports of the commissioner appointed under the Interception of Communications Act. There is the same careful language and quiet professionalism, with no effort being made to grab headlines or attract attention. The commissioner could be described as a watchdog, but a watchdog with no desire to bite anyone. The lack of independence, the lack of any responsibility to Parliament, and the ability of the prime minister to censor the commissioner's report prior to publication, all go to support this conclusion. This is not to suggest that the commissioner will not carry out his role with integrity, nor is it to suggest that having some form of review is not a step forward, but it is to suggest that this is a minimal form of oversight.

The Tribunal is a body of lawyers of not 'less than ten years' standing' to be appointed by royal warrant. People on such appointments can only be removed on a motion approved by both Houses of Parliament. This gives them a greater degree of independence than that enjoyed by the commissioner, who can be dismissed by the prime minister alone. The main task of the tribunal is to investigate whether MI5 had reasonable grounds for investigating the complainant. Such grounds may not only involve the issue of whether an individual is properly the subject of an investigation but also whether a category of person can reasonably be described as 'subversive'. The tribunal may also investigate whether the vetting of people for various government posts has been properly carried out and whether any material resulting from the vetting process has been improperly disclosed. Individuals who believe that, while carrying out its duties, the Security Service has caused damage to their property may also complain although in this instance complaints are investigated by the commissioner. Any person or any groups of persons is able to complain. The tribunal is bound to investigate unless it believe the complaint is frivolous or vexatious. It can be argued that avoiding the appearance of being frivolous, or even vexations, may be difficult given the degree of secrecy that surrounds such activities. However, it is also the case that some members of the public see it as a matter of prestige to believe that they are of sufficient importance to be of interest to the Security Service.[43] The power of the tribunal to call for papers and people is extremely wide; it is entitled to see anything or anyone. This contrasts with other external review bodies such as the US Congressional Intelligence Committees that must negotiate with their intelligence services in order to gain access to information. Being seen as an 'insider' body can be a disadvantage when gaining public legitimacy but it can make it easier to gain quick and full access to the facts.

One of the most controversial aspects of the legislation is the way it legitimates the activities that Peter Wright describes in colourful language: 'For five years we bugged and burgled our way across London at the State's behest.'[44] The Security Service Act states: 'No entry or interference with property shall be unlawful if it is authorised by a warrant issued by the Secretary of State under this section.'[45] Such warrants may be issued if the information to be obtained will be of 'substantial value', 'it cannot reasonably be obtained by other means', and the information obtained is subject to proper safeguards against improper disclosure. This section does at least require the secretary of state to make a judgement concerning the importance of the action, and the alternative means available, which is an improvement upon Wright's claim that bugging and burglary were carried out not only to obtain information, but 'for fun'.[46]

The 1989 Act contained no mechanism of review or oversight although, as we shall see, this was changed in the Intelligence Services Act 1994. The reasons for this will be developed in the next chapter, but it is worth nothing that the nature of MI5 had radically altered with the end of the cold war.[47] For MI5, whose principal tasks had been counter-espionage and counter-subversion, the demise of the main ideological enemy, the Soviet Union, threatened its very existence. For example, in the 1970s about 20 per cent of MI5 officers dealt with 'subversive activities'; today it takes one half of one person's time.[48] MI5 would have struggled to persuade the government, let alone informed opinion, that it was a cost-effective organisation were it not for terrorism and serious crime. Without these activities MI5 would appear to have no function other than dealing with bits and pieces of espionage, and this 'threat' would be of little significance to either politicians or the public. Managing a domestic intelligence service in the Britain of the 1990s is a *very* different business from doing so in the 1970s. A service which deals with problems stretching across major departments (Northern Ireland); which is beginning to experience the problems of being tasked instead of being self-tasked (by law enforcement agencies); and which is geared more to commercial than to political espionage, poses very different management and co-ordination problems – problems which probably could not have been solved without placing MI5, and its sister agencies, on a statutory footing. My argument, that such changes have relatively little to do with democracy and accountability to the public, may disappoint some people who wish to believe in 'progress' and other forces of 'good', but no government will consider such changes until the costs of secrecy outweigh those of openness. It is true that the government stood to gain some political advantage from 'opening up' intelligence and appearing to alleviate public anxieties about MI5, but the principal motive was to meet government concerns; to provide the legal framework for domestic intelligence in the twenty-first century.

10 The Democratisation of UK Intelligence?

1994 was the year in which the Secret Intelligence Service and the Government Communications Headquarters were placed on a statutory basis and all intelligence agencies made subject to a form of oversight. Although there is inevitably debate over the extent and significance of the reform process, even the critics see certain changes, such as the increasing crossover between law enforcement and intelligence agencies, as profoundly important.[1]

PARLIAMENT AND INTELLIGENCE

The only window on to an understanding of the apparently dramatic changes enshrined in the Intelligence Services Act 1994 is the extensive parliamentary discussion of the Act that took place during 1994 and 1995.[2] The Conservative government did not produce a White Paper or attempt to carry out the equivalent of a Defence Review. The only explanation as to why the Secret Intelligence Service (MI6) and the Government Communications Headquarters (GCHQ) were not only acknowledged but also placed on a statutory footing is that offered during debate. Perhaps even more surprising was the decision to place all the intelligence agencies, MI5, MI6, and GCHQ under a form of parliamentary oversight. This was something that all previous governments had said was impossible. However, with the collapse of the Soviet Union and peace talks in Ireland and the Middle East, the impossible was becoming probable.

The UK Parliament was traditionally not allowed to debate intelligence, so the only topics that were discussed were allegations of treachery and, more rarely, abuse of power. It was these topics that impinged most directly on the public sense of well-being (security) and few people expressed any interest in the organisation, efficiency or effectiveness of British intelligence. The dual, but contradictory, myths of incompetence (riddled with traitors) and omnipotence (James Bond) seemed to satisfy most appetites. However, most members of the public are unlikely to see activities such as tasking, remote sensing, analysis, and dissemination, as impinging on their interests. The issues that generate public attention are always control, accountability, and the collecting of information about fellow citizens. These issues remain dominant in recent parliamentary discussion. However, such issues are not only generated by public concerns but also because many of the MPs who express, or are seen as having, a special interest in intelligence, became interested in the subject because of their involvement with cases of injustice. This topic would certainly give someone a degree of familiarity with policing, including Special Branch, and perhaps with the Security Service, but would provide little or no incentive to study the history or activities of GCHQ. Of course, any lack of knowledge among parliamentarians does not merely reflect their interests, or lack of interest, but also reflects a long tradition of deliberate obsfucation and mystification by successive governments. The existence of MI6 was not even officially acknowledged until 1992.[3]

What makes the Act surprising was that only five years before, during the debate on the Security Service Act, the government had denied that any form of parliamentary oversight was desirable.[4] However, this does not mean that the government had a sudden change of heart. It was, as we shall see, all a matter of managing change.

The major parliamentary debates, as is normal practice, took place during the Second Reading of the Bill and during the Committee stage in the Commons.[5] The Foreign Secretary, Douglas Hurd, opened the debate on 22 February 1994. He argued that the legislation reflected the government's commitment to 'greater openness' but also its desire to protect national security and operational matters associated with intelligence and security. However, despite the absence of a White Paper, he still saw no need to provide any clear rationale for the Bill or for the apparent change in the government's attitude. He did, however, refer to three factors that contributed to the legislation:

- the work of the agencies has changed because the threats facing the United Kingdom have changed;
- the views of the agencies towards legislation and oversight have changed;[6]
- the Government has been able to observe the actual working of the measures which were introduced in the Interception of Communications Act 1985 and the Security Service Act 1989.[7]

However, although examples of the changed role of the intelligence services were given, most of them were not very new or very changed.[8] He also did not tell the House what led to the change of heart by the agencies. Informed sources certainly acknowledge the impact of visits from the Canadian and Australian agencies describing the virtues, as well as the drawbacks, of oversight. Having a channel by which to communicate with the public, other than by leaks, is a major benefit. Oversight bodies can become advocates as well as critics and this is extremely valuable when fighting for resources, even for organisational survival, in a rapidly changing environment. Also, Parliament was not given any concrete examples of how experience supposedly reduced anxiety in Whitehall; there is no reference to the practical operation of the earlier 1985 or 1989 legislation. However, if the government's exposition of the reasoning behind the Bill was inadequate, it is also true to say that the Opposition did not offer any alternative rationale. The Opposition did tease the government about having undergone a change of heart in allowing a form of oversight but they did not put forward any coherent alternative vision of the role, organisation, or purpose of intelligence.

Further criticisms of the legislation focused on the traditional issues of preventing misuse of intelligence, preventing harm to the citizen, and ensuring satisfactory oversight. The only other specific issue that the Opposition raised was the failure of the government to restore trade union rights to the employees of GCHQ.[9] No doubt this was an important issue, but hardly central to the legislation before the House.

Further criticism focused on the claim that the legislation did not go far enough in providing safety features for the intelligence machinery. Although there were several amendments tabled for discussion, only the main, contentious issues will be discussed.[10]

The Opposition spokesperson on Foreign Affairs, Dr John Cunningham, accepted the principles behind the Bill and made a major concession by agreeing that 'no Parliamentary Committee of whatever nature should be involved in operational matters.'[11] Dr Cunningham did not attempt to follow Mr Hurd's lead by discussing the need for intelligence other than to state in general terms that 'Britain retains global interests and internationally shared responsibilities ... to prevent terrorism, nuclear proliferation, the weapons trade and drugs trafficking.'[12] His main criticism of the legislation concerned the nature and size of the oversight committee. Both in the House, and in Committee, the Opposition parties argued that the oversight committee should take the form of a Select Committee and that it should be nine, rather than six, in number. This last point was accepted and was incorporated into the final legislation.[13]

Dr. John Gilbert, a Labour MP, in one of the better speeches on the Bill, argued that a Select Committee need not threaten legitimate interests in secrecy and security. Although membership of the committee would require the approval of the House, this could be done by prime ministerial resolution. This would mean that the power of nomination would remain with the prime minister, but the House could veto any candidate that did not meet with its approval. Gilbert also claimed that no Select Committee would publish a report 'containing sensitive passages that the Government say should not be published. I consider that absolutely inconceivable.'[14] However, despite the efforts of the Opposition during the debates, and in Committee, the Government accepted only one minor change, that concerning the size of the committee.

THE INTELLIGENCE SERVICES ACT 1994

The Intelligence Services Act 1994 places both MI6 and GCHQ on a statutory basis. It also places all of the secret services, that is SIS, GCHQ and MI5, under a form of parliamentary oversight. However, despite this innovation the legislation very much follows the style and content of the two previous pieces of legislation dealing with intelligence activity, the Interception of Communications Act 1985 and the Security Services Act 1989.[15] However, the 1994 Act has one new feature and that is the creation of an oversight mechanism in the form of the Parliamentary Intelligence and Security Committee. The nature and effectiveness of this form of parliamentary oversight will be discussed in more detail after an outline of the other main sections of the legislation.

The Act consists of twelve sections and four schedules. The arrangement of the sections falls neatly into four main topics:

- establishment of the duties and organisation of SIS;
- establishment of the duties and organisation of GCHQ;
- mechanisms for the issuing of warrants and approving 'certain other actions'; and
- establishment of a form of oversight.

The schedules outline the procedures to be adopted by the tribunal, commissioner, and parliamentary committee.

The first section of the legislation deals with SIS. The role of SIS is defined as being the collection of information and performance of 'other tasks' relating to persons 'outside of the British Islands' which affect national security interests, economic well-being or the prevention or detection of serious crime.[16] The key concepts are left undefined in that there is no attempt made to define 'other tasks', 'national security', 'economic well-being', or 'serious crime'. The fact that no attempt is made to define these terms means that there is a lack of restriction on either the government, or indeed its critics, speculating over what might or might not be allowed. Leigh and Lustgarten[17] and Michael Supperstone[18] both make the charge that the concept of national security is so vague, and has been so abused, that it does not provide a secure footing for secret state activity. The uncertainty of meaning is so great, they argue, that the term provides little restriction on intelligence activities and this uncertainty may be exploited by the government of the day to carry out activities that could not be justified in public.

The second section of the Act concerns the role of the Chief, popularly known as 'C', who is responsible for the efficient running of the service and for ensuring that it operates within its mandate.[19] The Chief is also given the legal obligation not to act 'to further the interests of any United Kingdom political party'.[20]

The role of GCHQ is defined as being to monitor electronic communications and to provide assistance and advice concerning languages and cryptography. These tasks can only be performed on behalf of the government if they are exercised in connection with the same tasks assigned to SIS, that is, national security, economic well-being and serious crime. There is not only the same language, but also the same lack of definition. The same language is also used to describe the duties of the GCHQ director, namely that he or she is responsible for efficiency, ensuring it acts in accordance with its mandate, and that it does not act to further the interests of any political party.[21]

The legislation then goes on to state that: 'No entry or interference with property or with wireless telegraphy shall be unlawful if it is authorised by a warrant issued by the Secretary of State under this section.[22] As with MI5, this section gives the agencies the power to commit what would otherwise be criminal offences such as telephone tapping, breaking and entering, and theft. Such methods can only be used when the secretary of state thinks it necessary; that is, when:

- they substantially assist MI5, SIS or GCHQ in carrying out their tasks under the 1989 and 1994 Acts;[23]
- the task cannot 'reasonably be achieved by other means;[24]
- arrangements have been made to secure proper handling of the information as required by the 1989 and 1994 legislation;[25]
- it authorises the Security Service to carry out the terms of a warrant issued under the Act on behalf of SIS or GCHQ even though such action may not be a part of the Security Service's mandate.

A warrant can be issued either by the secretary of state or by a senior official who has been authorised to issue such warrants in 'urgent cases'. A warrant lasts for six months but can be renewed or revoked if the secretary of state so wishes. The legislation also gives immunity under UK law for any act committed whilst carrying out an action authorised by the secretary of state.

The final sections of the legislation create a tribunal and commissioner to investigate complaints. Both the tribunal and commissioner are modelled on the previous legislation, that is the Interception of Communications Act 1985 and the Security Service Act 1989. The commissioner has the responsibility of reviewing the exercise of the powers granted to the secretary of state, particularly the issuing of warrants, and to make an annual report to the prime minister. The commissioner may also report to the prime minister, at any time, on any matter that concerns the discharge of his or her functions. The tribunal has the responsibility of investigating all complaints, excepting those complaints that concern property, from individuals or organisations. The commissioner must deal with complaints concerning property.

INTELLIGENCE OVERSIGHT AND ACCOUNTABILITY

As stated earlier, many of the provisions echo those of previous legislation but there is one genuinely innovative feature of the legislation and that is the creation of a form of parliamentary oversight. The Intelligence and Security Committee is given the task of examining the 'expenditure, administration and policy' of the three intelligence agencies. The committee, consists of nine individuals who must be members of either the House of Commons or the House of Lords and must not be ministers. However, membership of the committee is not determined by Parliament but by appointment by the prime minister after consultation with the Leader of the Opposition.[26] The Committee's remit is obviously wide, and potentially far-reaching, but such a remit would appear to require unfettered access to people and papers and considerable research resources. However, it only has a staff of three and its powers are heavily constrained. Information can be denied to it either by the director of an agency or on the grounds that the secretary of state has determined that it should be withheld.[27] Information can be withheld as 'sensitive' on the grounds that it could be properly withheld from a Parliamentary Select Committee or on the grounds of national security. In this case, however, the concept of national security is given some clarification in that Schedule 3, Section 4 states:

> the following information is sensitive for the purposes above –
>
> (a) information which might lead to the identification of, or provide details of, sources of information, other assistance or operational methods available to the Security Service, Intelligence Service or GCHQ;
> (b) information about particular operations which have been, are being or are proposed to be undertaken in pursuance of any of the functions of those bodies; and
> (c) information provided by, or by an agency of, the Government of a territory outside of the UK where that Government does not consent to the disclosure of the information.

The committee can also be denied access to information, not because of any UK interest or national security requirement, but by any of its intelligence allies who choose to mark (and which of them will not?) information which they communicate as being 'not for disclosure'. There are few surprises in the above list of 'exemptions'. They are the typical categories given protection in most democracies, that is, intelligence sources and methods.

Once again, as with all new monitoring or review bodies, there is the question of whether it feels the need to announce its presence by issuing dramatic statements or whether it will try and establish itself as a 'safe pair of hands'. The ISC has published several reports that provide the basis for an assessment.

The first report published by the ISC was an interim report in which it stated that it held weekly meetings and claimed that it was 'now operating within the "ring of secrecy"'.[28] This was given meaning by the announcement that it had held a series of meetings with Whitehall personnel and had begun to set an agenda; an agenda which included issues such as the end of the cold war, the fall-out from the *Ames* case, and the police/intelligence relationship. These were topics that came to dominate its reports over the next two years.[29] It is of particular interest to note that this, its first report, dealt with MI5's work against organised crime.[30] The report was a response to a government announcement that it intended to increase MI5's role in the fight against crime. It was therefore a 'political' response to a political proposal and indicated that the committee was prepared to flex its political muscles.

The report begins by identifying 'some very important decisions' which the government needs to make.[31] However, despite the clearly political nature of the agenda it hesitates to identify what the rest of us would call 'concerns'. Although the report identifies the issues, what it calls the principles and arrangements covering the work of MI5 in the field of crime, there is little air of excitement, controversy, or 'playing to the public gallery'. The report is couched in the anodyne language and style of a civil service briefing and is the very opposite of sensationalist. Its audience was clearly the government and legislators and not the media or general public. It was a form of a 'pre-emptive strike' against the government being tempted to take what the ISC calls 'simple' options.[32]

The issues that concern the committee are:

- MI5 should not be self-tasking when countering 'conventional' crime; that is, crime that does not have significance for national security nor the 'economic well-being of the state'. These latter are part of M15's traditional remit under which, as the committee correctly argues, it is 'essentially self-tasking'.[33]
- MI5 should be tasked by law enforcement organisations and work *in support of* them (the Committee's emphasis).
- 'Organised' crime and 'serious' crime are not the same thing and the justification for M15 involvement needs to be made for each.
- The 'accountability issues' will need to be resolved.
- The authorisation of interception of communications and interference with property will also need to be resolved.[34]

However, unlike the later report (see below), there is a distinct shortage of concrete recommendations. What is even more disappointing is that there is no effort to balance competing values or to assign any kind of weight to differing interests. This interim report was an important statement that the committee intended to be more than a rubber-stamp, but the message that it sent was: we are going to be independent and play a political, as well as quasi-legal role, but we are 'safe'.

The next report from the ISC was the annual report for 1995.[35] Some of the issues discussed in the earlier report are raised again, but the annual review is obviously broader in scope. The main issues dealt with are

1. the ISC itself and its mandate
2. the way in which the agencies have responded to the end of the cold war
3. the relationship between the agencies and law enforcement work against 'serious crime'
4. the tasking of intelligence agencies
5. the nature and dissemination of the damage assessment following the revelation that Aldrich Ames was a Soviet agent
6. the nature of security and vetting procedures within the agencies
7. the briefing of ministers by agencies (see also concern over the *Ames* case – issue 5 above).

Some of the concerns expressed are merely echoes of the anxieties expressed in the interim report discussed above. However, there are some new clues to the way in which the committee will function. It expresses a general satisfaction with itself, stating that: 'the system of oversight by a small Committee of Parliamentarians is appropriate to the task it has been given and is capable of meeting the purposes which government and Parliament intended.'[36] However, it would be wrong to accuse the committee of complacency, since it does reflect on its mandate and hints – one could not express it more strongly – that it may even seek to stretch its mandate. When discussing how other countries, particularly the USA, manage oversight, the report states that there are two main differences between oversight in the UK and elsewhere:

> [First,] while we do not have responsibility for the initial allocation of resources [the budget], we do have clear responsibility to ensure that the Agencies have access to adequate resources and that those resources are used in a cost-effective way. The second is the US Agencies' obligations to keep their oversight committees informed of their activities as opposed merely to responding to requests for information. While the legislation which established our Committee is different, we have told the Agencies that this Committee expects to be kept properly and promptly informed.[37]

Given that neither the legislation, nor government statements to the House of Commons, gave any hint that the intelligence agencies would be required to seek prior approval from the committee for any operations, one wonders what the phrase 'promptly and properly informed' is meant to imply. Given its context, a discussion of US oversight and the requirement for 'prior approval', it would seem to suggest that the committee is asking for contemporaneous information about some operations. This raises the question: when does the present become the future? The committee is certainly putting pressure on the heads of the intelligence agencies to contact them if they are about to carry out operations that *might* raise policy issues at a later date. If the committee is more than a rubber-stamp, and the evidence from its reports is that it is more than this, then any intelligence chief would be wise to develop a continuous and close working relationship with it. Much of the success of the committee depends on the qualities of the chair person, but the opinion in Whitehall[38] is that Tom King is a very active chairman, who expects 'not to be surprised' by later events; he wishes to know in advance what the awkward issues are likely to be.

The committee's concern over the *Ames* case relates not only to significance – has the damage assessment exercise been rigorously and fully carried out? – but to the dissemination of the results of the exercise. The Scott Inquiry into arms sales raised similar concerns over the effectiveness of dissemination and the extent to which Ministers paid full and proper attention to the intelligence they were receiving.[39] It seems that the old intelligence problem – decision-makers' use of intelligence – has not been solved in the UK despite the system of close relationships between producer and consumer departments.[40]

Finally, there is the issue of tasking and the relationship between law enforcement and intelligence agencies. The committee concludes that

> it will be insufficient simply to add the countering of serious organised crime to the Security Service's responsibilities . . . the Service is essentially a 'self-tasking organisation'. The legislation needs to make it clear that, in respect of work that the Service will be doing *in support of* the law enforcement organisations, it will not be self-tasking [emphasis in original].[41]

It also states that the differences in legal powers to interfere with property and intercept communications between the MI5 and the police service must be resolved. The fact that MI5 must seek a warrant from the secretary of state whereas the police only require the approval of a senior officer means that 'there will be clear problems if these different systems are being operated side-by-side'.[42]

The government has responded to these points by introducing new legislation. The first Bill amended the Security Service Act 1989 to read

> (4) It shall be the function of the Security Service to act in support of the prevention and detection of serious crime.[43]

The government has also introduced new legislation covering police intelligence activities. This Bill, which was passed along with about 40 other measures on the last day of the last Conservative government, became the Police Act 1997.[44]

The Act gives the police the right to enter property and intercept communications.[45] Initially the proposals were given a guarded welcome by then opposition party, the Labour Party, but when it became clear that the legal profession, civil liberties' groups, the media, and other opposition parties were all opposed to the Bill, the Labour Party also decided to oppose it.[46] However, it was in the House of Lords that the legislation came under serious attack from former Home Secretaries, senior judges, and a majority of peers.[47] The main criticisms centred on two issues. The first was whether the system of review by a commissioner, which was the formula used in other 'intelligence' legislation, should be replaced by a requirement that the police gain prior approval for intrusive surveillance from a judge. The second issue centred on the argument that surveillance of certain premises, for example the offices of solicitors and doctors, should certainly require prior judicial approval even if all such operations did not. The government response was to amend its Bill to require 'all authorisations to be notified to the Commissioner as soon as practicable' and to require the commissioner to scrutinise 'particularly sensitive cases within 48 hours'.[48] However, although the Labour Party opposed the Bill, it is unlikely to alter its provisions now that it is in power.

The latest annual report from the ISC covers many of the issues previously discussed but it is worth noting that it continues to identify this area, police/intelligence relationships and powers, as one 'we will continue to follow with particular interest.'[49] However, it also states that although some cases have been developed by the Security Service based upon requests from law enforcement agencies, the resources devoted to such activities 'are likely to remain relatively small'.[50] The report also states, in its conclusion, that it will continue to monitor the new arrangements as to whether the agencies are 'pursuing their supporting roles effectively'.[51]

The above discussion raises the very interesting question of whether the ISC has been a powerful influence on government policy in this area despite its relatively short time in office. To have virtually formulated the law and procedures in this vital new area, intelligence and the fight against crime, would obviously be a major achievement. However, private sources state that this is something of an exaggeration. Although the committee formulated its own view and recommendations, this was not done in a vacuum. In addition to developing its own views it obviously can act as a channel for expressing the strongly held views of key players in Whitehall. It is contrary to British political tradition for officials to air their views about any government policy, let alone proposed legislation. The battles take place behind closed doors in Whitehall committees and corridors and the public is not privy to these discussions except via 'private' briefings to journalists. However, the existence of the ISC has created a new avenue for influencing opinion – if you can manage to convince the committee that your proposals are the right ones, it will do the advocacy for you! The ISC may become another instrument to be used and – if it is not careful – manipulated by those engaged in Whitehall power struggles. There is no unity of view on issues of intelligence policy in the intelligence community, departments, cabinet office or ministers, and the existence of a body like the ISC provides a new weapon in the policy-making process.

However, the ISC did influence the legislation on crime and the Security Service and this is greatly to its credit. It showed a degree of maturity at birth which compares very favourably with experience in other countries such as the United States or Canada who focused on immediate public concerns and civil liberties issues, and took a long time to realise that a well-managed and efficient service is a far greater protection against 'abuse' than any number of laws or oversight bodies. Effective management and control, a clear sense of purpose, is a far greater protection of the rights of citizens than a multitude of inquisitive oversight staff 'investigating' intelligence. They are only likely to find out that things have gone wrong after the event, which means that it is too late: the rights of citizens have already been damaged. The aim must surely be to prevent such infringements through effective and efficient management. Exposing abuses does little to prevent them if intelligence officers are 'out of control'. In fact it may undermine morale, creating an 'I do not care attitude' that actually increases the probability of rogue operations. By its emphasis on high quality management, co-ordination and tasking procedures, the committee has shown that it has already gone through its 'steep learning curve'.

CONCLUSION

The obvious conclusion to be drawn is that Britain has moved some distance in lifting the secrecy that traditionally covered intelligence issues. It must also be conceded that placing UK intelligence on a legal footing has not meant that it is subject to the kind of constraints found in the USA or Canada. The legislation is designed to be permissive rather than restrictive – it is minimalist and can be viewed as an attempt to prevent anything more drastic being imposed as a result of scandal, rulings of the European Court or by change in government. But what made even this necessary? I believe that the legislation is a form of risk management. Both the Secret Intelligence Service and the Security Service will tell you that the world has changed – the environment and mandate have altered. Less so for GCHQ or MI6 than for MI5, but all of them see new opportunities opening as old ones close. One of the major changes has been the move into, or expansion of, activities concerning drug trafficking, proliferation of weapons of mass destruction, manipulation of the currency, and organised crime. This creates new audiences such as the courts and a greater interest in a much wider group of consuming departments. In order to 'manage' such intelligence activities they had to be placed on a statutory footing. In the past, when things went wrong secrecy, deniability, was the best protection, but if private individuals are to be brought before courts of law then your 'deniability' is only as good as others will allow. To conclude, the argument is that once the agencies lost control over their monopoly of information, then the balance between the 'dangers' of openness and secrecy shifted. The legislation is the result of this process of 'risk management'.

Will a Labour government choose to alter the 'balance' in a more civil-liberties direction? I do not believe it will. Although it may come under pressure from some of its supporters to reform these statutes, there would seem few incentives to do so. There will still be contrasts made with overseas experience, and this will remain a useful focus of debate but it has been, and will continue to be, domestic factors that drive reform. There is no evidence to support the view that reform was inevitable or that all democracies have arrived at some common democratic goal. The UK was not driven by scandal or the politics of revelation and its system of intelligence accountability is unlike any other. Rather, changes in the pattern of political and operational risk associated with intelligence activities seem far more important than any 'democratic logic'.

11 Overseas Experience: FOI in Canada, Australia and New Zealand

As we have seen, other countries' experience of open government and freedom of information is often taken as a model to be followed. This has become even more attractive as more and more countries have introduced freedom of information legislation. This is so because *the greater the diversity of cases, the greater is the range of types of government that can be shown to be compatible with some form of FOI*. The range of examples seems to severely dent, if not erode, the argument that there is some element or elements about country X's system of government that prevents it from introducing FOI. However, although this argument does have merit, it is not quite the knockout blow that it may appear. The argument does not explain some important variations:

1. in the *timing* of the introduction of FOI – why some nations have been more reluctant than others to enact legislation;
2. in the *form* of FOI – why some nations have been more or less enthusiastic in the kind of access they have allowed and to what;
3. in the *manner* in which FOI is applied – and therefore the degree to which it actually changes what is often described as its main priority, the culture of secrecy; and
4. in the *degree to which FOI is a part of something that might be called 'open government'* – that is, the degree to which the process of policy-making, political decision-making, is 'open'.

It must be conceded at once that to undertake such a task is beyond the scope and resources of this study. Indeed it is a task that no single person has contemplated or achieved, in that it would require a team of scholars working within an agreed framework. Where comparisons are made it is generally between the statutes rather than on their implementation or effect.[1] This pattern is largely followed below. Although some attempt is made to comment on the circumstances of the introduction of FOI legislation, it is the variations in statute which form the basis of comparison. In order to maximise the comparison, the countries selected are all from the 'Old Commonwealth', those countries that share what is often described as a common 'Westminster' tradition. This excludes not only the USA (1966) and Sweden (1776), which I covered in my earlier work, *Public Secrets*, but also fellow members of the European Union such as France (1978), Denmark (1970), and Holland (1978). Although British commentators used to concentrate on the US model, this is beginning to change as familiarity with Commonwealth experience grows. A good example of this is the recent Select Committee Report on Open Government, which examined FOI practice in New Zealand, Canada and Australia.[2]

The committee begins by arguing that drawing lessons from overseas experience is not new.[3] For example, the Franks Committee on Official Secrecy (1972) and the Labour Government (1979), when considering reform of the official Secrets Act, both commissioned studies of overseas practice.[4] However, the issue that impresses the Select Committee is that other commonwealth countries, with what are said to be 'Westminster-style systems' have introduced freedom of information legislation. The committee does not analyse in any detail what is meant by a Westminster-style constitution but it does argue that 'certain constitutional conventions, such as a neutral civil service and Cabinet collective responsibility', are common.[5] Its main concern is an examination of the various FOI statutes and their impact. The committee identifies two key benefits: the impact on personal records; and the quality of decision-making. It states:

> [T]here was a consensus in Australia and New Zealand that the right of access had resulted in far greater objectivity in the recording of information. It used not to be uncommon to find subjective and even abusive comments on file. That had ended with FOI legislation.[6]

The committee also seems to accept the claim that: 'Standards of administration had improved in that FOI had encouraged objective, reasoned and defensible decision-making.'[7] This rather rhetorical statement is made somewhat more credible by the admission that such improvements were also the result of: 'outside scrutiny, the requirement to give reasons for decisions and of the review and appeals system, established in the 1970s'.[8] The committee also believes that FOI has led to 'greater public participation in policy debate'.[9] However, it is in danger of confusing access with open government. Firstly, although FOI may have an impact on the quality of administrative *records*, this does not mean that it can also be assumed that it has had an equal impact on the *quality of decisions*. Secondly, although

FOI may improve the process of administrative decision-making, it cannot be assumed that this necessarily improves the quality of political decisions. Access provisions normally give the right to information only after decisions have been made – and internal documents, along with cabinet papers, are, as we shall see, explicitly excluded from Australian and Canadian FOI provisions.

So what can we learn from comparing Australian, Canadian and New Zealand experience?

1. The introduction of FOI was a response to a particular set of circumstances that could be called a 'crisis of legitimacy'. Certainly this can be argued in the case of Canada and Australia. In both of these countries there had been argument over FOI for many years, even decades, but without success. It was only when the state was accused of grossly abusing its own citizens, in *secret*, that FOI legislation was passed.[10]
2. FOI did not happen in isolation but was part of a larger process of change in governance covering public administration, judicial review, the introduction of ombudsmen, and the 'restructuring of the state'.
3. Although Canada and Australia can both be described as following a Westminster model there are important differences. Both have federal systems and this has created, particularly in Canada, important tensions that provide an incentive for the regions to challenge the secrecy of the centre.
4. There are variations in the content of FOI legislation that reflect their effort to solve the problem of applying a US model within their own particular constitutional tradition. Even a strong British advocate of reform, Patrick Birkinshaw, argues that the comparison demonstrates that there are 'enormous differences' between them.[11]

CANADA

During the 1970s both parliamentary committees, and interest groups such as the Canadian Bar association, called for the introduction of FOI legislation. The Liberal government, under Pierre Trudeau, promised legislation but it never materialised. In their election campaign of May 1979 the Conservatives promised to introduce FOI but this too failed to materialise before another election in 1980 that restored

Trudeau. This time the Trudeau government did introduce FOI legislation, but McCamus states that

> the passage of the Bill proved to be both long and controversial. Committee hearings which began in March of 1981 continued on and off for more than a year and, in early 1982, it was widely rumoured that the government would not proceed with the Bill. However, after revision it was enacted on June 28 1982.[12]

Given the influence of the USA on British attitudes towards FOI, it is somewhat surprising that Canada took so long and displayed such an ambivalent attitude towards the introduction of FOI.

Few commentators point out the conjunction between the introduction of FOI and the problems of the Federal government, particularly over Quebec. The late 1970s was the period of the McDonald Commission on 'Freedom and Security under the Law' which examined the Federal, particularly the RCMP, response to the Quebec issue.[13] Its report, which was finally published in August 1981 after being held back for several months, concluded that the RCMP Security Division should be disbanded and that this function should be handed over to a new, civilian, agency. Again the government was uncertain how to react. It was seen by some that the RCMP had only 'done its job', and that if it had acted unlawfully it was with the understanding, if not instruction, of senior politicians. Others saw the record of the RCMP as reflecting a history of government abuse targeted against so-called subversive organisations. However, although the CSIS Act (1984) follows the Access Act (1982) the impact of the scandals associated with the Quebec Crisis had an impact on both. It was during the 1970s that the press reports and official inquiries on the Quebec Crisis were at their height. The cumulative affect of these reports was to undermine public confidence in government and therefore contribute to the demand for FOI legislation.

The Canadian Access to Information Act (1982) provides a right of access to Federal government records whatever the form in which they are held. It therefore includes paper files but also sound recordings, films, computerised data and E-mail.[14] However, although all Federal departments and 'other government bodies' are included as a part of 'government', many important agencies such as the Canadian Broadcasting Corporation, Air Canada and Canadian National Railways are excluded. The Act also requires all government record-holders to compile a register which describes the records kept, their probable location, any other information likely to assist someone in identifying records, and all administrative manuals used by employees in performing their duties.[15] The last of these is particularly valuable as an attack on 'secret law'; the practice whereby decisions are based on internal documents that offer interpretations of the law and actually constitute the basis upon which decision are made. One of the main complaints against British administrative practice was that departments such as the Inland Revenue and Social Security refused to publish the manuals issued to employees and yet such manuals were crucial to understanding the decisions made in individual cases.[16]

Crucial factors affecting the operation of FOI legislation are the time and cost of applying for records and in appealing against denials of access. There was considerable debate in Canada over the charges to be levied on applicants. Initially the government wished to levy a charge of C$25.00 to cover copying and the first five hours of searching, with an additional payment for each extra hour.[17] However, the Canadian Bar Association objected to this charging structure, arguing that people could face unknown bills only to be told that their application was denied. It also provided an incentive to departments to spend as long as they wished on a particular case, knowing that all costs incurred by delay or dithering could be passed on to the applicant.[18] The Bill was subsequently amended to exclude the time spent in considering an application from the allotted 'five hours' and only an initial deposit of C$5.00 must be paid before a request is considered. A decision must also be made within 30 working days, although this can be extended if the request is complicated or third parties need to be consulted.[19] The second element, the process of appeal, is equally vital to the success of FOI. If litigation, requiring the employment of lawyers and lengthy court proceedings, is involved, then applicants are likely to be dissuaded from exercising their rights. Effectively the agency is in control, since a refusal is tantamount to a challenge – accept our decision or risk huge and unknown costs. Canada has reduced this risk by using the mechanism of an information commissioner (IC). The IC is a form of 'ombudsman' whose role is to review the decisions of departments – although, as with most ombudsman, the decision of the IC is advisory and does not constitute a definitive ruling; if the applicant is not satisfied with the ruling he or she may still appeal to the Federal Court of Canada.[20]

Another important set of factors associated with FOI is the nature of the exemptions, that is, those categories of documents that are excluded from access. Some of the exemptions have been described as 'traditional' by commentators – that is, they cover the same ground as the seven basic exemptions under the US FOI legislation – but others are undoubtedly unique to Canada. The 'common' exemptions cover areas such as international affairs and defence, 'working papers', commercial information, personal information, law enforcement records, and material withheld under other statutes.[21] The more specific exemptions relate to cabinet records and to information that could 'reasonably be expected to be injurious to the conduct of... Federal–provincial affairs'.[22] The exemptions for cabinet and internal working papers are extensive and detailed. Section 69(1) states that 'the Act does not apply to confidences of the Queen's Privy Council for Canada', which means that all proposals, background papers, agendas and minutes of Committees relating to the 'policy-making process are excluded', McCamus concluding that this creates immunity for the 'inner circle' of Canadian government and that the Canadian FOI Act has produced 'the most secretive executive privilege rules to be found in the western world'.[23] The exemptions for advisory, working, and cabinet papers clearly reflect the influence of the British tradition, with its fear of civil service interference in 'politics' and its concern to maintain the authority of ministers.[24]

The impact of the Canadian freedom of information legislation is hard to assess, but there certainly does appear to have been some resistance in overcoming the notion that applicants were 'adversaries' seeking to make life difficult for ministers and civil servants.[25] The IC was even concerned for a time that the government might try to modify or even repeal the Act:

> I think a number of ministers and public servants believe the Access Act goes too far... While I doubt that the electorate would tolerate a repeal of the Act or that a government would repeal the Act, I repeat that the Government's response to the Parliamentary Committee's report places the rights in considerable jeopardy.[26]

However, such attitudes are not new. As we saw, the Canadian political elite did not have a uniform attitude to the introduction of FOI and demanded a degree of 'protection', for the process of government, hence the exclusion of consultative and cabinet papers, for the core political process. We can see that Canada has implemented a version of 'freedom of information' but by no means the full, radical vision, contained in ideals such as open government. Although the normative ideal may have provided one motive for change, the way in which Canada implemented the ideal is very much conditioned by its history and circumstances. As we shall see, this pattern, the common ideal disguising substantial variation in practice, is repeated in Australia and New Zealand.

AUSTRALIA

We shall see that despite common timing there is no identity between the Canadian, Australian, and New Zealand legislation. This is perhaps unexpected given that all appear to have been inspired by US experience and were attempting to solve a common problem, namely, how to make FOI 'fit' the Westminster model. However, the circumstances giving rise to FOI in Australia have some important parallels with Canada. Australia also experienced a 'crisis of legitimacy', not only because of intelligence, particularly domestic intelligence, activities but also because of the crisis associated with the dismissal by the Governor General of Australia, Sir John Kerr, of the Labour prime minister, Gough Whitlam, in 1975. Allegations of interference centred on the role of the United States, the CIA, and 'international capital'.[27] The Whitlam crisis is rooted in the history of suspicion among many Labour politicians over the Australian Security Intelligence Organisation's (ASIO) 'meddling' in Australian politics: the Petrov Affair of 1954; the split in the Australian Labour Party in 1954; and ASIO contacts with the Catholic, virulently anti-communist, wing of the labour movement, the Democratic Labour Party. This culminated in a rather bizarre incident in 1972 when the newly elected Labour Attorney General mounted a raid against his own intelligence organisation's (ASIO) headquarters on the grounds that he was being denied access to information.

By 1974 the prime minister, Gough Whitlam, had decided to set up a Royal Commission (chaired by Mr Justice Hope) to investigate the organisation, role, and effectiveness of the Australian Security and Intelligence services. However, the report is notable for two features: the absence of any evidence to support the more conspiratorial charges; and the concentration on the ASIO compared to any other member of the community.[28] The latter issue reflects the concern found in many Western democracies during the 1970s and 1980s that domestic intelligence agencies were operating in a 'repressive' manner against radicals, critics, dissenters, and those with 'unconventional views'. The charge was that such agencies were using labels such as 'subversive', communist, and terrorist, to carry out illegal, undemocratic and unconstitutional activities designed to preserve the 'establishment'. The notion of their being a 'realm', a state or body representing the public interest and therefore worthy of protection, had all but disappeared. The claim to protect the public interest was seen as a mask disguising the protection of some narrow, sectional interest such as class, race, gender, international capitalism, the military–industrial complex, or whatever.[29]

However, as well as inspiring the Hope Commission into security and intelligence agencies, the series of events referred to above also inspired the Australian Labour Party to commit itself to open government. In 1973 the Whitlam government created an inter-departmental cabinet committee to adapt US experience of FOI to an 'Australian constitutional and administrative structure'.[30] However, the published report was subject to 'strong criticism' from those who argued that it had failed in its main task and had not given sufficient weight to those aspects of the Australian system limiting the scope for FOI. This issue continued to vex politicians and commentators for the next eight years. One of the ways that this manifested itself, which is also found in New Zealand, is the debate over the 'ministerial veto'. The argument was that in a parliamentary system ministers are required to take individual and collective responsibility for decisions and so must have the right finally and conclusively to determine whether a document could or could not be released. Critics argued that no minister should be allowed to be judge and jury in his or her own case when issues of personal or political embarrassment might weigh more than constitutional considerations. However, under the Act passed in 1982, and even after its amendment by the Hawke (Labour) government in 1983, ministers retain the power of veto.[31] To give an American president, let alone a member of the US cabinet, the unfettered power to veto the disclosure of information, would be unimaginable. To Congress, it is precisely such institutions that constitute the 'enemy'.

The Australian Freedom of Information Act 1982 creates a right of access to documents held by public bodies unless such documents fall into an exempt category. However, in addition it also requires that all public agencies issue a description of the activities they perform and publish their previously confidential internal manuals. The latter echoes the Canadian stress on removing 'secret law', the practice whereby decisions where based upon purely internal interpretations of the law unavailable to the public.

In Australia the right of access is to documents and not to information but it does include access to data held in electronic or mechanical form. The right applies only to documents created after 1977 except in the case of records of personal information if access to earlier records is necessary to provide a proper understanding of the file.[32]

Otherwise earlier documents are covered by the Archives Act 1983, under which records are available only after 30 years. This means that, in 1999, non-personal documents created between 1969 and 1977 are not accessible. The agency also has the right to refuse requests that 'would substantially and unnecessarily divert the resources of the agency'. An agency must process a 'reasonable' request within 30 days.[33] All such requests must be accompanied by an A$30.00 application fee and agencies may recover their administrative costs by charging a A$15.00 per hour search fee and a A$20.00 per hour fee to cover the cost of making a decision.[34] An applicant can apply to have the fee waived or reduced on the grounds of personal hardship or the public interest. The Australian Law Reform Commission report on FOI legislation recommended that agencies should not be allowed to charge for personal information and that they should not be able to charge for time spent in arriving at a decision. Both seem improvements that would bring Australia into line with experience elsewhere.[35]

In the event of a refusal the applicant has the right to appeal. An applicant can apply for an internal review but if this is unsatisfactory, or takes longer than 30 days, the applicant may appeal to the Administrative Appeals Tribunal (AAT). However, although the applicant need not be legally represented – the review is meant to be conducted with as little formality as possible – an application to the AAT costs A$300.[36] The Law Commission found that many applicants considered that the cost of appealing, given the costs already incurred, was an effective barrier to pursuing a request.[37] The AAT has also been criticised because it is a general administrative law body and does not consider only FOI cases. This means that it may be slower than the appeal bodies of other countries in developing the expertise and understanding with the agencies that can bring about 'cultural' change. However, the Law Commission argued that although there might be merit to these criticisms, the AAT did bring a wide range of expertise and independence (many of its members are judges) to its deliberations and that this outweighs any disadvantages there might be.[38] However, as we shall see in the discussion of exemptions which follows below, there is one area in which the AAT is seriously handicapped: it cannot overrule a ministerial veto.

Most of the exemptions under the Australian FOI are the usual categories, such as defence, international relations, law enforcement and public safety, the national economy, commercial secrets, privacy and legal privilege. However, as in the case of Canada, the Act exempts all cabinet and internal working documents.[39] If a minister signs a certificate stating that a document is a cabinet document, or that the disclosure of a working document would be contrary to the 'public interest', then such certificates are absolute. Only if the decision were unreasonable would there be any grounds for challenge.[40] The role this gives to ministers is rather reminiscent of the recommendations of the UK Franks Committee on the Official Secrets Act that a ministerial certificate certifying that a document had been properly classified was conclusive. It is interesting to see ministers continuing to enjoy such a role under the 'Westminster model'.

It is clear that Australia, like Canada, sees itself as having important constitutional differences between itself and the United States and that such differences mean that special protection must be given to ministerial deliberations, particularly in cabinet. It is also clear that the pattern of applications is centred on requests to see personal information. Over 90 per cent of requests were to the four government departments most directly concerned with the public: the ATO, Veteran's Affairs, Social Security, and Immigration. It is also clear that the number of applications is relatively low. In 1993–4 547 requests were made to 91 government agencies. Of these, 74 per cent were granted in full, 19.8 per cent in part, and 5.3 per cent were refused. No records are kept as to what constitutes the basis for refusal, but only 4 per cent of refusals were appealed. Perhaps it is the absence of impact that has finally made this idea a possibility in the UK.

NEW ZEALAND

The New Zealand Official Information Act 1982 is unusual in its scope, in that the right of access is to information (undefined) and not to documents, records or to any specific medium. The courts have interpreted the lack of any definition to mean that Parliament intended the word to have its everyday meaning and that the right of access extends beyond 'written material'. There have even been occasions when the ombudsman has asked a participant at a meeting to provide an account of what was said at the meeting, even though no formal minutes were taken.[41] The right of access is granted not only to citizens but also to anyone who is resident in New Zealand and to any organisation with a place of business in New Zealand.[42]

The New Zealand Act is also comprehensive in the range of organisations to which it applies. It covers not only all departments of state but also all state-owned enterprises – except where the government owns less than 50 per cent of the shares or the corporation is in the process of privatisation. The status of state-owned enterprises under the FOI was the subject of some debate in New Zealand. There were those who argued that the desire to create public corporations that could compete with the private sector on a 'level playing field' was undermined by requiring public bodies to be more 'transparent' than their private counterparts. However, even after the large-scale 'agencification' of public bodies in New Zealand, under the State-Owned Enterprises Act of 1986, a Parliamentary Select Committee decided that such bodies would remain subject to FOI.[43]

New Zealand is less generous than Canada in the assistance it provides to the public to discover which documents are held in which departments. Although public bodies are required to publish their manuals and a directory of their functions and organisation, they are only obliged to publish a 'general' description of the categories of documents that they hold. This seems to contradict the requirement that a requester give a reasonable description of the information requested. Where a requester is unable to identify the information required from the directory, there is an obligation on departments to provide assistance, but there would seem to be some room for 'creative avoidance' in these circumstances.

Another important element concerns the time and cost of applying. Originally the Act contained no set time limits for the processing of requests, but simply required that requests be dealt with 'promptly' or within 'a reasonable time'. However, the 1989 amendments have now added an upper limit, in that all requests must be replied to within 20 working days. An extension can be granted to this period if large quantities of information are requested or if consultations with other bodies are necessary in order to process the request. Charges can be levied on requests, except for requests for personal information, which are free. Charges must be reasonable and can cover labour, materials and 'extra' costs such as responding to an urgent request. However, all such charges are reviewable by the ombudsman. Any such charges must be notified to the requester before actioning the request so that the requester knows in advance what their request will cost. Departments are not allowed to charge for the time taken to process a request, although they are allowed to charge for the time spent in reading or reviewing information. Eagles rightly points out the apparent conflict that this creates since how is a department to process a request (exempt from charges) except by reading and reviewing information (chargeable)? In 1987 the cabinet issued a set of guidelines on charges, although they do not have the status of law.[44] However, departmental charging decisions remain reviewable by the ombudsman.

The next important issue concerns the exemptions, those categories of documents to which there is no right of access. The basic principle underlying the New Zealand approach is the desire to avoid making too many absolute exemptions and to require that each request be weighed against the balance of public interest in disclosure versus confidentiality. However, as with Canadian and Australian FOI exemptions there are difficulties that are said to reflect the 'Westminster tradition'. New Zealand was concerned to maintain what it saw as its core constitutional arrangements such as the individual and collective responsibility of ministers, the political neutrality of officials, and the confidentiality of advice tendered to ministers; but it did not, as in Canada, wish to exempt all cabinet or 'internal' working documents. Rather, the New Zealand legislation requires that each request be judged as to whether it breaches, goes to 'the heart of', a particular convention.[45] These core conventions are listed in the Act, although there is some dispute as to whether the list is exhaustive and conclusive, providing a complete listing of what one would traditionally call 'the public interest', or whether ministers and the courts have the flexibility to argue that conventions not listed in the statute can also be 'core'.[46]

What is clear is that within a so-called 'Westminster system' the attempt to create a statutory listing of core conventions runs counter to the absence of a written constitution. It seems very odd to try to create one through the back door via a Freedom of Information Act. However, giving ministers a role in decisions concerning the protection of core conventions seems less than satisfactory. It either places too much power in the hands of ministers, making them judges in their own case, or it gives too little protection to genuine interests because ministers will be politically incapable of exercising their right to secrecy because of their fear of the political consequences of protecting secrecy. One can hear opposition parties demanding that ministers explain 'what they have to hide' each and every time they invoke a constitutional convention.

The other exemptions are fairly straightforward, covering the usual grounds of law and order, national security, privacy, international relations, commercial and economic interests, and legal privilege. However, Eagles makes the important point that the New Zealand

Act only uses the language of 'rights' when giving individuals the right to see information about themselves.[47] This right is less constrained by the 'test of harm' and the only grounds for refusing individuals the right to see official information about themselves are that: it involves disclosing information about another person either living or dead; it is information supplied in confidence and commenting on another's merits, such as a reference; disclosure would be likely to prejudice their mental or physical well-being; it would affect the safety or security of prisoners; it would breach legal professional privilege. In addition there is also a general exemption covering frivolous, vexatious or trivial requests. It was originally designed to protect against 'excessive' requests, a quantitative judgement, but the ombudsman has interpreted it to refer to motivation, a qualitative judgement, which has made it virtually redundant. It is now of little importance given that a civil servant would seem wiser to provide the information than to tell someone they are being frivolous or vexatious! The next important dimension is the process of adjudication when disputes or appeals arise concerning access to information.

In New Zealand the ombudsman has the power to rule on refusals, charges and delays. However, under the OIA the ombudsman is more akin to a court, in that the rulings are legally binding unless a veto is issued by order of council, than to an Ombudsman. In practice the ombudsman acts as an appellate body adjudicating cases and establishing precedents rather than as an officer of Parliament acting as a kind of 'independent MP' trying to resolve disputes on behalf of citizens. In adjudicating an appeal against a refusal of access the ombudsman has full access to all information and files unless the Attorney General rules that security or cabinet deliberations may be prejudiced. In the case of refusal the ombudsman has the duty to engage in informal discussions with the department to try and resolve the dispute – only if this fails is a formal report made. Between 1982 and 1987 the main role of the courts was to review the decisions of any of the agencies involved including the ombudsman, ministers or departments. An appeal to the court can only be made after the ombudsman has made a ruling except in the case of personal information when a requester can go directly to the High Court. However, given the cost involved in appealing to court, the ombudsman is obviously the favoured route. Since 1987 there is an automatic right for an appellant to seek a judicial review of any order in council that vetoes a recommendation from the Ombudsman that information should be disclosed. The cost of such appeals being meet from the public purse.[48]

Assessing the impact of FOI is particularly problematic in the case of New Zealand because of the changes that have taken place in its system of government. The 1980s and 1990s have seen the public sector transformed by privatisation, contracting out and joint public/private enterprises. This process, although similar to that which occurred in the UK, is seen by most commentators as being even more radical because, from 1945 to 1984, New Zealand was even more public-sector dependent.[49] Although there can be no direct relationship between this restructuring and the introduction of FOI – FOI dates from 1982 whereas restructuring begins with the election of a radical Labour government in 1984 – the two processes have affected each other. As we saw above, there have been concerns about the impact of FOI on the confidentiality of the 'commercialised' state enterprises. However, the relationship between a state enterprise and its market is only one side of the equation – there is also the relationship between such enterprises and the political process, i.e. accountability. Eagles *et al.* point out that ministers may not be able to invoke the exemption covering 'internal advice' if they are communicating with state-owned enterprises since the State-Owned Enterprises Act of 1986 states that Ministers cannot exercise direct control over such bodies. However, one can equally reverse this argument and state that a Minister would seem to have little reason to keep confidential matters for which they have no responsibility. If they were attempting to interfere in ways prohibited by law then disclosure would certainly be embarrassing, but in this case (let us be generous) it may be the ambivalence in their relationship with state-owned enterprises that creates the desire for secrecy. In other words clear lines of responsibility will create a powerful incentive for secrecy, clear lines of non-responsibility for disclosure and ambivalence, on balance, for secrecy. If ministers feel that they may, on occasions, need to interfere, to explore the ambivalence, then they are likely to wish to veil such relationships in the cloak of secrecy for, once lifted, it is difficult to replace. However, further research should be undertaken to explore the relationship between FOI and governance in New Zealand.

CONCLUSION

This brief summary of the various Commonwealth FOI legislation highlights several points. The first is that they although the principle of access is found in all three instances there are significant deviations from the ideal. All of them struggle to find a way of implementing the principle of universal access, with their 'Westminster-style' system of government. This is particularly important when considering the difference between open government, the transparency of policy-making, central decision-making and the right to see administrative files. Although the division between administration and policy is, as we have seen, somewhat arbitrary, it is a concept with enough teeth to make FOI a hard nut to crack! The lesson from Commonwealth experience is surely that, although there are problems in adapting FOI to a Westminster system one can succeed to a degree if one is prepared to recognise the real nature of FOI: it is about personal access to personal files as a part of a process of managing grievances. Provided that one recognises that it has little to do with opening government or democracy, but much more to do with managing the complexity of contemporary government, then an accommodation can be reached.

12 Freedom of Information in the UK

This chapter examines both the Labour government proposals for Freedom of Information legislation and the previous Conservative government's open government initiative. Discussion of Citizen Charters and codes of practice may seem rather dated now that a Labour government, committed to freedom of information legislation, has been elected but experience with the Code has influenced the legislation and Charters remain in place in many public bodies.[1] Before discussing the Labour plans for FOI it is important that we understand why a Conservative government became attracted to a form of public access and the problems associated with this experiment.

THE CONSERVATIVE GOVERNMENT'S EXPERIMENT WITH FOI

The measures undertaken by the Major government were welcomed by few and described as inadequate by many. Seen in isolation the Major approach to openness seems nothing more than a brief flickering of light before the inevitable fulfilment of the democratic ideal through the enactment of a right of access to government information. However, there is more to the story than this. As we have seen there had been a series of measures affecting the secret state and so the question – where did the Conservative policy on open government fit into the pattern of change in British government? – remains interesting.

Prior to the open government initiative, Conservative governments, under Thatcher and Major, had introduced several changes to legislation affecting the secret state: data protection (1984), greater access to local government (1985), interception of communications (1985), access to personal files (1987), reform of official secrecy (1989), and a new statutory basis for the secret intelligence services (1989 and 1994). This would suggest that the open government initiative was part of a cumulative process of 'liberalising' British government. However, such an interpretation is hardly likely to appeal to liberals since they consistently condemned all of these measures as half-hearted at best. Liberal opinion is much more likely to argue that the measures reflected the little boy with his thumb in the dike trying to resist the flood of liberal democratic opinion. The measures are seen as 'forced' upon a reluctant and unwilling government that is anything but committed to liberalising British government. There is undoubtedly some truth in this view. A series of adverse rulings from the European Court of Human Rights triggered at least some of the legislative changes. However, it is a somewhat complacent view. It is clear that there have always been those in government who genuinely wish to see greater liberalisation and who were motivated by a desire to 'modernise' what they saw as antiquated approaches to secrecy. For many years there have been people in all political parties, and in senior positions in the civil service, arguing for reform. So the question remains – why did such views succeed in bring about change between 1988 and 1998 when they had not done so earlier? Some would argue for a 'drip' effect gradually eroding traditional attitudes to secrecy. Others would point to external sources such as lobby group, commercial and European pressures for change. However, none of these arguments seems a wholly convincing explanation of either the extent of change or the timing of change. The reforms must be placed against a wider background of a changing world and a changing system of government.

Discussion of the open government initiative must begin with a discussion of the Citizen's Charter programme of 1991 since it was this initiative that made a commitment to improving the availability of information about public services. The aim of the Charter was to improve 'quality, choice, standards and value'. The Charter programme was designed to enhance the power of the consumer in the expectation that this would promote greater efficiency and effectiveness in the public sector. The government believed that there was an imbalance in power between the citizen and government given that many of the services are monopolies. The Charter programme is a recognition that contracting out and privatisation can only have a modest role in enhancing consumer power. The aim was therefore to set standards against which all providers of services would be judged irrespective of whether they were monopolies, quangos or privatised agencies. However, in order to judge whether public bodies are delivering a quality service the consumer requires greater access to information. The publication of targets, standards, would be of no value if the consumer had no way by which to judge whether they were being reached. In addition the Charter further aims to 'empower' consumers by requiring public bodies to improve their complaint procedures and by appointing 'adjudicators' to resolve disputes.[2] The Charter programme was followed, in November of 1991, by the paper *Competing for Quality*, which was designed to improve the mechanism for compulsory tendering and by extending competition to the provision of professional and technical services. Although it can be argued as to whether there was a coherent vision of the relationship between the citizen and government during the early Thatcher years, there was no doubt that there was such a vision by the beginning of the 1990s.

There is no doubt that this programme had the backing of the then Prime Minister, John Major. Not only did he chair a series of seminars on the application of Charter principles to various public bodies, he also appointed William Waldegrave to head up a unit in the Cabinet Office, the Citizen's Charter Unit, and ensured this responsibility would have Cabinet status. In addition the Prime Minister appointed a panel of advisers who would monitor the development of the Charter and award Chartermarks to public bodies who met the published criteria. Finally, the Charter programme was announced with a fanfare of publicity and statements to the House of Commons to the effect that it was 'the most comprehensive programme ever to improve public services' and that it would 'improve the life of every citizen in the land'.[3] Initially, the proposal was seen as having some merit by the opposition parties; indeed, the Labour Party claimed to have thought of it first and to have published its own version shortly before the White paper.[4]

Whatever commentators feel about the virtues of establishing quality services or privatisation there is consensus that the Charter programme can only work if there is greater access to information. This was recognised by the government, which made 'openness' one of the six main Charter principles. In its 1996 Report on the Charter programme the government stated that

> Full and accurate information should be readily available about how services are run, perform and who is in charge. The introduction of performance tables...has allowed people to find out about their services and ask questions about their performance.

To repeat an earlier point, one cannot judge unless one has 'the facts'. However, the kind of information revealed by the Charter process is about the delivery of services and not about policy-making or decision-making. Knowing how many patients have been treated or how many trains arrived ten minutes late may be valuable but it only enables one to see the surface of the iceberg, visible outcomes, and not what lies hidden, the process of determining policy and resources. The key point is that the stress is on making the *deliverers* reveal information; the government remains as hidden as ever. The logic of separation between us (policy – the government and Whitehall mandarins) and them (those who deliver – schools, hospitals, railways, etc.) is reflected in that we, as consumers, are entitled to know about 'them' but not, as citizens, about the government (us). However, if the Charter programme does little to open up Whitehall, what of Prime Minister John Major's open government initiative?

It is worthwhile noting that in the volume on the Citizen's Charter edited by Chandler the examples discussed all come from what I have described as the 'them' part of the public sector. They are: the National Health Service; education; public housing; the railways; and local authorities. There is no Charter setting standards for the Foreign Office, though there will, no doubt, be some document requiring doorkeepers and telephonists to be polite and helpful!

Norman Lewis sees the Charter programme as being potentially more significant than many commentators who treated some of the grandiose claims made at its launch with some scepticism.[5] However, he does raise a fundamental issue that goes to the heart of the potential effectiveness of the programme: How can you judge the delivery of services if either policies, resources, or lines of responsibility, are unclear? If the railway service is inadequate is this a product of: government failure to develop an integrated transport policy, government failure to provide resources, a badly framed contract, or railway management failing to deliver a service? If the Charter proposals are to work effectively then none of the above uncertainties can be tolerated. If those kind of certainties are tolerated then the Charter is relatively meaningless – those subject to criticism can always find someone else to blame and buck-passing will become institutionalised. Lewis also argues that setting standards can either be a wholly internal process, may involve some consultation with the usual 'special interests', or could be a more wide ranging process involving what he calls 'oppositional discourse'.[6] Such discourse requires greater transparency in policy-making and a consultation process in which the widest trawl of views is undertaken with mechanisms that force governments to 'respond to countervailing points of view'.[7] It is not entirely clear what Lewis has in mind here, other than greater openness and breadth of consultation, but he does cast admiring glances at the US policy-making process which he sees as more legalistic and therefore as 'requiring' genuine discourse. He also argues that the combination of reforms, Next Steps and the Charter programme, would be best served by much clearer 'isolation of responsibility for the performance of different tasks' particularly the need for policy-making agencies as well as service delivery agencies.[8] Finally, he concludes that a new regime of public law, including the roles of monitoring and supervisory agencies such as the ombudsman, need to be reassessed in the light of these developments. The role of the 'regulator' becomes much more important when delivery is at a distance and when public confidence depends upon the independence, powers and remedies available to such regulators. Ethics take on a new importance when the mechanisms of the market, contracting out, privatisation and agencification become the norm. The First Division association and other civil service trade unions have been arguing for some time that there is a need to institute, perhaps in law, a new code of ethics for the civil service.[9] Such debates are obviously relevant to the question of openness, leaking and whistleblowing.

If the Charter programme is focused on assisting the consumer, was John Major's 'open government' initiative also designed to assist the consumer or was this initiative focused on the citizen?

The aim of the *Open Government* White Paper is stated in very broad terms – 'open government is a part of an effective democracy'[10] – but there are very different senses to the term 'open government'. The most common interpretation is that it is synonymous with 'freedom of information' and 'a right to know'. However, it is worth repeating the argument that it is preferable to keep these concepts distinct since otherwise there is a loss of meaning and a resultant loss of clarity of communication. The right to know refers to the general claim that, in a democracy, the citizen has a right to be informed. The right to 'be knowledgeable' depends not only upon what government does or does not do but on the whole range of mechanisms and processes by which the citizen acquires information. It therefore not only includes Hansard and other official sources of information but also a whole range of processes by which the citizen becomes informed. Amongst these, there are far too many to list, are: a 'free' and active media, access to public libraries, and the right to meet with others and exchange information. It therefore goes beyond the 'passive' process of being a recipient of official data or statements and implies the right and opportunity to learn through participation in the political life of the nation. From this general right one can derive two further rights:

Freedom of Information – a statutory right of access to official information, mainly documents, and normally enforceable in a court of law.
Open Government – the right to participate in, be consulted about, government decisions.

Although the White Paper refers to all of these aspects its main thrust is quite clear. In its explicit reference to the Citizen's Charter it states that

> This White Paper builds on the Government's commitment to make government more accountable... Greater openness under the Citizen's Charter is already leading to better service for the citizen. The Charter is providing everyone with more essential information.[11]

The main purpose of the Major government's initiative was (a) to supply factual information so allowing the 'consumer' to make judgements on services and (b) to enhance the ability of citizens to pursue grievances against public bodies. Those that did have some such role, the proposals to grant statutory rights of access to personal and health and safety information, were not presented before the end of the Conservative Parliament in May 1997.

If open government means access to, and participation in, the *business of government*, and not merely the receipt of information after the fact, what impact, if any, do these proposals have on decision-making? One may certainly think that they have when one reads statements such as 'The Government accepts that openness in Government means not only providing information about Government policies and activities but developing a culture of openness throughout the Civil Service.' However the very next sentence reads: 'The aim is to ensure that there is a continual and refreshing interchange between the Civil Service and other organisations.'[12] The idea that greater openness and changing the culture of the Civil Service involves a few more people tooing and froing between Whitehall and Industry is so absurd that one wonders whether the document was not written by Sir Humphrey Appleby![13] One's expectations are again raised by the next paragraph which states that 'the Government believes in the value of consultation in developing policies'.[14] However, this time the opportunity is taken to commend the established practice of publishing White Papers – the only 'extra' being offered is that, in *some cases* (the White Paper suspiciously refers to only one example) *some of the submissions* made by organisations and individuals will be made available in the House of Commons and British libraries![15] As we shall see below, the access provisions also do not provide much assistance to the citizen seeking to influence decisions.

To summarise so far, in the key area of what I call open government, participation in decision-making, the White Paper had little to offer.

But what did the Code give access to? As already stated, the White Paper did promise to introduce new rights of access in the areas of personal records and Health and Safety but such measures fell with the Government. Without any new statutory rights of access, any improvements in public access to information or documents become dependent upon government blessing. One can ask, but one does not always receive.

The Code of Practice committed the government to providing information, though importantly not documents, in the following areas: after policies and decisions are announced, facts, and the analysis of facts, departmental handbooks, rules, procedures, etc., relating to its dealings with the public; reasons to those affected by administrative decisions; full information about the costs, redress procedures, targets, standards, etc., concerning all public services covered by the Citizen's Charter, and finally, changes in all departments, in response to specific requests.[16]

The fact that release decisions are entirely a matter for the government and that such decisions cannot be reviewed by a court of law meant that most critics dismissed the scheme as irrelevant. This sense of irrelevance may have been intensified by the contrast between its modest, if not timid, approach to access and its radical approach to other civil service reforms. A government engaged in the persistent destabilisation of bureaucrats, what must have felt to civil servants as virtual permanent revolution, decided that the 'culture of secrecy' was to be merely tinkered with. However, what if anything does it tell us about the future direction of change?

The right to apply for information is not restricted in any way by the code so that anyone, whether citizen or not, can make an application. Any request must be 'reasonable', that is, it must not be too general, too vague, or too difficult, to fulfil.[17] However, departments can make charges to cover the costs of processing requests. These may take the form of 'standard' charges for routine requests to the levying of an additional charge to cover 'reasonable costs' where a request is complex or requires extensive searching of records. Uncertainty over costs is one of the most unsatisfactory provisions in the Code. This has been of concern to the parliamentary select committee on the ombudsman, which argued that all departments should allocate the same, standard, blocks of 'free time' and maximum hourly fees to the processing of requests. However, in its response the government rejected this recommendation, arguing that departments must be allowed discretion in 'accordance with their financial procedures' and the 'particular circumstances' of the request.[18] However, the lack of predictability will inhibit citizens from exercising their right to make requests. The basic rule of administrative life is that any criteria are preferable to complete discretion since criteria allow the citizen to make an informed decision and to formulate an appeal. They also allow easier, and more effective, monitoring.

However, the Code of Practice is only a code and there are no statutory rights of access. The code only expressed an intent to grant citizen's requests under certain conditions that the government determined; any commitments made are unenforceable in law. However, the Code had somewhat more teeth than this would imply because the implementation of the Code was subject to review by the Parliamentary Commissioner for Administration (PCA – Ombudsman). The PCA had responsibility for reviewing decisions to withhold information and for the levying of charges.[19] The PCA has issued several special reports on open government.[20] The reports are critical and imply that, at least in the beginning, the Major government was not very serious about making open government work.[21]

In another case the PCA states that 'there are staff who do not know about the obligation to release information under the Code'.[22] The PCA also found that, despite the commitment by the Ministry of Agriculture and Fisheries to release all 'handbooks, rules and procedures', it had never made public its procedures to compensate farmers whose imported cattle had to be slaughtered because they were found to be infected with foot and mouth disease.[23]

Such cases led the Select Committee on the PCA to hold inquiries on open government.[24] Two general themes remain relevant. One is its discussion of overseas experience[25] and the other is its decision to advocate a Freedom of Information Act for the UK.

The committee were clearly impressed with the argument that FOI legislation was beneficial and that it had, at the very least, not harmed the workings of government in other countries. However, before looking at the Committee's conclusion it is worth identifying its main criticisms of the operation of the code. These may show us the kind of problems that Labour will face when it introduces FOI.

One can illustrate the problems of the Code by examining several cases. One example being the Treasury. One change was the publication of the meetings between the Governor of the Bank of England and the Chancellor. Although the record of the meeting was not published until six weeks later, it was eagerly awaited by the media and political commentators in order to see whether there was any disagreement that could be exploited for news or political advantage.[26] In addition the Treasury also highlighted its decision to publish a great deal of information relating to government economic policy, including: the background to the Budget; the reports of the panel of 'Wise Men' (a group of economic experts who proffer advice to the Chancellor); and papers relating to internal management including their expenditure and management reviews. The Treasury also pointed to its adaptability in that, although it had initially denied access to its annual report on financial malpractice in the civil service, it altered its view following criticism from the PCA and such reports are no longer restricted.[27]

The Department of Transport, which had been the subject of four PCA investigations, testified that it had changed its policies on disclosure as a result of the Code. It has decided that it can release the reports of public inquiries on roads even when the Minister has not yet made a final decision. However, this was done only following 'a debate with the PCA' who persuaded the Department that one inspector would not be influenced by knowing the views of a predecessor.[28]

The Permanent Secretary at the Department of Social Security stated that '50% more codes of guidance (documents giving guidance to DSS staff on interpretation of the law) are available now than before'.[29] This was the subject of questioning by a Committee member, Dr Wright, who asked the Permanent Secretary to provide more details of her claim. Mrs Botwell subsequently supplied a detailed list of those available and those still restricted.[30] The criteria used to determine disclosure was whether disclosure would provide information that may assist fraud or other abuse of the system such as avoidance of National Insurance contributions. Mrs Botwell also stated that the Department processed 43 million benefit requests every year and that such assessments are determined by information fed into and processed by computer. To provide an individual assessment of each case would be (a) too expensive in administrative time, and (b) too slow. This demonstrates the problems of providing access. The public may feel entitled to expect a personalised and individual assessment of their circumstances, they are unique, whilst the DSS is concerned with balancing entitlement against cost. In such cases the really crucial decision concerns the way in which each applicant is processed rather than what information to disclose. Information cannot be supplied if it is not there. Complaints may well be based on the view that information ought to be there, rather than whether it is being made available to them. This highlights the dilemma posed by an information rich department; it can function only through depersonalising its processes.

The committee concludes that the Code 'is an important step forward which is already resulting in greater openness from government'.[31] Few observers disagree with that conclusion but this then leaves the interesting question – why did the committee (with two dissenters) decide to support FOI legislation?

The main benefit of FOI legislation, the Report argues, would be 'to change governmental culture'.[32] The committee is afraid that the Code, like the Fulton Report, and Croham Directive of 1976,[33] will be ignored, avoided, quietly forgotten or otherwise rendered ineffective. The fear is that without the force of law both ministers and civil servants will be able to alter or manipulate the code to suit their interests. Such a situation can only be avoided, under the Code, by vigorous policing by the PCA, but he has many other duties and his recommendations are advisory, not compulsory. However, even the Campaign for Freedom of Information admits that departments have generally felt obliged to accept the PCA's ruling.[34] So what convinces the committee that FOI legislation is necessary? The key argument is that the government undermined its own case against FOI when it announced its intention to introduce new rights of access to personal, health and safety, and environmental data. To place some rights on a statutory footing and under the jurisdiction of the Data Protection Registrar, whilst others are 'voluntary' and under the jurisdiction of the Ombudsman, creates confusion and potential conflicts. The Report concludes:

> The Ombudsman and the Code would be left with the 'rump' of government information, sometimes obstructed or overruled by the impinging of statutory judgements on their own remit. This system seems complicated and effectively to cancel the very advantages of the [Code]. [A single Freedom of Information Act] would preserve the Ombudsman's important role, maintain the consistency of open government judgements and ensure that the various considerations that inform any decision on access all carry similar statutory weight.[35]

There is a great deal of merit to this claim. A multitude of rights of access, a mix of statutory and voluntary obligations, would risk confusion both for the public and civil servants. The government has tried to avoid creating a single statutory framework because of the complexities that this would involve but it has, in turn, created another form of complexity, this time for others. The more rights of access that are created then the more this will conflict with the 200 Acts of Parliament that prohibit the release of specific categories of information.[36] The more mechanisms of enforcement, data protection registrar, PCA and the Courts, the more inconsistency there is likely to be on how to balance competing interests. The more diversity there is in the methods by which the public apply for access the more time and effort is likely to be wasted. The public is more likely to apply under the wrong provision, or by using the wrong form, and this is bound to be a source of considerable irritation. The government, by recognising that the nature of administration had changed, legitimated the destruction of its own Code. This process was completed with the election of a Labour government, committed to introducing FOI, in May 1997.

THE LABOUR GOVERNMENT'S WHITE PAPER ON FREEDOM OF INFORMATION

The opening sentence of the Labour Government's White Paper, *Your Right to Know*, states that

> Unnecessary secrecy in government leads to arrogance in governance and defective decision-making. The perception of excessive secrecy has become a corrosive influence in the decline of public confidence in government. Moreover, the climate of public opinion has changed: people expect much greater openness and accountability from government than they used to.[37]

The next paragraph then goes on to describe the practical changes the government has made by setting up a Food Standards Agency and by requiring non-departmental public bodies, the old name for which was 'quango', to produce annual reports. This rhetorical style is in striking contrast to the justifications found in overseas freedom of information legislation. The absence of any reference to democratic ideals is striking. Rather it stresses the view that FOI is important because of its practical and symbolic affects. Other nations have taken the view that even if FOI were to produce no results whatsoever that it is an important right which any democracy ought to have.

The scope of the proposed British FOI is very wide covering all government departments, executive agencies, the National Health Service, local authorities, schools and higher education, and public service broadcasting. However, the government has decided to exempt one category of government body, the intelligence services. All of the intelligence agencies are exempt from the proposals so that none of their records, even those concerning their purchase of paper or pens, will be accessible. It is also intended to be very broad in what is covered in that it will provide access to 'information *or* records' with records being interpreted to cover all forms of recorded information including electronic records, film tape, etc. The White Paper is also radical in that, unlike most other countries, the Act will apply to all records whenever they were created. This means that memorandum or other documents written prior to the Act, and with no thought of the Act in mind, will be accessible.[38]

However, less clear are the obligations on authorities to publish guides describing their records, their internal manuals, a description of their functions, and a list of officers and their responsibilities. The White Paper states that all bodies will be encouraged to 'actively provide information' but no details are provided of how the applicant is meant to identify the records they wish to see. Given the enormous range of records and the diversity of possible data holders, given that many records will be held by more than one agency, it is hard to see how the public will know what to request or to whom to make the request. Access laws depend upon agencies having a reasonable idea of what records they do hold and in providing reasonable guidance to the public of what is available. Putting public records on some form of accessible index will be a long and tedious job. It is one that the White Paper does not even envisage.

Other important factors affecting the utility of FOI legislation are the cost in applying and the delay in processing requests. The Labour proposal is that all applicants will pay a standard fee of £10. This would also be the maximum fee chargeable to someone requesting their own, personal, information, although no details are provided of charges for copying or recovering administrative costs. However, the White Paper does say that all charges must be reasonable.[39] The White Paper argues that costs should fall on 'heavy users', rather than on 'normal' applicants and that the Government may charge higher fees to commercial and corporate users. It also states that no charge will be made for any review or appeal process. The White Paper makes no mention of any target times by which requests should be processed. This is something that the eventual legislation must include.

We know from American experience that one of the main factors inhibiting people from making requests is cost of rejection. This does not refer to the initial cost of applying, or to any psychological feeling of being unwanted, but to the cost of the appeal process. All applicants presumably feel that they 'have a right to know' when they apply so a refusal can place them in an uncomfortable dilemma: should they assert their 'rights' and risk the cost of an appeal or do they abandon their 'legitimate' quest? As we have seen there are considerable variations in the mechanism of appeal ranging from the, generally considered, overly legalistic and formalistic US approach to the Canadian model of an Information Commissioner. The UK intends to follow the Canadian model and appoint an Information Commissioner (IC). The task of the IC is to resolve what the government has called its key principle; namely that there is a presumption of openness such that information should be disclosed except when its disclosure would cause harm.[40] The decision of the IC will be binding on the agency and, as we shall see later, on the applicant. This contrasts with previous codes in that the ombudsman may only recommend disclosure but has no power to force release. In order to arrive at a decision the IC will have a right of access to any record, held by an agency subject to the Act, and will even have the right to apply for a warrant to search premises and seize papers if he believes records are being unlawfully withheld or are at risk of being destroyed. However, the main function will be one of adjudication and the IC will be encouraged to mediate between requestor and agency to try and resolve disputes quickly and informally. This desire to keep litigation out of the process of appeal is taken one step further. The White Paper states that 'We do not propose that there should be a right of appeal to the Courts.'[41] This certainly contrasts with experience elsewhere. The argument for removing a right of appeal to the Courts is that litigation is expensive and that agencies can use the prospect of litigation as an effective weapon against applicants. Applicants may be told, 'What is the point of appealing, it will only go to Court and you won't wish that expense, will you?' The possibility of Court action may be invoked at a very early stage to dissuade applicants from seeking review or from appealing to the IC. However, there is a delicate balance between acknowledging that allowing appeals to the Courts may entail the risk of expense and delay, and denying a fundamental right to someone who feels that neither internal review, nor the IC, have correctly interpreted the law. This view may also reflect a fear, reflected in the desire to charge corporate applicants a higher user fee, that commercial and corporate applicants may dominate FOI usage, particularly the appeal's process, because of their vastly greater resources.

As stated above, the main task of the IC will be to make judgements on the balance of harm. This will require weighing the stated presumption in favour of disclosure against the possible harm that could be caused to a series of specified interests. The government proposes that, instead of having a set of categories that will be totally exempt from FOI, the aim is to identify the interests that could be harmed by disclosure.[42] The list of interests, against which requests will be tested, are

- National security, defence and international relations
- Law enforcement
- Personal privacy
- Commercial confidentiality
- Safety of the individual, the public and the environment
- Information supplied in confidence
- The integrity of the decision-making and policy advice processes in government

The list, when compared to experience elsewhere, is a fairly standard one. However, there are some complex issues associated with several of the 'interests.'

The White Paper recognises that there is a possible tension between FOI and personal privacy. Other countries have experienced cases in which an individual has sought legal protection from the courts by arguing that a proposed disclosure would endanger their right to privacy. The British proposals certainly create such a possibility in that the White Paper states that

> The right to privacy cannot be absolute – there may be circumstances where disclosure of personal information may be in the public interest...this may require a mechanism to allow third party appeals against impending disclosure.[43]

If the government envisages releasing information about an individual that may affect their right to privacy a mechanism allowing for third-party suits is essential. However, this raises the important question of whether people will be happy to have such suits determined by the IC given that their right to appeal to the Courts has been denied. This would seem to place the IC in an invidious position in having to adjudicate, not only between the government and a requestor, but between the government, an applicant and a third party. How can the integrity of the IC's position be maintained in such circumstances? Similar problems can arise with 'commercial confidentiality'. A competitor may request release of data about a contract and the successful party may attempt to seek to oppose the application. The discussion of the issues associated with government contracts and the operation of 'contracting-out' is less than satisfactory. It is vague in that it identifies dilemmas but does nothing to show how they can be resolved. Which interest, when two collide, does the government consider should dominate? This cannot be resolved on a purely case-by-case basis. There are important issues of public policy and the public, and the IC, will need answers.

However, the most problematic of the interests is the protection of the 'integrity of government.' The White paper states that

> government needs space and time to assess arguments and conduct its own debates with a degree of privacy [*sic* – *i.e.* secrecy] . . . [Policy decisions] can be damaged by random and premature disclosure of its deliberations under Freedom of Information legislation.[44]

The government argues that it could have adopted the canadian solution of making all cabinet deliberations totally exempt from FOI and that it has adopted a more open strategy by making all government information available subject only to the test that such disclosures should not harm the 'integrity of government'. However, the test that will be applied is not 'substantial harm', as with the interests above, but only 'harm'. It is true that this test will be applied to each document requested, and does not involve exemption for all documents marked 'confidential', or even 'top secret', but this seems more a matter of presentation than substance. How is the IC to determine that release would harm the process of deliberation other than by consulting Ministers or senior officials? Is the IC supposed to have such a detailed understanding of the complexities of government that he or she is capable of determining each case on its merits? These propositions are unbelievable. The 'Westminster model' of centralised decision-making by a government composed of ministers who are members of the directly elected chamber has shown itself to be more important than any principle of openness. This point can be highlighted by examining how the test of harm will work in practice. The IC is meant to examine each record or computer file in order to see whether some or all of it can released. Each request will be tested against the set of interest as defined in the legislation. If there is a reasonable case that harm may be caused to the integrity of government then a decision must be made as to whether any part of the file can be released or whether a part of the document can be released. In the latter case, this may involve removing some pages or blanking out some lines. However the kind of nice judgements that this implies seem beyond the scope of any 'independent' adjudicator. The result will be effective exemption for all internal working documents and for all advice offered to and from ministers. Background and factual papers will be released, as under the previous code of practice, but nothing of 'political' interest. Anything that may generate a story in the next day's newspapers will be exempt. I do not find this either surprising or a matter for condemnation. Rather it merely reflects the structure of power and interest found under the British system of government.

13 Conclusion

The reality is that freedom of information legislation fails to provide the revitalisation, the purification, of government that the public seem to expect and that politicians sometimes promise. One only has to consider that in the USA Watergate occurred after the FOI Act of 1966, and that, although the Act was then strengthened in 1974, this did not prevent the Contra Affair, the arms to Iran scandal, or allegations of sleaze in the White House. In my opinion one could go through the list all of the main scandals that have affected an American president since the Second World War and show that FOI was irrelevant to every single one.

The complaint in Canada, Australia and New Zealand is that even though the public can supposedly obtain the information they want, the legislation is inadequate, irrelevant or, at the very least, requires strengthening. This is because there are two types of information the public wishes to know and FOI only really affects one of these: access to personal files. The information the public wishes to know about high politics is not available under FOI legislation. No FOI gives access to the private papers of ministers or presidents, far less does it give us the right to tape record their private conversations or photograph their private dinners and meetings. And yet it these events that interest the media and attract an audience.

If we take a few more examples from recent British experience we can further illustrate the problem. The last Conservative government under John Major suffered considerable damage from allegations concerning 'sleaze'. These centred on allegations concerning 'cash for questions' and allegations of sexual misconduct. The Major government was also damaged by divisions in the party over Europe to the extent that the prime minister is said to have referred to some of his own backbench MPs as 'the bastards'. These MPs, opposed to any accommodation with Brussels, were said to be willing to give an interview to any journalist willing to listen. They were also willing to complain about the weakness of Major's leadership. Major was placed in an impossible position as a result. If he acted against them he risked losing crucial votes in the House of Commons, but if he failed to act then he was vulnerable to the accusation of being indecisive and weak. These were the issues that dominated press and public comment, and which were efficiently exploited by the opposition parties, but no FOI

Act would have provided any useful information on these 'great debates'. The reality is that no government is immune from controversy and FOI is irrelevant to the resolution of such controversies. It may have a role to play in clarifying events but only too late for this to be of any interest other than to historians.

The argument that one can solve or prevent any perceived crisis in democracy through FOI is unworthy of serious consideration. However, FOI is not valueless. It can assist governments in managing the complexities of the information greedy state. It helps ensure that records are more accurate, which is of benefit to governments; and fairer, which is of benefit to citizens. The problems arise when this modest but worthwhile reform is confused with open government. FOI is not an important part of creating more open government, making the process of political decision-making more transparent and more open to citizen participation. There are quite other mechanisms that do this. The creation of a more federal structure, with competing centres of decision-making, is far more important to this process. Britain's relations with Europe and the creation of devolved government in the UK with assemblies in Wales, Scotland and Northern Ireland, will prove far more significant to 'opening' up government. Another important element is the increasing privatisation and agencification of the process of delivering outputs, the services that government provides to the nation. The Swedish model of open government, that was so attractive to the Fulton Committee,[1] is built on a clear separation of 'administration' and 'politics'. The model does not reflect the values of the contemporary world, enhancing the consumer and increasing efficiency and effectiveness, but the tradition of the 'legal state' in which administration is performed by independent boards, legally and institutionally cut off from ministers. This is the root of its 'goldfish bowl' style and not any notion of democracy.[2] It is also clear that Canada, Australia, New Zealand and the UK have all been unable to emulate the US approach to FOI because the legislature of a Westminster model is not separate from the executive. The British, and other similar cabinets, are not appointed by a directly elected president who claims to be the 'tribune of the people'. There is no competition between Number 10 Downing Street and the leadership of Parliament because they are one and the same thing. However, this means that the prime minister is able to influence, even control, the investigative function of Parliament. Of course there are scandals that lead to tribunals of inquiry or Select Committee reports, but these inquiries are designed to discover what went wrong rather than to attach blame, the Scott Inquiry into arms sales to Iraq being a classic example.[3] In the United States, Congress would have had a much more enjoyable time embarrassing the White House than Scott had being balanced and judicious.

FOI has much more to do with the increased sense of individual rights than with traditional notions of power countering power or with the powerless confronting the powerful. One does not need to believe in 'postmodernism' to recognise that technology and education have created a much more fragmented and diverse population. As individuals we expect not only that governments are fair, are socially just, but also that they are fair to *us*. One way that this desire expresses itself is in the demand to see the files that relegate our lives and determine the benefits we receive. The root cause of FOI does not lie in democratic theory but in our reaction to the bureaucratic state. The spread of the idea reflects our unwillingness to accept a state in which decisions by civil servants about education, passports, licences, unemployment and disability allowances and so on determine our opportunities and that such decisions are taken in a paternalistic form, in the dark.

The enactment of FOI legislation was often stimulated by a sense of crisis associated with a loss of faith in the secret state but this is more important to the explanation of timing than to the basic cause of FOI. The fact that Britain did not experience the public furore associated with ASIO or the RCMP might have meant that it could delay FOI until the balance of interests within Whitehall had changed. The restructuring of the British civil service during the 1980s and 1990s was a slower, but equally important factor, in explaining the advent of FOI experiments in the UK. New Zealand, as we saw, seems to be a mixture of the two ingredients although more research needs to be done before it can be finally located.

In this book I have been arguing both a negative and a positive case: the negative being to reject both the normative and surveillance theory approaches as inadequate to understanding state secrecy; while the positive was to assert the importance of power and interests in explaining the minimalist response to secrecy reduction found in most democratic nations. In my earlier work on this subject I argued that the comparative evidence demonstrated that there was little or no relationship between democracy, its values and ideals, and secrecy. This involved an examination of the historical development of information policy in the USA, Sweden and the UK. The evidence demonstrated that Sweden's more open style emerged during the eighteenth and nineteenth centuries, long before democracy was a part of the political culture; and that Britain's more secretive approach was a product of the particular relationship between civil servants and ministers that was also well-established prior to democracy. In the USA the argument also held, in that although presidents had striven to protect national secrets, Congress had been unwilling to provide that protection, not because of differences in views about democracy but because Congress feared the emergence of the 'Imperial Presidency'. It was the structure of power, between administration and cabinet and between legislatures and executives, that determined government information policy.

This review of the contemporary scene has not produced any reason to change that thesis. Although democratic ideals are often listed as the main reason for change in each case, there has in fact been a deeper and more compelling reason for reform: the interests of government in managing information. It is true that the nature of the problems of managing information have changed between the nineteenth century and the present day, but the logic of power is unchanged.

Can one eliminate secrecy from politics? My answer must be no. It may be possible to reduce secrecy but this would require much more radical measures than the introduction of FOI. It would require a radical restructuring of the bureaucratic state, which does have its advocates on both the left and the right. Replacing 'big government' with a more market approach would affect government secrecy but might merely transfer it from one realm, the public, to another, the private. However, I know of no 'libertarian' who has attempted an analysis of the effect of the market on secrecy reduction. There are writers on the left who advocate the restructuring of democracy. Paul Hirst's concept of 'associative democracy', with its emphasis on community and devolved government, is an attempt to offer a radical vision of democracy.[4] Secrecy would certainly be much less of a problem if politics were more participatory and more local. However, given that these radical visions seem likely to go the way of all others, one can only conclude that FOI is a worth while, though modest, gain for the citizen, but that secrecy will remain in the interests of our rulers.

Notes

1 Introduction

1. K. G. Robertson, *Public Secrets: A Study in the Development of Government Secrecy* (London: Macmillan; New York: St Martin's Press, 1982) p. 3.
2. A. P. Tant, *British Government – the triumph of elitism – a study of the British political tradition and its major challenges* (Aldershot: Dartmouth, 1993).
3. For some interesting arguments on 'democracy', including the view that democracy is legitimated on the grounds that it contributes to 'sound decisions' (that is, good government) see Joseph Raz, *Ethics in the Public Domain: essays in the morality of law and politics* (Oxford: Clarendon Press, 1994) ch. 4.
4. Robertson, *Public Secrets*, ch. 3.
5. Ibid., p. 196.
6. See David Held, *Democracy and the Global Order: from the modern state to cosmopolitan governance* (Oxford: Polity Press, 1996); Barbara Misztal, *Trust in Modern Societies: the search for the bases of social order* (Oxford: Polity, 1996); Claus Offe, *Modernity and the State: East, West* (Oxford: Polity, 1996); Robert E. Goodin, 'Political ideals and political practice', *British Journal of Political Science*, 25 (1): 37–56; Paul Hirst, *Associative Democracy: new forms of economic and social governance* (Cambridge: Polity, 1994); Joseph Raz, *Ethics in the Public Domain*; Robert Blackburn (ed.), *Rights of Citizenship* (London: Mansell, 1993); R. J. Dalton and M. Kuechler (eds), *Challenging the Political Order – new social and political movements in Western Democracies* (Oxford: Polity, 1990); Paul Hirst, *Representative Democracy and its Limits* (Cambridge: Polity Press, 1990); Jürgen Habermas, *Between Facts and Norms: contributions to a discourse theory of law and democracy* (Oxford: Polity, 1996).
7. For an excellent series of articles summarising much of this debate see Paul Heelas, Scott Lash and Paul Morris (eds), *Detraditionalization: critical reflections on authority and identity* (Oxford: Blackwell, 1996).
8. For an analysis of the postmodern concept of risk, see Ulrich Beck, *Risk: towards a new modernity* (London: Sage, 1992).
9. Campaign for Freedom of Information, *Open Government Seminar: a seminar on the Open Government White Paper* (London: Campaign for Freedom of Information, 1993); Peter Hennessy and Chris Westcott, *The Last Right? open government, freedom of information and the right to know* (Glasgow: University of Strathclyde, Dept of Government, Strathclyde Papers on Government and Politics no. 12, 1992); Clive Ponting, *Secrecy in Britain* (Oxford: Blackwell, 1990); Peter Hennessy, *Whitehall* (London: Martin Secker & Warburg), 1989); Peter Thornton, *Decade of Decline: civil liberties in the Thatcher years* (London: NCCL, 1989); Paddy Hillyard and J. Percy-Smith, *The Coercive State* (Fontana, 1988); David Hooper,

Official Secrets – the Use and Abuse of the Act (London: Secker & Warburg, 1987); Clive Ponting, *Whitehall – tragedy and farce* (London: Hamish Hamilton, 1986).

10. A. P. Tant, 'Leaks and the nature of British government', *Political Quarterly*, 66: 197–209; Patrick Birkinshaw, *Grievances, Remedies and the State*, 2nd edn (London: Sweet & Maxwell, 1994); Yvonne Cripps, *The Legal Implications of Disclosure in the Public Interest*, 2nd edn (London: Sweet & Maxwell, 1994); Christopher Dandeker, 'National Security and Democracy: the United Kingdom experience', *Armed Forces and Society*, **20** (3): 353–74; Charles D. Raab, 'Open Government: policy information and information policy', *Political Quarterly*, 65 (Jul./Sep.): 340–7; Patrick Birkinshaw, 'I only ask for information' – the White Paper on Open Government *Public Law*, 1993 (Winter): 557–68; Tant, *British Government* – Norman S. Marsh, *Public Access to government-held information – a comparative symposium* (London: Stevens, 1992); D. Oliver, *Government in the United Kingdom: the search for accountability, effectiveness and citizenship* (Milton).

2 The Morality of Secrecy

1. Books on constitutional/legal arguments about secrecy are included under the heading of 'politics'. The sociological approach is dealt with under the heading of surveillance in the next chapter.
2. For an example of the normative approach to fundamental issues such as sovereignty and citizenship see Paul Craig, 'Public Law, Sovereignty and Citizenship', in Robert Blackburn (ed.), *Rights of Citizenship* (London: Mansell, 1993).
3. Sissela Bok, *Secrets – on the ethics of concealment and revelation*, (New York: Pantheon, 1982). I have selected Bok because most philosophers discuss what I would call 'personal secrecy' (that is, privacy). See Michael Oakeshott, *On Human Conduct* (Oxford: Clarendon, 1975); Stuart Hampshire (ed.), *Public and Private Morality* (Cambridge University Press, 1978); Sissela Bok, *Lying*, esp. ch. 11 (Hassocks, Sussex: Harvester Press, 1978); Privacy, *Nomos*, vol. 13 (1971); Alan F. Westin, *Privacy and Freedom* (New York: Atheneum, 1967); R. Bronaugh (ed.), *Philosophical Law, pt IV* (Westport, Conn.: Greenwood 1978); R. Wacks, *The Protection of Privacy* (London: Sweet & Maxwell, 1980).
4. Bok, *Secrets*, p. 6.
5. Ibid., p. 9.
6. Ibid., p. 20.
7. Ibid., p. 23.
8. Ibid., p. 23.
9. Ibid., pp. 25–6.
10. Ibid., p. 26.
11. Ibid., p. 24.
12. Ibid., p. 110.
13. Ibid., ch. 11, pp. 171–90.
14. Ibid., p. 173.

15. Ibid., p. 176.
16. Ibid., p. 192.
17. Ibid., p. 193.
18. She says this about Nicholas Katzenbach's argument that covert operations to influence political results in foreign countries should be abandoned:

    > Others [secret practices] are equally injurious indirectly because of their capacity to backfire and to invite abuse. Thus Nicholas Katzenbach has argued that the case against using covert operations in friendly countries – such as paying friendly party leaders or trying to damage hostile ones – is so strong that the practice should be abandoned. (S. Bok, ibid., p. 203)
    > (The article referred to is N. Katzenbach, 'Foreign Policy, Public Opinion, and Secrecy', *Foreign Affairs*, 52 (Oct.).

19. Ibid., p. 204.
20. This concept is explored in Michael Herman, *Intelligence Power in Peace and War* (Cambridge University Press, 1996) ch. 20.
21. There is a little-known book by a British Labour MP, Peter Shore, which argues that 'the tradition of total secrecy encourages irresponsibility in government', but I have seen not one single reference to this book in any subsequent publication: Peter Shore, *Entitled to Know* (London: Macgibbon & Kee, 1966).
22. Clive Parry, 'Legislatures and Secrecy', *Harvard Law Review*, 67 (5): 737–85.
23. D. G. T. Williams, *Not in the Public Interest* (London: Hutchinson, 1965).
24. Walter Gelhorn, *Security, Loyalty and Science* (Ithaca NY: Cornell University Press, 1950); E. Shils, *The Torment of Secrecy – the background and consequences of American security policies* (London: William Heinemann, 1956); Francis Rourke, *Secrecy and Publicity* (Baltimore: Johns Hopkins Press, 1961 and 1966);. H. H. Ransom, *Can American Democracy Survive the Cold War?* (Garden City NY: Anchor, 1964).
25. *The Civil Service: vol. 1: Report of the Committee (Chairman Lord Fulton)* (London: HMSO, Cmnd 3638, 1968); *Departmental Committee on Section 2 of the Official Secrets Act 1911: vol. 1: Report*; also *Vols 2, 3 and 4, Written and Oral Evidence (Chairman Lord Franks)* (London: HMSO, Cmnd 5104, 1972). Hereinafter *The Franks Report*.
26. Clive Parry, 'Legislatures and Secrecy', pp. 737–85.
27. Ibid., p. 741.
28. as quoted in ibid., p. 754.
29. Ibid., p. 773.
30. In practice they simply ignore him altogether.
31. Williams, *Not in the Public Interest*, p. 11.
32. Ibid., p. 211.
33. *The Franks Report*; for a discussion of the Franks Report see pp. 86–7 below.
34. Ronald Wraith, *Open Government – the British Interpretation* (London: Royal Institute of Public Administration, 1977); R. K. Middlemas, 'Cabinet Secrecy and the Crossman Diaries', *Political Quarterly*, 47 (1); Joe Jacob, 'Some Reflections on Government Secrecy', *Public Law*, 1974

(Spring); W. Birtle, 'Big Brother Knows Best' – the Franks Report and Section 2 of the OSA', *Public Law*, 1973: 100–12. Jonathan Aitken, *Officially Secret* (London: Weidenfeld & Nicolson, 1971).

35. See Wraith, *Open Government*.
36. Judith Cook, *The Price of Freedom* (London: New English Library, 1986); Des Wilson, *The Secrets File: the case for freedom of information in Britain today* (London: Heinemann, 1984); Trevor Barnes, *Open Up: Britain and Freedom of Information* (London: Fabian Society, 1980); Stuart Dresner, *Open Government: lessons from America* (London: Outer Circle Policy Unit, 1980); Outer Circle Policy Unit, *A Consumer's Guide to Open Government: techniques for penetrating Whitehall* (London: Outer Circle Policy Unit, 1980); David Leigh, *The Frontiers of Secrecy: closed government in Britain* (London: Junction Books, 1980); Stan Cohen and Laurie Taylor, *Prison Secrets* (London, NCCL, 2nd edn with postscript, 1979); Anthony S. Mathews, *The Darker Reaches of Government: access to information about public administration in the United States, Britain and South Africa* (Berkeley, Calif.: University of California Press, 1978); Justice (British Section of the International Commission of Jurists), *Freedom of Information* (London: Justice, 1978); Colin Seymour-Ure, 'Great Britain', in Itzhak Galnoor (ed.), *Government Secrecy in Democracies* (New York: Harper Colophon, 1977); Barry Cox, *Civil Liberties in Britain* (Harmondsworth: Penguin, 1973); Bernard Schwartz and H. W. R. Wade, *Legal Control of Government: administrative law in Britain and the United States* (London: Oxford University Press, 1972).
37. For reviews of such campaigns, see: James Michael, *The Politics of Secrecy: confidential government and the public right to know* (Harmondsworth: Penguin, 1982); Norman S. Marsh, 'Access to Government-held Information in the UK', in Norman S. Marsh (ed.), *Public Access to Government-held Information – a comparative symposium* (London: Stevens, 1992) and A. P. Tant, *British Government – the triumph of elitism – a study of the British political tradition and its major challenges* (Aldershot: Dartmouth, 1993).
38. Patrick Birkinshaw, *Open Government, Freedom of Information and Local Government* (London: Weidenfeld & Nicolson, 1986); *Freedom of Information – the law, the practice, the ideal* (London: Weidenfeld & Nicolson; 1988); *Government and Information – the law relating to access, disclosure and regulation* (London: Butterworth; 1990); *Reforming the Secret State* (Milton Keynes: Open University Press; 1990).
39. Birkinshaw, *Reforming the Secret State*, p. 67.
40. Ibid., p. 67.
41. Birkinshaw, *Freedom of Information*, p. 20.
42. John Baxter, *State Security, Privacy and Information* (Hemel Hempstead: Simon & Schuster, 1990).
43. Ibid., p. 7.
44. Ibid., p. 1, *passim*.
45. Rosamund Thomas, *Espionage and Secrecy – the Official Secrets Act 1911–1989 of the UK* (London: Routledge, 1991).
46. David Hooper, *Official Secrets – the Use and Abuse of the Act* (London: Secker & Warburg, 1987).

47. Thomas, *Espionage and Secrecy*, p. 2.
48. Ibid., p. 234.
49. Ibid.
50. Tant, *British Government: Constitutional aspects of official secrecy and freedom of information – an overview* (Colchester, Essex: Dept of Government, University of Essex, Essex Papers in Politics and Government, no. 52, 1988); 'The Campaign for freedom of information: a participatory challenge to elitist British government', *Public Administration*, 68 (Winter): 477–91; 'Leaks and the nature of British government', *Political Quarterly*, 66: 197–209.
51. Tant, *British Government*, p. 45 and p. 71; and on p. 90 he states: 'What has not been effectively questioned (in the UK) is whether government, in whatever guise, has the right to make decisions independently and on behalf of the people'.
52. Ibid. p. 241.
53. Laurence Lustgarten and Ian Leigh, *In from the Cold* (Oxford University Press, 1994).
54. Ibid., p. 35.
55. Ibid., p. 14.
56. Ibid., p. 23.
57. Ibid., p. 35.

3 Surveillance and Secrecy

1. Max Weber, *Economy and Society* (Berkeley, Calif.: University of California Press, 1978).
2. The Translator's Note, Michel Foucault, *Discipline and Punish* (trans. Alan Sheridan, London: Allen Lane, 1977).
3. Ibid., pp. 141–9.
4. Ibid., pp. 149–56.
5. Ibid., p. 173. Foucault repeats the point on p. 201, when he states 'the major effect of the Panopticon: to induce in the inmate a state of conscious and permanent visibility that assures the automatic function of power.'
6. Ibid., p. 203.
7. Ibid., p. 214.
8. Ibid., p. 218.
9. Ibid., pp. 213–14.
10. For example, Peter Gill, *Policing Politics: security intelligence and the liberal democratic state* (London: Frank Cass, 1994); David Lyon, *The Electronic Eye: the rise of surveillance society* (Cambridge: Polity, 1994); Christopher Dandeker, *Surveillance, Power and Modernity* (Oxford: Polity, 1989); and Anthony Giddens, *The Nation-State and Violence* (vol. II of *A Contemporary Critique of Historical Materialism*) (Cambridge: Polity, 1985).
11. Giddens, *The Nation-State and Violence*.
12. Ibid., p. 2 and pp. 7–17.
13. Ibid., p. 14.

14. Ibid., pp. 12–13.
15. Ibid., pp. 17–20.
16. Ibid., p. 47.
17. Ibid., pp. 174ff.
18. Ibid., p. 203.
19. Ibid., p. 209.
20. Ibid., p. 295. In the actual quotation Giddens uses the incredibly clumsy: 'Totalitarianism is a tendential property of the modern state.' It escapes me as to what having the property of tending towards something means as opposed to the simpler phrase, 'a tendency to'.
21. Ibid., p. 303.
22. Ibid., p. 309.
23. Dandeker, *Surveillance*.
24. Ibid., p. 37.
25. Ibid., p. 41.
26. Ibid., p. 50.
27. Ibid., p. 51.
28. Ibid., p. 59.
29. Ibid., p. 131.
30. *The Times*, 11 August 1995, p. 7.
31. Lyon, *The Electronic Eye*, p. ix.
32. Ibid., p. 3.
33. Ibid., p. 4.
34. Ibid., p. 18 quoting from Mark Poster, *The Mode of Information* (Cambridge, Polity, 1990) pp. 97–8.
35. Ibid., p. 19.
36. Ibid.
37. Ibid., p. 31.
38. Ibid., p. 25.
39. Lyon, *The Electronic Eye*, p. 185.
40. C. J. Friedrich, *The Pathology of Politics* (New York: Harper & Row, 1972).
41. Lyon, *The Electronic Eye*, p. ix.
42. Ibid., see pp. 196.
43. Ibid., pp. 214–17.

4 The End of Whitehall?

1. For an interesting argument that it was more Major than Thatcher, see B. W. Hogwood, 'The Machinery of Government, 1979–97', *Political Studies*, 45 (4): 704–15.
2. Geoffrey, K. Fry, *Policy and Management in the British Civil Service* (Herts., UK: Prentice-Hall, 1996) p. ix.
3. R. A. W. Rhodes, 'The hollowing out of the State: the changing nature of public service in Britain', *Political Quarterly*, 65 (2): 138–51; Ewan Ferlie, Lynn Ashburner, Louise Fitzgerald *et al.*, *The New Public Management in Action* (Oxford University Press); Robert Pyper, *The British Civil Service* (London: Prentice-Hall, 1995); Gavin Drewry, 'The Civil Service: from

the 1940s to "Next Steps" and beyond', *Parliamentary Affairs*, 1994: 581–95; A. Grant Jordan, *The British Administrative System: principles versus practice* (London: Routledge, 1991).

4. Elizabeth Mellon, 'Executive Agencies in Central Government', in Anthony Harrison (ed.), *From Hierarchy to Contract* (Hermitage, Berks: Policy Journals, 1993) p. 33.
5. Keith Dowding, *The Civil Service* (London: Routledge, 1995) p. 105.
6. Barry J. O'Toole and A. Grant Jordan (eds), *Next Steps: improving management in Government?* (Aldershot: Dartmouth, 1995) pp. 8–9.
7. Colin Campbell and Graham Wilson, *The End of Whitehall: death of a paradigm?* (Oxford: Blackwell, 1995).
8. Hugh Heclo and Aaron B. Wildavsky, *The Private Government of Public Money: community and policy inside British politics* (Berkeley, Calif: University of California, 1981).
9. For a description of the interview methodology see Campbell and Wilson, *The End of Whitehall*, pp. xiii–xiv.
10. Ibid., pp. 294 ff.
11. For accounts of the Northcote–Trevelyan reforms (1850s) and those associated with Warren Fisher (1920s) see G. Kitson Clark, 'Statesmen in Disguise: reflections on the history of the neutrality of the Civil Service', *Historical Journal*, 2 (1): 19–39; Henry Parris, *Constitutional Bureaucracy: the development of British central administration since the Eighteenth Century* (London: George Allen & Unwin, 1969); Geoffrey K. Fry, *Statesmen in Disguise: the changing role of the Administrative class of the Home Civil Service 1853–1966* (London: Macmillan, 1969) and Peter Hennessy, *Whitehall* (London: Martin Secker & Warburg, 1989).
12. Andrew Shonfield, *Modern Capitalism* (Oxford University Press, 1965); E. M. Nicholson, *The System* (London: Hodder & Stoughton, 1967); Hugh Thomas (ed.), *Crises in the Civil Service: Vol. 1: Report of the Committee 1966–68 (Chairman Lord Fulton)* (London: HMSO, Cmnd 3638, 1968). (Hereinafter *The Fulton Report*.)
13. 'All in all, the Fulton Report was a failure': Dowding, *The Civil Service*, p. 20; 'None of them [the reforms following Fulton], with the possible exception of the setting up of the Civil Service Department [itself abolished in 1981], affected substantially the structure or functions of the bureaucracy': James B. Chistoph, 'High civil servants and the politics of consensualism in Great Britain', in Mattei Dogan (ed.), *The Mandarins of Western Europe: the political role of top civil servants* (New York: John Wiley & Sons, 1975) p. 54. See also Peter Kellner and Lord Crowther-Hunt, *The Civil Servants: an inquiry into Britain's ruling class* (London: Macdonald, 1980).
14. *The Fulton Report*, paras 145ff. and 188ff. See also Fry, *Statesmen in Disguise*, and Parris, *Constitutional Bureaucracy*, for a discussion of nineteenth-century administration.
15. See Geoffrey K. Fry, *Policy and Management*, pp. 39ff.
16. Richard Crossman, *The Diaries of a Cabinet Minister*, vols 1 and 2 (London: Hamish Hamilton and Jonathan Cape, 1975); Leslie Chapman, *Your Disobedient Servant* (London: Chatto & Windus, 1978). See Kevin

Theakston, *The Labour Party and Whitehall* (London: Routledge, 1992) ch. 2 for an interesting discussion of Labour Party experience with 'the mandarins' during its periods in office prior to 1997.

17. W. A. Niskanen, *Bureaucracy and Representative Government* (Chicago: Aldine-Atherton, 1971); W. A. Niskanen, *Bureaucracy: Servant or Master?* (London: Institute of Economic Affairs, 1973).
18. Fry p. 38 quoting From Lady Thatcher's memoirs, *The Downing Street Years* (1993) pp. 6–7.
19. However, as we shall see later, this is by no means a reliable test of whether a 'revolution' in the civil service has really occurred.
20. *The Fulton Report*, vol. 1.
21. For the background to Next Steps and discussion of earlier reforms, see Richard Common, 'The agencification of the civil service', in Maurice Mullard (ed.), *Policy-making in Britain: an introduction* (London: Routledge, 1995) pp. 136–59; Patricia Greer, *Transforming Central Government: the Next Steps Initiative* (Milton Keynes: Open University Press, 1994); Spencer Zifcak, *New Managerialism: administrative reform in Whitehall and Canberra* (Buckingham: Open University Press, 1994); Gavin Drewry and Tony Butcher, *The Civil Service Today* (Oxford: Blackwell, 2nd edn, 1991).
22. See Greer, *Transforming Central Government*, pp. 23–4.
23. The office was originally located in the Prime Minister's Office though it was later located within the Cabinet Office and then, in 1992, in the new Office of Public Service and Science under the Chancellor of the Duchy of Lancaster.
24. HC 236, vol. 1, para. 19, 1981/82.
25. Pyper, *The British Civil Service*, refers to savings of £1.5–2 billion and to the generally favourable reviews of the unit by the National Audit Office (1986) and the Public Accounts Committee of the House of Commons (1986).
26. Michael Heseltine, *Where There's a Will* (London: Hutchinson, 1987) pp. 20–1.
27. Ibid., p. 22.
28. *Efficiency and Effectiveness in the Civil Service* (London: HMSO, Cmnd 8616, 1982) para. 13.
29. Fry, *Policy and Management*, p. 66.
30. Pyper, *The British Civil Service*, p. 64.
31. For a discussion see Ferlie *et al*., C. Pollitt, 'Antistatist reforms and new administrative directions – public administration in the United Kingdom', *Public Administration Review*, 56 (1996): 81–7 and Dowding, *The Civil Service*.
32. Rhodes states, 'The simple fact that there has been a continuous stream of reforms clearly shows that they "underachieved" ': Rhodes, 'The hollowing out of the State', p. 138.
33. For a discussion of the Treasury's reaction, and that of Chancellor Lawson, see O'Toole and Jordan (eds), *Next Steps*, p. 9 ff.
34. Zifcak, *New Managerialism*, pp. 48–54; and Common, 'The agencification of the Civil Service', pp. 147–8.
35. Zifcak, *New Managerialism*, p. 53.

36. For example, all three military services had different and independent ways of producing the required numbers of false teeth. See also Sifcak, *New Managerialism*, pp. 34–45.
37. *Efficiency Unit Report: Improving Management in Government: the Next Steps* (London: HMSO, 1988).
38. *Improving Management in Government*, para. 44.
39. Drewry, 'The Civil Service', states: 'the Fulton Report anticipated changes that were destined to resurface, in a new disguise, during the Thatcher years. In particular, the desirability of hiving off departmental functions anticipated the Next Steps initiative launched twenty years later', p. 587.
40. Colin Talbot, 'The private government of public agencies? – evaluating the impact of "Next Steps"', Political Studies Association Annual Conference, April 1997, pp. 5 and 14 (unpublished).
41. Rhodes gives the example of the contracting out of office cleaning under the Labour Government of Harold Wilson which produced an estimated saving of 35 000 jobs and £500 000. Rhodes 'The hollowing out of the State', p. 140.
42. Ibid., pp. 141–2.
43. Mellon, 'Executive Agencies in Central Government'.
44. Ferlie *et al.*, (eds), *The New Public Management*, p. 174.
45. Ibid.
46. Ibid.
47. Anthony Harrison, 'Conclusion', in (ed.), *From Hierarchy to Contract*.
48. Talbot, 'The private government of public agencies?', p. 12.
49. F. F. Ridley, 'Political neutrality and the British civil service', in Bernard Williams *et al.*, *Politics, Ethics and Public Service* (London: Royal Institute of Public Administration, 1985) pp. 38–9.
50. F. F. Ridley, 'Using power to keep power – the need for constitutional checks', *Parliamentary Affairs*, 44 (4): 447. See also Ridley, 'Political neutrality, the duty of silence and the right to publish in the civil service', *Parliamentary Affairs* 39 (1986): 437–48.
51. Kevin Theakston, *The Labour Party and Whitehall* (London: Routledge, 1992) p. 42.
52. Eric Beston's evidence to the Scott Inquiry.
53. Campbell and Wilson, *The End of Whitehall*, pp. 62–3.
54. Diana Woodhouse comments that since the Second World War, (parliamentary questions) 'are frequently used as an opportunity for scoring party points and for launching personal attacks rather than for providing information' (Woodhouse, *Ministers and Parliament: accountability in theory and practice* [Oxford: Clarendon, 1994]) p. 24).
55. Crossman, *Diaries*; see also Tony Benn, *Against the Tide: Diaries 1973–76* (London: Arrow, 1990).
56. Pyper, *The British Civil Service*, p. 85.
57. For example Woodhouse, *Ministers and Parliament*, '[the idea of] a clear split between administration and policy and a presumption that any policy content can be isolated – [is] a dubious proposition' (p. 126).
58. T. Burns and G. M. Stalker, *The Management of Innovation* (London: Tavistock, 1961).

59. Campbell and Wilson, *The End of Whitehall*, pp. 41ff.
60. See Ferlie *et al.*, O'Toole and Jordan (eds), *Next Steps*; Zifcak, Harrison (ed.), *From Hierarchy to Contract*; Philip Giddings (ed.), *Parliamentary Accountability: a study of Parliament and Executive Agencies* (Basingstoke: Macmillan, 1995); Ian Colville, K. Dalton and C. Tomkins, 'Developing an understanding of cultural change in HM Customs and Excise: there is more to dancing than knowing the steps', *Public Administration*, **71** (Winter): 549–66.
61. Ferlie *et al.*, *The New Public Management*, p. 233.
62. For a report see *The Times*, 20 May 1997.
63. House of Commons, *Hansard*, 19 May 1997, col. 401.

5 Accountable Government?

1. See Chapter 4.
2. For a discussion of this debate see K. G. Robertson, *Public Secrets: A Study in the Development of Government Secrecy* (London: Macmillan; New York: St Martin's Press, 1982) pp. 80 ff.
3. For example, there are no indexed references to accountability in: David Hooper, *Official Secrets – the Use and Abuse of the Act* (London: Secker Warburg, 1987); James Michael, *The Politics of Secrecy: confidential government and the public right to know* (Harmondsworth: Penguin, 1982); Ronald Wraith, *Open Government – the British Interpretation* (London: Royal Institute of Public Administration, 1977); Anthony S. Mathews, *The Darker Reaches of Government* (Berkley: University of California Press, 1978); Stanley de Smith, *Constitutional and Administrative Law* (Harmondsworth: Penguin, 1975); T. C. Hartley and J. A. G. Griffiths, *Government and Law* (London: Weidenfeld & Nicolson, 1973); E. C. S. Wade and A. W. Bradley, *Wade and Philips on Constitutional Law* (London: Longman, 1970). However, there is an exception to this pattern in that the Campaign for Freedom of Information Handbook contains several references to accountability. It is a matter of some speculation as to why the Freedom of Information Campaign is something of an exception, but it may reflect the fact that 'accountability' has a harder edge than the more traditional concept of 'responsibility'. 'To be responsible' implies acting reasonably and in accordance with the rules. It concerns the relationship between master and agent and whether the agent is acting in accordance with due process and within the bounds of authority. However, 'to be accountable' implies that one group can force another to justify its actions – it implies that others can challenge the merits of what one does.
4. Dawn Oliver and Gavin Drewry, *Public Service Reforms: issues of accountability and public law* (1996), p. 3.
5. R. V. Ericson, 'Rules for police deviance', in C. D. Shearing (ed.), *Organisational Police Deviance* (Toronto: Butterworth, 1981) pp. 83–110; R. V. Ericson, *Making Crime* (Toronto: Butterworth, 1981); R. V. Ericson, *Reproducing Order* (Toronto: Butterworth, 1982); R. V. Ericson, 'Patrolling the facts – secrecy and publicity in police work', *British Journal of*

Sociology 1989 (40): 205–26; R. V. Ericson, *Negogiating Control* (Milton Keynes: Open University Press, 1989).
6. Ericson, 'Rules for police deviance', p. 86.
7. Ibid., p. 85.
8. Nevil Johnson, *In Search of the Constitution* (London: Methuen, 1977), p. 85.
9. Keith Dowding, *The Civil Service* (London: Routledge, 1995), pp. 154–5.
10. The most comprehensive discussion of the 'traditional' concept of accountability, ministerial responsibility, can be found in Diana Woodhouse, *Ministers and Parliament: accountability in theory and practice* (Oxford: Clarendon, 1994), cf. 1 and 2.
11. *Report of the Inquiry into the Export of Defence and Dual-Use Goods to Iraq and Related Prosecutions, The Rt Hon. Sir Richard Scott, The Vice Chancellor, House of Commons Papers 115* (London: HMSO, 1996). (Hereinafter *The Scott Report*.)
12. *Scott Report*, D3. 124.
13. Robertson, *Public Secrets*, p. 27.
14. S. Walkland and M. Ryle (eds), *The Commons in the Seventies* (Glasgow: Fontana/Collins, 1977); and see also Robertson, *Public Secrets*, pp. 27ff. for a discussion of earlier attempts at reform of parliament.
15. Robertson, *Public Secrets*, p. 30.
16. Patricia Day and Rudolf Klein, *Accountabilities: five public services* (London: Tavistock, 1987); Dawn Oliver, *Government in the United Kingdom: the search for accountability, effectiveness and citizenship* (Milton Keynes: Open University Press, 1991); Spencer Zifcak, *New Managerialism: administrative reform in Whitehall and Canberra* (Buckingham: Open University Press, 1994); Philip Giddings (ed.), *Parliamentary Accountability: a study of Parliament and Executive Agencies* (Basingstoke: Macmillan, 1995); Andrew Massey, 'Civil Service reform and accountability', *Public Policy and Administration*, 10 (1): 16–33; Stuart Weir, 'Quangos: questions of democratic accountability', *Parliamentary Affairs* 48 (2): 306; *Public Service Committee: Ministerial Accountability and Responsibility: First and Second Report, HC 313 1 11* (London: HMSO 1996); P. Hoggett, 'New modes of control in the public service, '*Public Administration*', 74: 9–32; A. Wall, Mine, yours or theirs – accountability in the new NHS *Policy And Politics*, 24: 73–84.
17. For example, even the Fulton Committee in its Report on the civil service stated that the assumption that ministers have full knowledge and control of what takes place in their departments is 'untenable' (para. 238).
18. Oonagh McDonald, *The Future of Whitehall* (London: Weidenfeld & Nicolson, 1992).
19. McDonald, *The Future of Whitehall*, p. 146.
20. Peter Hennessy, *The Hidden Wiring* (London: Victor Gollancz, 1995): see particularly ch. on 'The Cabinet'.
21. See p. 59 above.
22. Diana Woodhouse is a representative of this school; see ch. 12 of *Ministers and Parliament*.

23. *Fifth Report from the Treasury and Civil Service Committee: Developments in the Next Steps Programme, HC 348, Session 1988–89* (London: HMSO, 1989) para. 55.
24. House of Commons Debate, 21 May 1990, cols 150–1.
25. *Treasury and Civil Service Committee, HC 481 Session 1989–90, Progress in the Next Steps Iniative* (London: HMSO; 1990) paras 68, 70.
26. John McEldowney, 'The control of public expenditure', in Jeffrey Jowell and Dawn Oliver (eds), *The Changing Constitution* (Oxford University Press, 1994) pp. 175–207.
27. Oliver and Drewry, *Public Service Reforms*, pp. 83. ff.
28. Ibid., p. 85.
29. Woodhouse, *Ministers and Parliament*, p. 249.

6 Data Protection, Privacy and Limited Rights of Access

1. C. Melors and D. Pollitt, 'The Data Protection Bill', *Political Quarterly*, 55(3). See also James Michael, 'Data Protection', *Public Law*, 1982.
2. Data Protection Act 1984, Part 1, Schedule 1.
3. Bryan Niblett, *Data Protection Act 1984* (London: Oyez Longman, 1984) p. 13.
4. The Data Protection Act sections 21–4 allows an individual to be denied access on the grounds of national security. Part II of the Act allows certain databases to be exempt even from the requirement to register. See Patrick Birkinshaw, *Government and Information: the law relating to access, disclosure, and regulation* (London: Butterworths, 1990) pp. 180–209; and Niblett, *Data Protection Act 1984*.
5. Directive 95/46EC: OJL 281/31, 31 November 1995.
6. See Home Office Press Release 085/96, 22 March 1996. The government also announced the publication of a consultation document on how to respond to this directive, the supposed cost to business being one of the main concerns. A copy of the consultation document can be found on the Internet at: http://www.open.gov.uk/home_off/ccpd/dataprot.htm.
7. For a discussion of these laws, see Patrick Birkinshaw, *Freedom of Information – the law, the practice, the ideal* (London: Weidenfeld & Nicolson, 2nd edn, 1996), ch. 6; James Michael, 'Privacy', in Christopher McCrudden and Gerald Chambers (eds), *Individual Rights and the Law in Britain* (Oxford: Clarendon, 1994) ch. 8; 'The Scope of Legal Privacy', in David Feldman (ed.), *Civil Liberties and Human rights* (Oxford, University Press, 1993); Linda Clarke (ed.), *Confidentiality and the Law* (London: Lloyd's of London Press, 1990); Raymond Wacks, *Personal Information* (Oxford: Clarendon, 1989).
8. Audit Commission, *Setting the Record Straight* (London: HMSO, June 1995).
9. Bill Hebenton and Terry Thomas, *Criminal Records* (Aldershot: Avebury, 1993) p. 85.
10. Hebenton and Thomas, *Criminal records*, p. 109. The figure of 85 000 is an estimate for the year 1992 (Hansard, House of Lords, 24.6.91, col. 436).

11. Police Act 1997 c. 50. pt V.
12. As reported in *The Times*, 11 July 1997.
13. *House of Commons, Criminal Records, Home Affairs Committee 3rd report Session 1989–90, 285* (London: HMSO, 1990) Minutes of Evidence, p. 13.
14. Ibid., para. 16.
15. For a highly critical account of the process of private and public vetting in the UK see M. Hollingsworth and R. Norton-Taylor, *Blacklist: the inside story of political vetting* (London: Hogarth Press, 1988).
16. Patrick Birkinshaw, *Freedom of Information*, p. 138.
17. Some rights to attend council meetings had been granted under the Public Bodies (Admission to Meetings) Act 1960 and the Local Government Act 1972, although these did not cover subcommittees. See Patrick Birkinshaw, *Open Government, Freedom of Information and Local Government* (London: Weidenfeld & Nicolson, 1986).
18. Local Government (Access to Information) Act 1985, Pt 1 paras 1–15.
19. Local Government (Access to Information) Act 1985, s. 100D.
20. The only monograph on this subject is an analysis of the law and subsequent legal cases. See Tim Harrison, *Access to Information in Local Government* (London: Sweet & Maxwell, 1988).

7 Listening In

1. This is discussed in Chapter 10.
2. Patrick Fitzgerald and Mark Leopold, *Stranger on the Line: the secret history of phone tapping* (London: Bodley Head, 1987) p. 115.
3. House of Commons, *Hansard*, 31 July 1952, col. 1665.
4. Fitzgerald and Leopold, *Stranger on the Line*, pp. 116 ff.
5. *Report of the Privy Councillors appointed to Inquire into the Interception of Communications*, Cmnd 283 (London: HMSO, 1957). The royal prerogative refers to those powers that the sovereign possesses as a result of 'position and dignity of Office'. Such powers have, over the centuries, been limited by statute and constitutional convention although they remain important in areas such as 'the defence of the realm'.
6. The High Court judge stated that this was an area of the law which 'cried out for legislation': [1979] 2 All ER p. 649. For other comment at the time see Carol Harlow, Comment – the Malone Telephone Tapping case', *Public Law*, 1980 (Spring): 1–6.
7. Publications of the European Court of Human Rights, series A, vol. 82, *Malone* (1984). For a discussion of this case see J. D. Baxter, *State Security, Privacy and Information* (Hemel Hempstead: Harvester Wheatsheaf, 1990).
8. Interception of Communications Act 1985, Section 2(2).
9. The Court ruled that the right to privacy could be interfered with under certain circumstances and found that German practice was in accordance with the Convention (*Klass* [1978], publications of European Court of Human Rights, series A, no. 28).
10. Laurence Lustgarten and Ian Leigh call this the 'Wednesbury test' after the ruling in the legal case of *Associated Picture Houses Ltd.* v. *Wednesbury*

Corporation [1948] 1 KB 223, 229 per Lord Greene, MR, In from the Cold (Oxford University Press 1994) p. 62.

11. The Commissioner has issued the following reports as of 1997: Interception of Communications Act 1985, Report of the Commissioner for 1995, Cm 3254 (London: HMSO, 1996); Interception of Communications Act 1985, Report of the Commissioner for 1994, Cm 2828 (London: HMSO, 1995); Interception of Communications Act 1985, Report of the Commissioner for 1993, Cm 2522 (London: HMSO, 1994); Interception of Communications Act, Report of the Commissioner for 1992, Cm 2173 (London: HMSO, 1993); Interception of Communications Act, Report of the Commissioner for 1992, Cm 1942 (London: HMSO, 1992); Interception of Communications Act, Report of the Commissioner for 1990, Cm 1489 (London: HMSO, 1991); Interception of Communications Act, Report of the Commissioner for 1989, Cm 1063 (London: HMSO, 1990); Interception of Communications Act, Report of the Commissioner for 1988, Cm 652 (London: HMSO, 1989); Interception of Communications Act, Report of the Commissioner for 1987, Cm 351 (London: HMSO, 1988); Interception of Communications Act, Report of the Commissioner for 1986, Cm 108, (London: HMSO, 1987).
12. For the latest Report from the Commissioner see Rt Hon. The Lord Nolan, Report of the Commissioner for 1996, Cm 3678 (London: HMSO, June 1997). The figures issued in the annex to the report show that the total number of warrants issued by the Home Secretary for the interception of telecommunications and for letters shows a steady rise over the last few years: 1985 – 286: 1990 – 515; 1995 – 997; 1996 – 1142.
13. Report of the Commissioner for 1987, Cm 351, (London: HMSO, 1988) para. 56.
14. Report of the Commissioner for 1996, Cm 3678 (London: HMSO, June 1997).
15. The powers, duties and composition of the tribunal are defined in Schedule 1 of the 1985 Act. For a brief account of the legislation see I. J. Lloyd, 'The Interception of Communications Act 1985', *Modern Law Review*, 49: 87–95.
16. Report of the Commissioner for 1996, para. 5.
17. Stephen Dorril, author and editor of *Lobster*, states that 'there is no effective sanction against illegal telephone tapping' (Dorril, *The Silent Conspiracy: inside the intelligence services in the 1990s* (London: Heinemann, 1993) p. 181. Even the generally calm Lustgarten and Leigh argue that 'the Commissioner (for the interception of communications) considered it unlikely that impropriety could be hidden from him. However, he also accepts that if it were taking place there would be no reason for it to come to his attention' (*In from the Cold* p. 62). This is the old 'bell that does not ring' argument, in that the lack of any evidence only confirms the existence of the plot. How could the commissioner know what he does not know?
18. *Statewatch*, 6(6): 1.
19. Police Act 1997 c. 50, s. 92.

8 Official Secrecy

1. Clive Ponting, who was acquitted after a famous Official Secret's Act prosecution, has written: 'in Britain, the governing elite hold the view that the whole process of government must be kept confidential' (Ponting, *Secrecy in Britain* [Oxford: Basil Blackwell, 1990]).
2. Patrick Birkinshaw, *Reforming the Secret State* (Milton Keynes: Open University Press, 1990); Patrick Birkinshaw, *Government and Information – the law relating to access, disclosure and regulation* (London: Butterworth, 1990); Stephanie Palmer, 'Tightening Secrecy Law: the Official Secrets Act 1989', *Public Law*, 1990 (Summer): 243–56; Stephanie Palmer, 'Analysis: In the interests of the State – the government's proposals for reforming Section 2 of the Official Secrets Act 1911', *Public Law*, 1988: 523–35; Peter Hennessy and Chris Westcott, *The Last Right? open government, freedom of information and the right to know*, Glasgow: University of Strathclyde, Dept of Government, Strathclyde Papers on Government and Politics no. 12, 1992; J. A. G. Griffiths, *Public Rights and Private Interests* (Trivandrum, India: Academy of Legal Publications, 1981).
3. Stephanie Palmer, 'Tightening secrecy law', p. 256.
4. The most relevant articles being: F. F. Ridley, 'Using power to keep power – the need for constitutional checks', *Parliamentary Affairs*, 44 (4); David Morgan, 'Media–Government Relations – the right to manage information versus the right to know', *Parliamentary Affairs*, 44 (4).
5. The election of a Labour government in May 1997, committed to introducing FOI, may change this, but it is not fair to judge on promises alone.
6. *The Fulton Report*, p. 91.
7. White Paper: *Information and the Public Interest* Cmnd 4089 (London: HMSO, 1969).
8. Kevin Theakston, *The Labour Party and Whitehall* (London: Routledge, 1992) p. 180.
9. The first such case, in 1971, involved the prosecution of a military officer and journalists during the Nigerian Civil War. All the defendants were acquitted and the judge commented that the Official Secrets Act ought to 'be pensioned off'. For a discussion of such cases see Rosamund M. Thomas, *Espionage and Secrecy – the Official Secrets Act 1911–1989 of the UK* (London: Routledge, 1991); and David Hooper, *Official Secrets* (London: Secker & Warburg, 1987).
10. Although there was a group formed in 1975, that won some initial support, entitled the 'All-party Committee for a Freedom of Information and Privacy Act', it emerged that all of its full-time activists were Scientologists. The organisation headed by Maurice Frankel, the FOI Campaign, was formed in 1984. See James Michael, *The Politics of Secrecy: confidential government and the public right to know* (Harmondsworth: Penguin, 1982) pp. 198 ff.; and A. P. Tant, 'The Campaign for Freedom of Information: a participatory challenge to elitist British government', *Public Administration*, 68 (Winter): 477–91.
11. See Chapter 11 for further details.

12. Geoffrey Prime (GCHQ) and Michael Bettaney (MI5) were also convicted of offences under the Official Secrets Act 1911 but will be dealt with later on in the chapter dealing with the Intelligence Services (Chapter 10).
13. For discussions of the Tisdall and Ponting cases, see Christopher McCrudden and Gerald Chambers (eds) *Individual Rights and the Law in Britain* (Oxford: Clarendon, 1994); Yvonne Cripps, *The Legal Implications of Disclosure in the Public Interest* (London: Sweet & Maxwell, 1986; 2nd edn 1994); David Feldman, *Civil Liberties and Human rights* (Oxford University Press, 1993); Geoffrey Robertson and Andrew G. L. Nicol, *Media Law* (Harmondsworth: Penguin, 3rd edn 1992); Rosamund M. Thomas, 'Espionage and Secrecy: the Official Secret Acts 1911–1989 of the United Kingdom', *Public Administration*, 70: 150–1; Rosamund M. Thomas, 'The British Official Secrets Acts 1911–1939 and the Ponting Case', *Criminal Law Review*, 1986: 491–510; 'Official duties: before and after Ponting', *Public Administration*, 63 (Summer): 125–31; Clive Ponting, *The Right to Know* (London: Sphere, 1985).
14. For discussions of the legal issues surrounding *Spycatcher* see: Ian Leigh, 'Analyis: Spycatcher in Strasbourg', *Public Law* 1992 (Summer): 200–8; Douglas Fairley, 'D Notices, Official Secrets and the Law', *Oxford Journal of Legal Studies*, **10** (3): 430–40; Eric Barendt 'Spycatcher and Freedom of Speech', *Public Law* 1989, (Summer); Yvonne Cripps, 'Breaches of Copyright and Confidence – the Spycatcher effect', *Public Law* (1989 Spring); Malcolm Turnball, *The Spycatcher Trial* (1988); R. C. Austin, 'The Wright affair – the wrong response: constitutional aspects of the Wright affair', *Parliamentary Affairs*, 40: 319–24; Laurence Lustgarten and Ian Leigh, *In from the Cold* (Oxford University Press, 1994).
15. See Michael Smith, *New Cloak, Old Dagger* (London: Gollancz, 1996) pp. 68 ff.
16. Section 1 of the old Act has been criticised for the way in which it has been used to prosecute people who were not accused of engaging in espionage. The most famous case involved a group of anti-nuclear protesters who were prosecuted under Section 1 for entering a 'prohibited place'. See ch. 8 of David Hooper, *Official Secrets: the use and abuse of the Act* (London: Secker & Warburg, 1987).
17. For a full discussion of this issue see K. G. Robertson, *Public Secrets: A Study in the Development of Government Secrecy* (London: Macmillan, 1982) chs 3–5.
18. In the case of defence, the protected categories are information concerning: (a) condition and organisation of armed forces; (b) equipment; (c) strategy and planning; (d) supplies and services required in time of war. In the case of crime, the protected categories are information that: (a) results in the commission of an offence; (b) facilitates an escape or impedes the prevention, detection or apprehension of offenders. The other Sections of the Act will be discussed in more detail below.
19. *The Franks Report*, paras 150–7.
20. For a discussion of the Ponting trial, see Rosamund M. Thomas, 'The British Official Secrets Acts 1911–1939 and the Ponting Case', pp. 491–510.

21. Dr David Owen MP argued that 'the balance of this legislation depends on there being a general interest defence. Without it, it is fatally flawed.' (HC Debate, *Hansard*, 29 June 1988, col. 373).
22. For a discussion of the Canadian Inspector General see Geoffrey Weller, 'The Canadian Security and Intelligence Service under stress', *Canadian Public Administration*, 31 (2). For the role of the US Inspector General see Frederick Kaiser, 'The Watcher's Watchdog', *International Journal of Intelligence and Counterintelligence*, **3** (1). For a recent overview of some of these issues see Glenn P. Hastedt (ed.), *Controlling Intelligence* (London, Frank Cass, 1991).
23. The current counsellor for intelligence staff is Sir Christoper France, a former permanent secretary at the Ministry of Defence, who was appointed in March 1995.
24. For a discussion of the pre-1994 mechanisms of accountability in the UK see K. G. Robertson, 'Accountable Intelligence – the British experience', *Conflict Quarterly*, 8 (1).
25. Carole Maychell, a part-time captain in the Intelligence Corps was the first person to be charged under Section 1 of the 1989 OSA. Section 1 deals with the 'life-long' duty of confidentiality imposed on all those connected to the intelligence services. However, although Maychell was detained in prison for four months, the Attorney General decided not to prosecute and issued a statement stating that there was 'insufficient evidence to ensure a realistic prospect of conviction'. See the *Guardian*, 25 September 1993. Tomlinson is therefore the second person to be charged under Section 1 of the 1989 Act, although the Attorney General has yet (November 1997) to decide whether to prosecute. The consent of the Attorney General is required for all OSA prosecutions. For reports on the case see *The Times*, 4 November 1997; *Guardian*, November 1997; and *The Sunday Times*, 9 November 1997. The only official secrets prosecution, trial and conviction of recent years concerned Michael Smith, a civilian employee of a defence contractor, who was convicted of passing military secrets to the Russians. However, Smith was convicted under Section 1 of the 1911 Act, which was untouched by the 1989 reforms. The statute dealing with espionage remains the Official Secrets Act 1911; the 1989 OSA repeals only Section of the 1911 Act.
26. For a discussion of the intelligence services tribunal, set up under the Intelligence Services Act 1994, see Chapter 10.
27. In the case of the recipient of a security or intelligence disclosure the prosecution must prove that one had reasonable cause to believe that it was such a disclosure. There is the requirement of *mens rea*, 'guilty knowledge', in the case of those handling leaks.
28. Yvonne Cripps, *The Legal Implications of Disclosure in the Public Interest* (London: Sweet & Maxwell, 2nd edn 1994) p. 1 (Introduction).
29. Ibid.
30. Ibid., p. 15.
31. Ibid. She also adds the following comment: 'In our society that assessment is often made, and in my view appropriately made, by judges.'
32. Cripps, *The Legal Implications of Disclosure*, p. 341.
33. Ibid., p. 342.

34. Ibid.
35. Ibid., p. 343.
36. Ibid.

9 Defending the Realm: MI5

1. For examples of books involving ‘leaks’ from insiders, particularly over the Hollis Affair, see: Chapman Pincher, *Traitors – the Labyrinths of Treason* (Sidgwick, 1987); Nigel West, *Molehunt – the full story of the Soviet Mole in MI5* (London: Weidenfeld & Nicolson; 1987); Anthony Glees, *The Secrets of the Service – British Intelligence and Communist subversion 1939–51* (Cape, 1987).
2. For example, see the constitutional critic J. T. Eliff, *The Reform of FBI Intelligence Operations* (Princeton NJ: Princeton University Press, 1979) and the more radical critic, Frank Donner, *The Age of Surveillance – the aims and methods of America's political Intelligence Service* (New York: Vintage, 1981).
3. As reported in *The Times*, 15 November 1987.
4. Mrs Thatcher, the prime minister, Debate on Blunt, 21 November 1979, *Hansard*, col. 408.
5. James Callaghan referring to his period as prime minister between 1976 and 1979, *Hansard*, cols 506–7.
6. Nigel West, *A Matter of Trust*: *MI5 1945–1972* (London: Coronet, 1982).
7. Statement by the prime minister in the debate on Security and the Denning Report, House of Commons, 16 December 1963, *Hansard*, cols 859–61.
8. Harold Wilson, Debate on Security and the Denning Report, *Hansard*, cols 879–81.
9. Oral Questions, House of Commons, 23 January 1964, *Hansard*, cols 1271–5.
10. Parliamentary Papers, *XXII*, *Report of the Security Commission* (London, HMSO, Cmnd. 2722, June 1965) para. 1.
11. The Reports of the Security Commission, by reference number and date only are: June 1965, Cmnd. 2722; September 1965, Cmnd. 2773; July 1966, Cmnd. 3151; June 1967, Cmnd. 3365; November 1968, Cmnd. 3856; May 1973, Cmnd. 5362; July 1973, Cmnd. 5367; May 1983, Cmnd. 8876; March 1984, Cmnd. 9212; May 1985, Cmnd. 9514. All are Parliamentary Papers, (London: HMSO). The ISC is discussed in the following chapter.
12. *Report of the Security Commission on Michael Bettaney*, May 1985, Cmnd. 9514.
13. Ibid., para. 1.6.
14. Ibid., para. 8.2.
15. Ibid., para. 8.5.
16. House of Commons, 26 March 1981, *Hansard*, col. 108.
17. See pp. 88, 105 for a discussion of this affair.
18. *The Times*, 3 November 1987.
19. See pp. 92–3 for a discussion of this case.

20. *Accountability of the Security Service*, Home Affairs Committee, First report, Session 1992–93, HC 265 (London: HMSO, 1992).
21. Ibid., Minutes of Evidence, paras 11 and 36.
22. *Public Records*, House of Commons, Education, Science and Arts Committee, Session 1982–83; and *Special Branch*, Home Affairs Committee Session 1984–85.
23. Appendix 4, Memorandum by the Home Office, Minutes of Evidence, *Accountability of the Security Service*, Home Affairs Committee, First report, Session 1992–93, HC 265 (London: HMSO, 1992) p. 20.
24. See Chapter 10.
25. Lord Denning, *The Resignation of Mr Profumo*, (London: HMSO, 1963) Cmnd. 2152, para. 238.
26. Ibid., para. 239.
27. For discussion of the JIC see Michael Herman, *Intelligence Power in Peace and War* (Cambridge University Press, 1996) and *Central Intelligence Machinery* (London: HMSO, 1993).
28. Confidential source.
29. See reports in *The Times*, 9 May 1992.
30. See reports in *Daily Telegraph*, 22 April 1992.
31. 'MI5's Official Secrets', *20/20 Vision*, Channel 4, 8 March 1985.
32. See *Independent*, 26 and 27 April 1990.
33. I. Leigh and L. Lustgarten, 'The Security Service Act 1989', *Modern Law Review*, November 1989, pp. 802–3.
34. See Chapter 7 for a discussion of the *Malone* case.
35. Security Service Act 1989, Section 1.
36. For example in Lord Denning, *The Resignation of Mr Profumo*, Cmnd 2152 (London: HMSO, 1963), the directive governing the activities of the Service was published and the government made a statement in the House of Lords on the meaning of subversion, *Hansard*, 357, HL Debates, col. 947, February 1975.
37. The Rt Hon. Lord Justice Stuart-Smith, *Report of the Security Service Commissioner for 1990*, Cm 1480 (London: HMSO, March 1991).
38. Ibid., para. 12.
39. Ibid., para. 10.
40. Ibid., para. 15.
41. Ibid.; *Security Service Act, Report of the Commissioner for 1991* (London: HMSO, Cm 1946, 1992); *Security Service Act 1989, Report of the Commissioner for 1992* (London: HMSO, Cm 2174, 1993); *Security Service Act 1989, Report of the Commissioner for 1993* (London: HMSO Cm 2523, 1994); *Security Service Act 1989: Report of the Commissioner for 1994* (HMSO, Cm 2827, 1995); *Security Service Act 1989, Report of the Commissioner for 1995* (London: HMSO Cm 3253, 1996); *Security Service Act 1989: Report of the Commissioner for 1996, Cm 3679* (London: HMSO, 1997).
42. Commissioner's report for 1997, paras. 30–3.
43. There is a Polish anecdote from the days of Communist rule in which a university professor arrives at work with a very sad expression. When asked by colleagues to explain his disposition he tells them that he did not see his normal secret police surveillance team on the way to university.

When they express surprise that this should make him sad, he replies 'If I am no longer under surveillance, it means I am no longer important.'

44. Peter Wright, *Spycatcher* (New York: Viking Penguin, 1987) p. 54.
45. Section 3(1), of the Security Service Act 1989.
46. Wright, *Spycatcher*, p. 54.
47. For MI5's own account of its functions see *The Security Service* (London: HMSO, 2nd edn, 1996 [1st edn 1993]). See also Stella Rimington, *Security and Democracy – is there a conflict?* (London: BBC Educational Developments, 1994).
48. Confidential source.

10 The Democratisation of Intelligence?

1. For some of the debates over recent changes to UK intelligence see: Stephen Dorril, *The silent conspiracy – inside the intelligence services in the 1990s* (London: Heinemann, 1993); James Adams, *The new Spies: exploring the frontiers of espionage* (London: Hutchinson, 1994); Peter Gill, 'Sack the Spooks: do we need an internal security apparatus?' *The Socialist Register* (1996); Michael Herman, *Intelligence Power in Peace and War* (Cambridge University Press, 1996); Mark Urban, *UK Eyes Alpha* (London: Faber, 1996); Michael Smith, *New Cloak, Old Dagger* (London: Victor Gollancz, 1996).
2. *Intelligence Services Bill, Second Reading, House of Commons*, 22/2/94, *Hansard*, cols 153–250 (1994); *Intelligence Services Bill, Second Reading, House of Lords*, 9/12/93, *Hansard*, cols 1023–79 (1994); *Intelligence Services Bill, Third Reading, House of Lords*, 14/2/94, *Hansard* cols 10–15 (1994); *Intelligence Services Bill, House of Commons, Standing Committee E*. Parliament, House of Commons, 3–29 March 1994; Intelligence Services [HL] A bill as amended in Standing Committee E, brought from the Lords 14/2/94. *Intelligence Services Bill, Second Reading, House of Lords, 2/2/94, Hansard* cols 153–250.
3. For the amusing contortions this created, see Smith, *New Cloak, Old Dagger*, p. 9.
4. Douglas Hurd, the Home Secretary, stated that:

   > Others have argued for a system of oversight... Others look to the Security Commission. These are serious proposals that deserve to be examined, but, having examined them, we do not favour them.' HC Debate on Security Service, *Hansard*, vol. 143 cols 1109–10 (1988).

5. The Bill was published in November 1993 and was debated as above (n. 2).
6. Hurd states this most clearly in the following: 'I have done so because the views of the agencies have changed and the kind of work which they do has changed.' (*Hansard*, House of Commons, 22 February 1994, col. 167).
7. Ibid., col. 161 where the secretary of state talks of the benefit of experience derived from the Security Service Act.
8. He gives three examples: (1) an ally who was alerted to their citizen's involvement in the construction of a plant for the manufacture of weap-

ons of mass destruction; (2) SIS monitoring of a drugs consignment; (3) the passing of information about the movements of a known terrorist to the police of a West European nation. However, at least two out of the three are examples of the traditional activities of SIS rather than of anything new.

9. The right to join a trade union was granted to GCHQ employees by the new Labour government in 1997.
10. The main amendments proposed were:

    - that the size of the committee should be increased from six to nine (accepted), Standing Committee E. col. 232;
    - that the legislation should include a list of 'democratic principles' which should govern the operation of the intelligence services as in the Canadian legislation (rejected), Ibid., cols 69–73;
    - that the concept of 'national security' should be defined (rejected), Ibid., cols 46–62;
    - to broaden the protection offered by Section 2(2) (b) that the head of the service shall ensure that an agency does not act to further the interests of any political grouping and should not seek to damage the interests of any political party (rejected), Ibid., cols 77–114;
    - that warrants granted under Section 5(1) allowing for interference with property etc. should be granted by the judiciary rather than the secretary of state (rejected), Ibid., cols 151–72;
    - that the oversight committee should be given the power to call for people and papers (rejected), Ibid., cols 235–55;
    - that the oversight committee should have access to the uncensored report of the commissioner and information about decisions of the tribunal (rejected), Ibid., cols 204–10;
    - that the prime minister should able to amend (censor) the report of the oversight committee only when the information was 'damaging to national security'. (rejected), Ibid., cols 265–73;
    - that the oversight committee should be protected by the Bill of Rights 1688 (rejected), Ibid., cols 257–65;
    - that trade union rights should be restored to GCHQ (rejected), Ibid., cols 282–321;
    - that the proceedings of the Committee should be protected by full parliamentary privilege, and not merely qualified privilege (rejected), Commons Debate, cols 179–80.

11. Standing Committee E, col. 166.
12. Ibid., col. 165.
13. The Intelligence Services Act 1994 10(2).
14. Commons Debate, 2 February 1994, cols 178–9.
15. Interception of Communication Act 1985, ch. 56, 1989; Security Service Act 1989, ch. 5, 1989.
16. Intelligence Services Act 1994, ch. 13, sec. 1.
17. Laurence Lustgarten and Ian Leigh, *In from the Cold* (Oxford University Press, 1994).
18. Michael Supperstone, 'The Intelligence Services Act 1994', *Public Law* (1994): 329–31.

19. Intelligence Services Act 1994, Sec. 2(2) (a).
20. Ibid., Sec. 2(2) (b).
21. Ibid., secs. 3 and 4 define the tasks and duties of the director of GCHQ.
22. Ibid., sect. 5(1).
23. Ibid., sect. 5(2 (a).
24. Ibid., sect. 5 ((2) (3).
25. Ibid., sect. 5(2) (4) refers to secs 2(2) (a) of the security Service Act 1989 and secs 2(2) (a) and sec. 4(2) (a) of the Intelligence Services Act 1994.
26. Ibid., sect. 10 and schedule 3.
27. Ibid., schedule 3(3)
28. Intelligence Security Committee, *Interim Report*, Cm 2873, (London: HMSO) May 1995.
29. Ibid., para. 10.
30. Intelligence and Security Committee, *Report on Security Service Work Against Organised Crime*, Cm 3065 (London: HMSO) December 1995. The Chairman of the Committee is a former Conservative Minister of Defence, the Rt Hon. Tom King.
31. Ibid., p. 1 (1).
32. 'The Committee believe, however, that there are certain key aspects that have not yet fully been resolved . . . the Committee are of the view that it would be insufficient simply to add the countering of organised crime to the Service's responsibilities under the 1989 Act.' (Ibid., p. 4 (paras 7 and 8).
33. Ibid., p. 4 (8).
34. All of the above points are made in very short order in a single paragraph of the report, p. 4 (8).
35. Intelligence and Security Committee, *Annual Report 1995*, Cm 3198 (London: HMSO) March 1996.
36. Ibid., p. 23, para. N.
37. Ibid., p. 21, para. 38.
38. Confidential sources.
39. The Rt Hon. Sir Richard Scott, *Report of the Inquiry into the Export of Defence and Dual-Use Goods to Iraq and related Prosecutions*, House of Commons Papers 113, 1996. See also Davina Millar, *Export or Die* (London: Cassell, 1996).
40. See Philip H. J. Davies, 'Organisational Politics and the Development of Britain's Intelligence Producer/Consumer Interface', *Intelligence and National Security*, 10 (4).
41. Intelligence and Security Committee, *Annual Report 1995*, p. 17, para. 28.
42. Ibid., p. 18, para. 28.
43. Security Service Act 1996, ch. 35.
44. The Police Act 1997, ch. 50.
45. The Police Act 1997, Part III, para. 92, states that: 'No entry or interference with property or with wireless telegraphy shall be unlawful if its is authorised by an authorisation having effect under this Part': 'this part' meaning an act approved by the commissioner appointed for the purpose of authorising such acts.
46. See *The Times*, 2, 25 and 29 November 1996; 14 and 17 January 1997.
47. *The Times*, 21 January 1997.

48. Home Office Press Release, *Strengthening Safeguards on Intrusive Surveillance*, 16 January 1997, Release no. 007/97. See The Police Act 1997, paras 97 and 98 for these provisions.
49. Intelligence and Security Committee, *Annual Report 1996*, Cm 3574 (London: HMSO) February 1997.
50. Ibid., para. 37.
51. Ibid., para. 54.

11 Overseas Experiment

1. There are relatively few truly comparative studies of government secrecy (and some of them are showing their age!) but see Robert Hazell, 'Freedom of Information in Australia, Canada and New Zealand', *Public Administration*, 67 (2) 1989: 189–210; James Michael, *The Politics of Secrecy: Confidential Government and the Public Right to Know* (Harmondsworth: Penguin Books, 1982); Norman S Marsh, *Public Access to Government-Held Information: A Comparative Syposium* (London: Stevens, 1992); K. G. Robertson, *Public Secrets: A Study in the Development of Government Secrecy* (London: Macmillan, 1982); Anthony S. Mathews, *The Darker Reaches of Government* (Berkley: University of California Press, 1978); Edward A. Shils, *The Torment of Secrecy: The Background and Consequences of American Security Policies* (London: William Heinemann, 1956); Itzhak Galnoor, *Government Secrecy in Democracies* (New York: Harper & Row, 1977).
2. *Select Committee on the Parliamentary Commissioner for Administration, Second Report, Open Government, HC 84* (London: HMSO, 1996).
3. Ibid., para. 7.
4. *Departmental Committee on Sch. 2 of the Official Secrets Act 1911: Vol. 1 Report; Vols 2, 3 and 4, Written and Oral Evidence (Chairman Lord Franks)* (London: HMSO, Cmnd 5104), 1972; *Disclosure of Official Information: A Report on Overseas Practice* (London: HMSO – Prepared by the Civil Service Department, 1979).
5. Select Co. on the PCA, Report on Open Government, para. 7.
6. Ibid., para. 15.
7. Ibid., para. 16.
8. Ibid., para. 16.
9. Ibid., para. 18. However, its only example of the effect on policy-making is the case of the New South Wales Public Interest Advocacy Centre, an Australian interest group, which 'had done important work on opening public debate on IUDs (intra-uterine devices) and human pituitary gland treatment'. However, no comparisons are done on the impact of similar groups in the UK where we do not have the benefit of FOI legislation.
10. There is a hint in Eagles that this may also have been a factor in New Zealand. He states that a Freedom of Information Bill was introduced in 1976 'prompted by a 1976 report by the Chief Ombudsman into the Security Intelligence Service'. Unfortunately no details are provided and other commentaries on the New Zealand FOI legislation fail to

mention this point. See I. Eagles, M. Taggart and G. Liddell, *Freedom of Information in New Zealand* (Auckland.: OUP; 1992) p. 1.

11. Patrick Birkinshaw, *Freedom of Information: the Law, the Practice, the Ideal*, 2nd edn (London: Weidenfeld & Nicolson, 1996) p. 50.
12. John D. McCamus, 'Freedom of Information in Canada' (originally published in *Government Publications Review* vol. 10, 1983, pp. 51ff.) in Robert Martina, G. Stuart Adam (eds), *A Source Book of Canadian Media Law* (Ottawa: Carleton University Press, 1991) p. 160.
13. One of the main allegations was that RCMP officers had broken into the offices of a left-wing press in Montreal and stolen a 'ton of documents'. Perhaps the most bizarre allegation is that RCMP officers set fire to a barn that *had been* used by the Quebec separatist organisation, the FLQ. For a summary of the allegations see Richard Cleroux, *Official Secrets: the Story behind the Canadian Security Intelligence Service* (Toronto: McClelland & Stewart, 1991) ch. 2.
14. Access to Information Act (1982) sections 3 and 4.
15. Ibid., section 31.
16. See Melanie Phillips, 'Welfare Benefits' in R. Delbridge and M. Smith (eds), *Consuming Secrets: How Official Secrecy Affects Everyday Life in Britain (A Report for the National Consumer Council)* (London: Burnett Books, 1982).
17. Access to Information Act (1982) section 11.
18. H. N. Janisch, 'The Canadian Access to Information Act', *Public Law*, 1982: 539–40.
19. Access to Information Act (1982) section 7.
20. Ibid., section 37.
21. For a brief, but useful, list of these exemptions see Patrick Birkinshaw, *Freedom of Information: the Law, the Practice, the Ideal*, p. 68.
22. Access to Information Act 1982, section 69 (Cabinet) and section 14 (federal–provincial relations).
23. McCamus, 'Freedom of Information in Canada', p. 160.
24. See K. G. Robertson, *Public Secrets: A Study in the Development of Government Secrecy* (London: Macmillan, 1982) chs 3–5 for an outline of the UK tradition and see The Report of the Commission on Freedom of Information and Individual Privacy, *Public Government for Private People* (Ontario Ministry of Government Services: Toronto Canada, 1980) ch. 5.
25. Information Commissioner of Canada, *Annual Report*, Ottawa, Ministry of Supply and Services, 1988, p. 3.
26. Information Commissioner of Canada, *Annual Report*, 1988, p. 5. The Parliamentary Report referred to is *Open and Shut: Enhancing the Right to Know and the Right to Privacy*, March 1987, to which the government gave a negative response in its reply *Access and Privacy: the Steps Ahead*, 1987.
27. For an account of these events with a strong 'conspiratorial flavour' see J. Coxsedge, K. Coldicutt and G. Harant, *Rooted in Secrecy: The Clandestine Element in Australian Politics* (Balwyn North, Australia: Committee for the Abolition of Political Police, 1982) ch 2, entitled 'Scenario for a Coup'.

28. Royal Commission on Intelligence and Security, chaired by Mr. Justice R. M. Hope, *Vols 1–4* (Canberra: Australian Government, 1977).
29. For relatively sensational accounts see: Morton Halperin *et al.* (eds), *The Lawless State: The Crimes of the US Intelligence Agencies* (Harmondsworth: Penguin 1977); Robert Dion, *Crimes of the Secret Police* (Montreal: Black Rose Books, 1982); J. Coxsedge, K. Coldicutt and G. Harant, *Rooted In Secrecy: The Clandestine Element in Australian Politics* (Balwyn North, Australia: committee for the Abolition of Political Police, 1982).
30. Peter J. Bayne, *Freedom of Information* (North Ryde, NSW: The Law Book Co. 1984) p. 4.
31. For further details see p. 134.
32. Australian Freedom of Information Act Sch. 12(1); see also Peter Bayne, *Freedom of Information* (North Ryde, NSW: The Law Book Co. 1984) p. 9.
33. The original 60-day time limit was reduced to 45 days in 1984. In 1986 the time limit was reduced to 30 days: *Freedom of Information Amendment Act 1983* Sch. 10(d).
34. A request for the applicant's own personal information must be accompanied by the standard $30 application fee. The hourly processing charges are, however, limited to a maximum of two hours. Applicants in receipt of a prescribed benefit or any other form of income support are entitled to relief from fees and charges in regard to requests for documents concerning decisions about their benefits. FOI (Fees and Charges) Regulations Reg 4, Sch. 1, Pt I, item 2A.
35. Australian Law Reform Commission, *Freedom of Information*, Discussion Paper 59 (Sydney: Australian Law Reform Commission, 1995), ch. 7.
36. This is the standard filing fee for AAT review and is prescribed in the AAT Regulations Reg. 19(1), (2).
37. Australian Law Reform Commission, *Freedom of Information*, 1995, p. 102.
38. Ibid., p. 105.
39. Australian Freedom of Information Act Schs 34–36.
40. Ibid., Sch. 58.
41. I. Eagles, M. Taggart and G. Liddell, *Freedom of Information in New Zealand* (Auckland: OUP, 1992) p. 21.
42. Previously the right was restricted to citizens and to businesses incorporated in New Zealand but these restrictions were removed in the Amendments of 1987.
43. Eagles *et al.*, *Freedom of Information*, p. 32.
44. As of 1990 the charges were 15 cents per page for copying and $25 per half-hour. Such charges may also be waived if (a) the charges cause hardship or (b) the Department considers it to be in the public interest.
45. Eagles *et al.*, *Freedom of Information*, p. 335.
46. Ibid., ch. 12 (B).
47. Ibid., p. 523.
48. There are two other elements of the New Zealand system worthy of brief comment; official secrecy and privacy. New Zealand is the only Commonwealth country that considered that it was necessary to repeal its secrecy laws and to replace them with a new statute covering the

Wrongful Communication of Official Information. The main change was a narrowing of the categories protected by criminal sanctions. Espionage remains an offence but the disclosure of information is only liable to criminal penalties when disclosure is likely to prejudice security, defence and law enforcement or to seriously damage the economic interests of New Zealand. In 1993 New Zealand introduced one of the most comprehensive systems of protection for personal data and privacy, in the democratic world; it covers both the public and private sectors and manual, as well as electronic, data. However, although complaints seem to have been evenly divided between the public and private sectors the Commissioner seems to have put the bulk of effort into regulating the public sector. On privacy see Rodney Haines, The Office and Function of New Zealand's Privacy Commissioner, *Government Information Quarterly* 1996, 13(3): 255–74.

49. For descriptions of this process see Graham Scott, Peter Bushnell and Nitkin Sallee, 'Reform of the Core Public Sector: The New Zealand experience', *Public Sector*, 13 (1991) (3); R. Laking, 'Developing a Culture of Success: Reflections from New Zealand Experience', *Public Administration and Development* 15 (1995): 283–94; S. Domberger and C. Hall, 'Contracting for Public Services: A Review of Antipodean Experience', *Public Administration*, 74 (1996): 129–55; R. G. Laking, 'The New Zealand Management Reforms', *Australian Journal of Public Administration*, 53 (1994): 313–24. In 1988 the public service employed 88 000 people, whereas in 1996 the number had fallen to 36 000 in a reduced number of 'core' departments.

12 Freedom of Information in the UK

1. After five years there were, according to a government review, 42 major charter schemes in place. See *The Citizen's Charter – Five Years on: A Report to Mark Five Years of the Charter Programme* (London: HMSO, Cm 3370, 1996).
2. Independent adjudicators were appointed, in 1993, to resolve disputes over taxation following the initial Taxpayer's Charter in 1992.
3. Statements made to the House of Commons by Francis Maude, then Chief Secretary to the Treasury, 15 November 1991.
4. See *The Guardian*, 25 March and 4 July 1991.
5. Norman Lewis, 'The Citizen's Charter and Next Steps – A New Way of Governing?' *Political Quarterly* 1993, 64: 316–26. In contrast Spencer Zifcak gives it only a passing mention, *New Managerialism: Administrative Reform in Whitehall and Canberra* (Buckingham: Open University Press, 1994).
6. Lewis, 'The Citizen, Charter', p. 320.
7. *Ibid*.
8. *Ibid*., pp. 320–1.
9. See *Treasury and Civil Service Committee, Seventh Report, Civil Servants and Ministers: Duties and Responsibilities, HC92 Session 1985–86* (London: HMSO, 1986); *Treasury and Civil Service Committee, Sixth Report,*

The Role of the Civil Service: Interim Report, HC390, Session 1992–93 (London: HMSO, 1993).

10. *White Paper on Open Government*, Cm 2290. (London: HMSO, Chancellor of the Duchy of Lancaster, Cabinet Office, Office of Public Service and Science, 1993) para. 1.1.
11. Ibid., paras 1–3, 1.4.
12. Ibid., para. 2.47.
13. Sir Humphrey Appleby is the fictional Permanent Secretary of the 'Department of Administrative Affairs' created by Jonathan Lynn and Anthony Jay for the BBC comedy programme *Yes Minister*. The series is available in book form as *The Complete Yes Minister* (London: BBC Publications, 1984). Sir Humphrey was notorious for blocking all attempts to reform the civil service.
14. White Paper on Open Government, para. 2.48.
15. Ibid.
16. *Open Government – Code of Practice on Access to Government Information* (London: HMSO, Cabinet Office, Office of Public Service, Citizen's Charter Unit, 1994) part 1 (3).
17. Ibid., section 11 (9).
18. *Select Committee on the Parliamentary Commissioner for Administration, First Special Report, Government Response to the Second Report of the Select Committee on the Parliamentary Commissioner for Administration, Session 1995–96 – Open Government, Session 1996–97 HC 75* (London: HMSO, 1997) para. 19.
19. *Code of Practice on Access to Government Information*, section 1 (11).
20. *Parliamentary Commissioner for Administration, Ninth Report, Session 1994–95, Selected Cases 1995 - Volume 4, Access to Official Information* (London: HMSO, Parliamentary Papers, 758, 1995); *Parliamentary Commissioner for Administration, Eighth Report, Selected Cases 1995 - Vol. 3, Access to Official Information, Session 1994 – 95*. (London: HMSO, Parliamentary Papers 606, 1995); *Parliamentary Commissioner for Administration, First Report, Selected Cases 1995–Vol. 6, Access to Official Information, Session 1995 – 96* (London: HMSO, Parliamentary Papers 86, 1996). See also *Parliamentary Commissioner for Administration, Fourth Report, Session 1995–96, Annual Report for 1995* (London: HMSO, Parliamentary Papers 296, 1996).
21. The case concerned a couple who had written to the Department of Transport requesting disclosure of the information given by the UK to the European Commission concerning an environmental assessment of a motorway-widening scheme. The DOT sent a letter stating that not all of the information could be disclosed on the grounds that it was exempt under provision 1 (b): it would be harmful to international relations. However, the PCA finds, on investigation, that all of the information, including that contained in the letter to be withheld, had, in fact, been given to the applicant. The PCA points out that the letter contained only factual information that had already been disclosed and that nothing was achieved by implying that something was being held back. The DOT relied on a general principle concerning candour and the confidentiality of exchanges with other governments to withhold the contents of the

letter to the EU (documents themselves are not provided) but since the *content* of the letter had already been disclosed in the DoT's reply, the claim that there existed a certain type of document the contents of which could not be disclosed merely created obsfucation and mystification. As the PCA states, 'it is paradoxical that the terms of the letter sent to the complainants left the impression that information was being held back'. The PCA goes on to state that he has not pressed the DOT to disclose the letter since 'the information contained in the letter has been released', and therefore, ironically, it has not breached the code! It is clear that such behaviour by the DOT merely excites suspicion. To imply that something is being withheld merely encourages people's fear that wrongdoing or incompetence have taken place and that such fears would be confirmed if only they could obtain the one bit of information still denied to them. In this case open government, far from satisfying anyone, exacerbated suspicion. See PCA Eighth Report, Access to Official Information, vol. 3, case A.3/94, 1995.

22. PCA Annual Report for 1995, 1996 para. 6.
23. Ibid., para 7.
24. *Select Committee on the Parliamentary Commissioner for Administration, Second Special Report on Open Government, Session 1995–96*. (London: HMSO, Parliamentary Papers HC 556, 1996); *Select Committee on the Parliamentary Commissioner for Administration, Second Report, Open Government, HC 84* (London: HMSO, 1996).
25. See the previous chapter for the committee's comments on other countries.
26. Procedures are now somewhat different since the Labour Chancellor made the Bank of England the independent authority with responsibility to meet Government inflation targets. This gave the Bank autonomy in setting interest rates.
27. Select Committee on the PCA, HC 84, Q. 350. In his evidence to the Committee the PCA, Mr Reid, states that details of the case can be found in his Eighth Report published in July 1995 (HC 606) but in fact it is discussed in his Ninth report, published in November 1995 (HC 758) pp. 11 ff.. It is comforting to note that even the Ombudsman has become subject to moments of confusion given the number of Reports and Committees he has been involved with!
28. Ibid., Minutes of Evidence, Sir Patrick Brown KCB, Permanent Secretary, Department of Transport, p. 64.
29. Ibid., Mrs. Ann Bowtell CB, Permanent Secretary, Department of Social Security, p. 69.
30. Ibid., Minutes of Evidence, Annex A, information supplied by the Department of Social Security, pp. 75 ff.
31. Ibid., para. 127.
32. Ibid., para. 121.
33. The Croham Directive was a policy statement issued, in July 1977, by the Cabinet Secretary of the Day, Sir Douglas Allen (later Lord Croham), that the analytical and factual basis of policy should be kept separate from advice and should be released. However, monitoring of the directive was dropped by 1979. See James Michael, *The Politics of Secrecy:*

Confidential Government and the Public Right to Know (Harmondsworth: Penguin; 1982), p. 216. The Select Committee report states that the directive was issued in 1976 but this is not strictly accurate. The Home Secretary, Merlyn Rees, issued a statement about reform of official secrecy in the autmn of 1976 but the directive was not issued by Lord Croham until 1977.

34. Select Committee on the PCA, HC 84, Minutes of Evidence, Maurice Frankel, Director, Campaign for Freedom of Information, paras. 189–191.
35. Ibid., para. 126.
36. The *White Paper on Open Government*, section 1.18, and Annex B and the Select Committee on the PCA, HC 84, para. 94.
37. *Your Right to Know: The Government's Proposals for a Freedom of Information Act*, Cm 3818 (London: HMSO, 1997) p. 1.
38. There is a limited exemption for records to which a statutory right of access has already been granted but where such rights have been granted only after a certain date: *Your Right to Know*, 1997, p. 7.
39. The parameters setting the criteria under which charges can be levied are likely to be set down in an order made under the Act. However, it is not clear whether upper limits are likely to be specified or whether it is up to each authority to interpret the criteria: *Your Right to Know*, 1997, pp. 12ff.
40. This is discussed below.
41. *Your Right to Know*, 1997, p. 29.
42. The exception to this being the exemption of all information or records held by MI5, MI6, GCHQ, and the Special Air Service (SAS) Regiment.
43. *Your Right to Know*, 1997, p. 17.
44. Ibid., p. 19.

13 Conclusion

1. See Chapter 4 above.
2. See K. G. Robertson, *Public Secrets: A Study in the Development of Government Secrecy* (London: Macmillan, 1982) chs 8 and 9.
3. See Chapter 5 above.
4. Paul Hirst, *Associative Democracy: new forms of economic and social governance* (Cambridge: Polity, 1994).

Index